C000225658

Saints on Earth

Let saints on earth in concert sing
With those whose work is done
For all the servants of our king
In heaven and earth are one.

Charles Wesley

Saints
on
Earth

A biographical
companion to
Common Worship

John H. Darch
Stuart K. Burns

Church House Publishing
Church House
Great Smith Street
London SW1P 3NZ

Tel: 020 7898 1451
Fax: 020 7898 1449

ISBN 0 7151 4036 1

Published 2004 by
Church House Publishing

Copyright © John H. Darch
and Stuart K. Burns 2004

The *Common Worship* Calendar
is copyright © The Archbishops'
Council, 2000 – 2004

All rights reserved. No part
of this publication may be
reproduced or stored or
transmitted by any means
or in any form, electronic
or mechanical, including
photocopying, recording, or
any information storage and
retrieval system without written
permission which should be
sought from the Copyright
Administrator, Church House
Publishing, Church House,
Great Smith Street, London
SW1P 3NZ
email: copyright@c-of-e.org.uk.

Printed in England by the
University Printing Press,
Cambridge

Contents

To the staff and students of
St John's College, Nottingham
– past, present and future

Introduction

In using the word 'saint' to described those commemorated in the Holy Days of the *Common Worship* calendar we are, of course, using it as a shorthand term. From a biblical perspective there is no difficulty in the use of the word, since it simply signifies those who are 'in Christ' – being dead is not a necessary part of the equation! In his epistles Paul uses the word extensively to refer to his fellow believers. But in common understanding 'saints' are exceptionally holy individuals who have been officially canonized by the Church. Yet, unlike the Roman Catholic Church, the Church of England has no machinery for doing this. Indeed, the very idea of the Church taking it upon itself to bestow 'sainthood' on some of its departed members is one that many Anglicans would find very difficult to accept. Even King Charles I, the only post-Reformation 'saint' to get into the 1662 Prayer Book (until removed in the nineteenth century), was never referred to as such, merely as a 'martyr'.

The increased profile given to the commemoration of the saints by the Oxford Movement created a difficulty in the nineteenth century. Since the 1662 provision was so inadequate, saints were borrowed from Roman Catholic and other sources. Responding to this need, the proposed Prayer Book of 1928 contained an Alternative Calendar with a much-improved selection of saints. Nevertheless these all came from the early days of Church history – the most modern being Catherine of Siena who died in 1380. The impression given was that 'saints' were those from the far distant past in the days when there were 'giants in the land'. We should not expect to see their like in the contemporary world! The unhelpful implication was that Christian holiness was an ancient, not a modern, phenomenon.

The Alternative Service Book 1980 introduced the concept of 'Lesser Festivals and Commemorations' as a means of commemorating individuals who had not been formally canonized by the Western Church before the Reformation. This enabled the commemoration of exemplary Christians from comparatively modern times and so, for the first time Anglican evangelicals, who had generally avoided all but the biblical saints' days (and sometimes not even those) began to relate to their own spiritual heroes from the Reformation onwards. A small but varied selection of 'saints' from all periods of church history and from differing Christian traditions made a welcome appearance. Saintliness, it seemed, was becoming both more modern and more relevant.

Common Worship incorporated many of the saints listed in *Celebrating Common Prayer* (published 1992 by the Franciscans and widely used by those of all traditions) along with a number of others. And the classification in ASB was further refined. After Principal Feasts (Christmas, Easter, etc.) and Principal Holy Days (Ash Wednesday, Maundy Thursday, Good Friday) came the Festivals, containing the biblical saints. Two new categories, the Lesser Festivals and the Commemorations were created (though the precise difference between the two is rather difficult to fathom) and these were concerned with heroes and heroines of faith from across the centuries of Church history, many comparatively modern (the most recent was martyred in 1980). It is those contained in these two latter categories with which this book is largely concerned.

Already Brother Tristam's *Exciting Holiness* (Norwich: Canterbury Press, second edition, 2003) has provided exhaustive liturgical provision for the saints' days and Robert Atwell's *Celebrating the Saints* (Norwich: Canterbury Press, 1998) is a most useful collection of additional readings. But the biographical information in these two volumes is, of necessity, very limited, and those in the latter 'largely reproduced' from the first edition of the former.

Our focus is purely biographical, seeking to aid those wishing to use the lives of these exemplary Christians for preaching and teaching purposes; indeed one of the proposed titles for this book was *Preaching the Saints*. We eventually settled on a more neutral title, however, since we did not want to give the misleading impression of providing a set of sermon outlines! It is for our readers to use the factual material in the way that God leads them. But it is designed to be used more widely than just for preaching and we hope that it will help to spark ideas for those leading intercessions on saints' days.

Also, since collective worship in church (and other) schools often focuses on the lives and achievements of inspiring individuals, our hope is that it will also prove a helpful source of material for teachers. With these purposes in the forefront of our minds we have tried to make the book as user-friendly as possible and to adopt narrative approaches to the brief biographies contained in this volume.

Our purpose is to make these men and women better known, for the *Common Worship* list of Holy Days includes, notably among the Lesser Festivals and Commemorations, many significant Christians whose stories are not widely known in the Church of England. Indeed, some are hardly known at all, for some it has been difficult to obtain information, and for some all that remains, like the smile of a long-faded Cheshire cat is the legend. But though we are both historians we certainly do not despise myth and legend, conveying as they do truths in different forms and from different ages. Nevertheless we attempt to offer not hagiography but history and biography. In some cases historically accurate information has revealed the hagiographical character of earlier biographies and the authors have had to face the choice of perpetuating a legend, or presenting verifiable history. For the most part we have chosen to rest with facts. Here are no plaster saints, but real flesh and blood human beings, warts and all, who despite the frailties of their humanity have much to teach us about the Christian life and the service and worship of God.

A word needs to be said on our choice of biographies since this book does not claim to be totally comprehensive. The major biblical saints are already very well known and with such a vast amount of easily accessible material available about them it would be superfluous to try to sum them up in short compass. On the other hand, some commemorations like the Week of Prayer for Christian Unity (18–25 January) and O Sapientia (17 December) defy biographical treatment altogether. Because of their largely non-biographical nature we initially decided to by-pass group commemorations, though we eventually modified this in the majority of cases – namely Japan, Uganda, and Papua New Guinea – since they are clearly defined and contain instructive stories of faith and sacrifice which deserve to be better known.

This book does not claim to be an original piece of research. All the information contained here is in the public domain – we have merely sought to collate and select that which is most helpful for the purposes of preaching and teaching. The authors have become increasingly aware while writing this book that acquiring information about all the people commemorated in *Common Worship* is a lengthy and time-consuming task. The major benefit of this book is that we have done the spade-work of tracking down the multiplicity of sources and presenting the information in easily accessible form under one cover.

Our grateful thanks go to Dr Stephen Travis who, from the detached standpoint of a Methodist layperson, observed that the Church of England had equipped itself with a whole new pantheon of saints but without a single work of reference to assist those who wished to use them for teaching purposes. Without his original idea this book would never have been written.

We are also grateful to those who have helped us in unearthing appropriate material, notably the Reverend Mother Superior CSJB for providing information on Harriet Monsell, co-founder of the Community of St John the Baptist, and Hugh Sheldon of Lea Hall, Derbyshire for information concerning Florence Nightingale. Thanks are also due to the Reverend Dr Dee Dyas of the Centre for Christianity and Culture at St John's for her insightful comments on the medieval commemorations, and to Christine Ainsley and Evelyn Pawley of St John's College Library for their valuable assistance. Thanks also go to Ruth McCurry for her comments on early drafts of the text.

We are particularly grateful to Kathryn Pritchard, our ever-helpful editor, who immediately recognized the potential of this project and has encouraged and guided us through the writing and editing process without ever losing her sense of humour. Finally, we record our gratitude to our wives, Madge and Joyce, for their support, encouragement and unfailing patience during the writing of this book.

We have sought to avoid any infringement of copyright, but if we have inadvertently done so, we should be grateful if the copyright holders would inform us so that due acknowledgement can be made in any subsequent edition. The verse from the Dietrich Bonhoeffer poem on page 49 is taken from 'Powers of Good' in *Letters and Papers from Prison* (The Enlarged Edition, SCM Press 1971, p. 400) and is reproduced by permission of SCM-Canterbury Press Ltd.

The small print concerning the lists of those individuals to be commemorated by the Church is instructive. ASB noted that 'diocesan, local and other commemorations may be added to this list' and *Common Worship* gives permission for 'diocesan and other local provision to supplement the national calendar'. In other words, the list is open-ended. Here are some examples of exemplary Christian lives – look out for others to celebrate, and be inspired by them also.

As members of a contemporary church with long roots in the past is the privilege of Anglicans, to celebrate the lives of those who have personally lived out the gospel, often at a great personal cost. Here is theology earthed in humanity. Our prayer is that, in some small way, this volume may help to unlock and enhance some of these rich resources for worship now provided for the Church of England in the Holy Days of the *Common Worship* calendar.

John Darch

Stuart Burns

The Feast of St Philip and St James, 2004

Basil the Great and Gregory of Nazianzus, Bishops, Teachers of the Faith, 379 and 389

Basil the Great, d.379

Basil was a bishop, a monk and a theologian. Along with his brother Gregory of Nyssa (see 19 July) and Gregory of Nazianzus he is one of the three 'Cappadocian Fathers' whose thought developed the Church's doctrine of the Holy Spirit and of the Trinity. Basil is not only honoured by the Church for his theological contribution, but also for his pastoral heart and for his care for the poor. He is known for his defence of the orthodox Nicene faith, particularly of the Trinity, and for the way in which he organized Eastern monasticism, emphasizing community life, liturgical prayer and manual work. His two collections of 'Rules' or 'guidelines' for monastic life, many of which were written as answers to questions that Basil was asked as he travelled on pilgrimages, are still influential today.

Born into an educated and privileged family, Basil never lost the love of classical literature, rhetoric and philosophy that formed his early training. He viewed Christianity as a faith that encompassed the great philosophies and cultures of the day rather than one which fought against them. His theology drew from the advances in thought of those around him, but clearly held to Christian principles and doctrine.

Basil initially lived as an ascetic, touring the monastic sites and communities of the East, before being ordained presbyter in 364 and then in 370 becoming bishop of Caesarea. During his tenure as bishop, Basil was in conflict with Arianism (which denied the full divinity of Christ) and with those who denied the divinity of the Holy Spirit. Basil is responsible for the insertion of the phrase 'and the Holy Spirit' into the Doxology, and his Liturgy is still used in the Orthodox Church throughout Lent.

As bishop, Basil established hospitals for the sick, homes for the poor, and hospices for travellers and strangers. Alongside his theological stance he was ceaseless in his efforts to bring unity to the Church, not only in the East, but also between East and West. He died two years before the Second Ecumenical Council at Constantinople, which brought order and unity to the Church and which was indebted to Basil for the theological and institutional foundations that he had laid.

For contemporary Anglicans Basil's influence can be seen most clearly in Eucharistic Prayer F in *Common Worship*:

> Look with favour on your people
> and in your mercy hear the cry of our hearts.
> Bless the earth,
> heal the sick,
> let the oppressed go free,
> and fill your Church with power from on high.

Gregory of Nazianzus, d.389

Gregory of Nazianzus (or Nazianzen) was born in Arianzus (Cappadocia) in 329. Along with Gregory of Nyssa (see 19 July) and Basil of Caesarea he is one of the three 'Cappadocian Fathers' whose thought developed the doctrine of the Holy Spirit and of the Trinity. He is honoured by the Church as a theologian of great distinction. Gregory expanded the idea that salvation is a progressive journey into the Godhead and stressed that the agent of this journey is the Holy Spirit. He proposed the term 'procession' to distinguish the nature of the position of the Spirit in the Godhead, and demanded that the Holy Spirit receive full worship and equal honour.

Gregory started out as an orator and finished as a reclusive poet. In between he attempted to live a life of solitude and reflection but was continually pressured by others to be involved in church politics and theological disputes. His sensitive nature was not up to the task and he was unsuitable for the cut and thrust of political life, forever seeking a place where he could fulfil his desire for solitude and contemplation. Yet Gregory also longed for recognition and honour from his fellow Christians.

In 364 at the age of 34, Gregory was ordained priest at the insistence of his father. Such was his lack of enthusiasm for this calling that he initially ran away. In 372 he was consecrated Bishop of Sasima at the insistence of Basil of Caesarea. Once again he initially fled. In 380 Gregory was made Bishop of Constantinople. This time he made no attempt to avoid the appointment, perhaps considering that finally the honour was deserved. It was during his time at the small orthodox church there that he produced some of his best known and theologically important work on the nature of God and of the Trinity.

The greatest moment of Gregory's life occurred in 381, when, as bishop, he presided at the opening of the Council of Constantinople. Unfortunately Gregory's triumph at Constantinople did not last long. He was criticized for moving from one bishopric to another, he was ill-advised in key council decisions, and became a victim of inter-party rivalry. All this combined to result in Gregory resigning from his post. He returned to his family estate in Arianzus, wrote poetry, and lived the ascetic life of which he had dreamed for so long.

And so, Father, grant to me,
by spirit and soul
by mouth and mind
in purity of heart
to give you glory. Amen.

2 January

Seraphim, Monk of Sarov, Spiritual Guide, 1833

In an age of industrialization, scientific progress and indifference to Christianity, Seraphim was revered as one who was clearly used as a vessel of the Holy Spirit, and whose life was fully devoted to God.

It was said of Seraphim that,

> It is now, when our Spiritual wings have atrophied and we have forgotten what possibilities are concealed in our spirit, that St Seraphim was sent to us . . . that we might remember our divine sonship and strive towards the limitless perfection of our Heavenly Father.

Born in the Russian city of Kursk in 1759, Seraphim started to live an ascetic life at the age of 19. First he lived at a monastery in Sarov, sharing in the ordinary life of the community before starting to live a life of seclusion in 1794. In 1825, Seraphim opened both the door of his cell and of his life and devoted himself to guiding others into the presence of God. So many stories and myths have grown up surrounding the deeds of this spiritual guide and 'Holy Man' that sometimes it is hard to tell where the kernel of truth lies. However, it can be said that he possessed the gifts of healing, discernment and prophecy and would reveal to his visitors the innermost secrets of their hearts. There is no doubt that Seraphim lived a live fully given to God, and was a living example of the way in which the Holy Spirit lives in and works through those devoted to him. Many thousands of Russians are believed to have come to him for advice and prayer during the last eight years of his life.

It has been said that 'He proved that the Church does not grow old, and that the grace of God is equally effectual in all ages and in all places.' In the Orthodox Church he is recognized as a 'Starets' or 'Holy Man' (someone who owes his authority to spiritual gifts). He is remembered as one who was severe in his personal asceticism, yet who was gentle to others, stressing the need for joy in the Christian life.

His teaching is summed up in his exhortation that 'The purpose of the earthly life is the acquisition of the Holy Spirit', and in his prayer, 'Warm me with the warmth of Your Holy Spirit'.

Vendanayagam Samuel Azariah, Bishop in South India, Evangelist, 1945

Born in 1874 in Vellalanvillai, Madras State, the son of a village priest, Azariah became an evangelist with the YMCA in 1895, later becoming its national secretary in India.

The prevailing attitude of the time was that mission was something done by Europeans to Indians. Azariah did not subscribe to this view and in 1902 was among the founders of the indigenous Indian Missionary Society. He also saw a need for indigenous leadership of the white-led Anglican Church in India if native Indians were to forsake their local religions to be attracted to Christianity.

In his thirties he was ordained and before he reached 40 he was consecrated bishop, the first Indian to reach episcopal rank in the Anglican Communion. But his appointment as Bishop of Dornakal was not without opposition. Many Indians looked down on his humble origins and many Europeans, even some of those who saw the wisdom of advancing Indians to positions of authority in the Church, thought it a premature step. He was fortunate in having a series of gifted archdeacons who did the administrative work of the diocese and freed him to travel and to teach, to inspire and lead the rapidly growing Church. During his 30-year episcopate, it is said that 100,000 people were added to the Church. His spiritual work needs to be seen against the political backcloth of the struggle for Indian independence led by Mahatma Gandhi.

A firm believer in cooperation between foreign and Indian church workers (on which topic he addressed the 1910 Edinburgh World Missionary Conference, asking for more equal treatment, including love and friendship, from European missionaries), he supported the development of an indigenous leadership in a united Indian Church. To this end he ordained able village catechists to Holy Orders. Though he strongly repudiated syncretism, Azariah encouraged the use of Indian cultural forms by the Church in order to make it truly Indian and not a European subsidiary.

He took a leading role in the conference at Tranquebar in 1919 which began the process of forging the major Christian denominations in South India (Anglicans, Methodists and the existing united Church which had previously brought together Congregationalists, Presbyterians, Lutherans and Reformed) into a united Church. His death in 1945 just preceded two major developments for which he had long waited – the foundation of the united Church of South India in1947, and India's independence from Britain in the same year.

William Laud, Archbishop of Canterbury, 1645

Laud was born in Reading in 1573, the son of tailor, and educated at St John's College, Oxford, becoming a Fellow in 1593. He was ordained in 1601 and in 1611 became president of the College. With powerful patrons in both Church (Bishop Neile of Durham) and State (the Duke of Buckingham), Laud soon rose to prominence. He occupied the following posts – Dean of Gloucester (1616), Bishop of St David's (1621), Bishop of Bath and Wells (1626) and Bishop of London (1628) – before becoming Archbishop of Canterbury in 1633.

Perhaps Laud was bound to be involved in conflict since he was an Arminian when the Church of England was overwhelmingly Calvinist in its belief, an advocate of greater sacramentalism in an age of preaching and a believer in the 'beauty of holiness' when plainness and simplicity in worship were the norm. Laud's belief that 'ceremonies are the hedge that fence the substance of religion from all the indignities which profaneness and sacrilege too commonly put upon it' did not seem so innocent to militant Puritanism. And when Laud encouraged the use of candles, frontals and copes, insisted on the use of surplices and holy tables set altarwise against the east wall of the church, and then used the full force of the law against any opposition, he put himself in the firing line.

Always a controversial figure, historians disagree on whether Laud or the Puritans were responsible for the religious (and later, civil) strife that engulfed England. And there is a real question as to how much Laud acted on his own initiative in his religious policy or how much he was simply implementing Charles I's wishes.

It was the destabilizing of Scotland after Laud's attempt to introduce an Anglican liturgy there in 1637 that led to revolt and war. Though impeachment for treason failed, Laud was condemned to death by a Parliamentary Act of Attainder and executed in 1645. He prayed on the scaffold:

> Lord I am coming as fast as I can, I know I must pass through the shadow of death, before I can come to see thee . . . Lord receive my soul and have mercy upon me, and bless this kingdom with peace and plenty, and with brotherly love and charity, that here may not be this effusion of Christian blood amongst them, for Jesus Christ his sake, if it be thy will.

Mary Slessor, Missionary in West Africa, 1915

Born to a poor family in Aberdeen in 1848, Mary Slessor came to faith as a teenager and engaged in outreach work amongst the deprived youth of Dundee. But she was already developing an interest in overseas mission work, still an unusual thing for a single woman in the mid nineteenth century. Like David Livingstone before her, Mary was born a Scots Presbyterian and spent her early life from the age of eleven working in the mills (in her case the linen mills of Dundee) for twelve hours a day, six days a week while at the same time studying in order to equip herself for mission work.

In 1876 she joined the Scots United Presbyterian mission, which had been founded by Hope Waddell at Calabar on the Niger Delta in West Africa. Able and independent, Mary became fluent in the local languages and showed both a humility and an understanding of Africans unusual in European missionaries of that generation. Instead of living in a European mission compound at a safe distance from the 'natives', Mary lived with her people. She gathered around her a household of outcast women and she adopted unwanted children, especially twins, who would otherwise be put to death according to the local superstitious practice. She also opposed other local practices, such as trial by ordeal, witchcraft and human sacrifice, eventually being successful in abolishing them altogether.

Unlike most missionaries of the nineteenth-century classical missionary societies, Mary adapted thoroughly to the culture of the people with whom she worked, eventually settling first with the Okoyong and later the Ibo people, in both cases doing much to assist their development. She encouraged the indigenous peoples with whom she worked to engage in trade, as much for its civilizing effects as for the financial benefits.

Mary earned the respect of both local leaders and the British colonial administration. She was often called upon to arbitrate in tribal disputes and in 1892 she was appointed as the British vice-consul – an unusual role for a missionary and a unique one for a woman. She was known as 'Ma Slessor' to her people, and became famous as 'the white queen of Calabar' to the British public, who read glamourized accounts of her exploits in books and magazines. Mary remained in Africa to the end of her life and died at Itu in 1915.

12 January

Aelred of Hexham, Abbot of Rievaulx, 1167

Aelred was born at Hexham in Northumberland in 1109 the son and grandson of married priests (at a time when clerical celibacy was not universally practised in the Catholic Church). At an early age he was sent to the Scottish court for an education that would ensure his future as a noble and courtier. Here he acted as a page to the young Prince Henry. King David of Scotland saw Aelred's potential, promoted him in the royal household and, it is speculated, may already have had the intention of making him a bishop.

But at the age of 24 Aelred turned his back on the opportunities that awaited him at court and entered the religious life in the newly-founded Cistercian abbey at Rievaulx in Yorkshire. Soon he was appointed master of novices, and gained a reputation for the quality of the pastoral care he exercised to those under his charge. In 1143, when a new Cistercian abbey was founded at Revesby in Lincolnshire, Aelred was sent from Rievaulx to be the first abbot.

He did not remain at Revesby for long, however, for in 1146 the Abbot of Rievaulx died and Aelred was elected abbot. He now found himself not just the superior of a community of 300 monks, but the head of the Cistercian order in England. His new responsibilities saw him travelling widely both in England and Scotland and also on the Continent – an ordeal for him as he suffered from a painful kidney complaint. But his influence was considerable and he is said to have been instrumental in persuading Henry II to attend a meeting with the Pope and King Louis VII of France in 1162. The following year he was present at Westminster Abbey, when Edward the Confessor's bones were re-interred there, and was inspired to write a biography of Edward.

Aelred's writings reveal a person of love and humanity who deeply valued, and encouraged among his monks, the cultivation of friendship, both with one another and with God. His two best-known works were *On Spiritual Friendship* and the *Mirror of Charity.* His writings and sermons (he left a considerable collection) indicated a love of Christ as Saviour and friend that was clearly the foundation of his faith and life. Aelred's writings constantly appealed to Scripture as his source of authority. His remarkable writings earned for him the epithet of 'the English St Bernard'.

Benedict Biscop, Abbot of Wearmouth, Scholar, 689

Benedict Biscop was a Northumbrian nobleman in King Oswy's court, who grew up under the influence of the Irish mission. At the age of 25, rather than accepting a land-grant from the king, he renounced his position in society, and began a life of travelling and pilgrimage.

Benedict visited Rome six times and stayed in 17 European monasteries, gleaning from them whatever he could about the monastic life. He finally returned to Northumbria where he founded the monasteries at Monkwearmouth (674) and Jarrow (682). The community at Monkwearmouth became very large (over 600) and very rich. Endowments were received from King Egfrith of East Anglia amongst others. Benedict imported masons and glaziers from Gaul, and on two further visits to Rome acquired books and pictures, building up the library at both his monastic communities. There was a great 'continental' flavour to the life of these communities. Benedict became totally loyal to the Roman Church, despite his upbringing in the Celtic tradition. He smoothed the transition from Celtic to Roman forms of worship and practice and, for example, he is recorded as having introduced a teacher of Roman chant. One of his students, Bede (see 25 May), was to become the foremost historian in the Saxon Church, and his learning shows the fruits of the library that Benedict established.

Benedict is one of the architects of the Romanization of the Church in Britain, accompanying Theodore, Archbishop of Canterbury (see 19 September) to Britain from Rome, and acting as abbot of his monastic community at Canterbury for a short time.

On his deathbed, Benedict reminded his monks of his 'rule of life'. These guidelines and principles by which he had lived his life were based upon the sixth-century Rule of St Benedict. He also stressed the requirement for his monks to select a new abbot on the basis of holiness of life rather than social class.

> He made no secret of his zeal for religion, and showed what ecclesiastical or monastic instructions he had received at Rome and elsewhere. He displayed the holy volumes and relics of Christ's blessed Apostles and martyrs, which he had brought, and found such favour in the eyes of the king, that he forthwith gave him seventy hides of land out of his own estates, and ordered a monastery to be built thereon for the first pastor of his Church.
>
> *Bede: The Lives of the Holy Abbots*

Hilary, Bishop of Poitiers, Teacher of the Faith, 367

Hilary became a Christian only after a prolonged period of study and enquiry. Initially an Orator, born of pagan parents, Hilary became disenchanted with pagan philosophy and started to investigate Christianity. He became a staunch defender of orthodoxy against Arianism, which denied the full divinity of Christ. He was made a bishop in 350.

As a bishop, Hilary was influential and vocal in theological debate, and many in the Western Church considered him to be a mischief maker and one who spread discord. Much of his reputation rests on his activity in councils and debates. On account of his teaching on the divinity of the Son, the Emperor Constantinus, an Arian sympathizer, had him excommunicated in 353. He was exiled to Phrygia in Asia Minor, albeit with freedom of travel. This resulted in him having the opportunity to encounter many Greek Christian theological writings for the first time, especially those of Origen, and this period saw him develop his theological understanding, strengthen his anti-Arian stance, and deepen his spirituality.

Hilary took part in the Council of Seleucia in 359, unsuccessfully campaigning against Arianism. In 360 he returned from exile to Gaul and was welcomed with great rejoicing, although he was not reinstated as bishop. He brought an orthodox theological understanding to the West, and was moderate in both discipline and doctrine, persuading many Western bishops of the validity of Eastern theology. He has been compared to Athanasius in the East, as a defender of faith and a campaigner against Arianism.

Hilary wrote many doctrinal and historical works, and also hymns. He is the first known writer of hymns in the Western Church, which before him sang only songs from a scriptural source. Hilary was impressed by the Eastern use of song as a means of spreading orthodox doctrine, and on his return to the West introduced such hymns to Western Christianity. Unsurprisingly Hilary's hymns develop Trinitarian themes and stress the relation of Christ to the Father. However, some of them are so intricate and precise in their theology that they were said to be difficult to sing!

> Oh you happy and glorious ones in the Lord, you who keep your confession of the perfect apostolic faith in your hearts and until now knew nothing of any written creeds! You did not need the letter because you were overflowing with the Spirit. Nor did you desire to use your hands for writing because for your salvation you confessed with your mouths and believed in your hearts.
>
> *Hilary, to the Bishops of Gaul,*
> *Germany and Britain*

Kentigern (Mungo), Missionary Bishop in Strathclyde and Cumbria, 603

Kentigern, also known as Mungo, was Bishop of the Strathclyde region of Scotland in the late fifth century. He was born the illegitimate grandson of a Saxon prince from the south of Scotland, and was brought up in a monastic school, close to the Firth of Forth, where he was taught by a Scottish bishop. 'Mungo' is a Celtic nickname, commonly given to those with the name Kentigern and it is said to mean 'darling'. The monastic way which he followed was of the Irish Celtic rather than Roman tradition, and when he was consecrated Bishop of Strathclyde it was by an Irish Celtic bishop, which served to emphasize Kentigern's freedom from Roman influence.

A casualty of the diverse and fragmented political landscape of Britain in the late fifth century, Kentigern spent time away from Scotland, possibly in Wales, where he is credited with the founding of the Church at St Asaph. This period away from Strathclyde has led to some historical confusion, and in the twelfth-century 'lives' that tell his story he is spoken of as being variously a native of Lothian, a Welshman and a Northumbrian.

When he returned to Strathclyde he lived in Dumfries, founded the Church in Glasgow, and re-established the memory of Ninian. Kentigern's legend includes the story of his comforting an unfaithful queen, who had given the king's ring to her lover. The king, on discovering the liaison, had thrown the ring into the sea, and demanded that the queen find it within three days, or face the consequences. As Kentigern comforted the queen, one of his monks caught a salmon, inside which was the ring. The work of Kentigern is acknowledged in the coat of arms of the city of Glasgow, which depicts the ring that was recovered from the salmon. Generally referred to as St Mungo's, the city's cathedral is dedicated to him.

13 January

George Fox, Founder of the Society of Friends (the Quakers), 1691

George Fox was born in 1624 at Fenny Drayton, Leicestershire, the son of a weaver. In 1643, when Fox was 19, he said that he received mystical revelations in which the voice of God told him to be directed by Christ alone. He described these revelations, which he took as a sign that everyone should be guided by their individual 'inner light', as coming to him while he waited in an absolutely calm frame of mind and as being preceded by violent physical agitation. He felt called to give up ties of family and friends and travelled in search of spiritual enlightenment.

In 1646, after many dead ends in his quest, he heard a voice which told him, 'There is one, even Christ Jesus, who can speak to thy condition.' In 1647 Fox began to preach openly his 'inner light' doctrine. He objected to political and religious authority, opposed war and slavery, and believed that all human actions should be directed by inner contemplation and a social conscience inspired by God.

On Pendle Hill in Lancashire George Fox experienced a vision of 'a people to be gathered to the Lord'. He made many converts and it was in the north-west that Fox's teachings had the greatest effect. In 1659 he made his home at Swarthmore Hall near Ulverston, owned by an influential supporter, Thomas Fell. When Fell died Fox married his widow, Margaret.

Fox's overt opposition to the established Church (whether Presbyterian or Anglican) resulted in frequent imprisonment – in 1649, 1650, 1653, 1656, 1664–6, 1673–5 – and it was the judge who sentenced him at Derby in 1650 who contemptuously described Fox and his followers as 'quakers' – a name which was to come into widespread use.

In 1666, though weakened by hardship and the effects of imprisonment, Fox began to devote most of his time to the organization of the Quakers as a Church. He was greatly assisted by Margaret Fell, whom he married in 1669, the year of the first great Quaker meeting. He also made missionary journeys to North America, Germany and Holland.

Fox spent his final years founding Quaker schools and communities and lobbying for passage of the Toleration Bill, which granted freedom of worship to all except Roman Catholics and Unitarians, that was finally enacted by Parliament in 1689. The Quakers registered under the Act as the 'Society of Friends'. He died in 1691 and his *Journal* was published posthumously in 1694.

Antony of Egypt, Hermit, Abbot, 356

Antony grew up in a wealthy family in Egypt, but at the age of 20, after the death of his parents, he gave all his possessions away and started to live as a recluse, among the local ascetics in his village. From 286 to 306 Antony lived in solitude, first in a tomb, and then in an abandoned desert fort. Later he moved to the Red Sea, where a monastery was formed, and he remained there until his death at the age of 105 in the year 356.

Antony did not spend all his life cut off from the world. In 311 he travelled to Alexandria to encourage Christians who had been imprisoned for their faith, and he journeyed there on a further occasion in 355 to confront the Arians whose teaching denied the full divinity of Christ. During this second trip he met Athanasius, who was so impressed by him that he wrote the story of his life. Within this *Life of Antony* Athanasius presents him as an example of the monastic way. His battles with demons in the desert, and the story of his great spirituality served to fuel the growing desire for an authentic Christian life which the Church, with her greater connections with the Empire and State, was beginning to lose. The *Life of Antony* was disseminated widely and was immensely influential in the growth of monasticism.

Antony was a leader almost by default. He sought a life of solitude and contemplation, but discovered that he became a beacon to others seeking an ascetic life. His retreat at Pispir, together with those at Nitria and Scete, quickly became colonies of monks, with Antony as their leader.

Although unable to read or write, Antony carried out correspondence not only with other monks, but also with emperors and officials. His replies to the letters he received (and which he never quite knew what to do with) reveal him as one who encouraged others to persevere, and stressed that the first obligation of the monk is to know himself, as only those that know themselves will be able to know God. The letters present the monastic life as a continual battle in which the believer is aided by the Holy Spirit, who guides him and opens the eyes of his soul.

Antony's fame spread far through his life and through his biography, and he is recognized as the founder of Western monasticism.

> [Antony] called his two companions . . . and said to them,
> 'Let your very breath be always Christ'.
>
> *Athanasius: Life of Antony XCI*

Charles Gore, Bishop, Founder of the Community of the Resurrection, 1932

Born in Wimbledon in 1853, Charles Gore was educated at Harrow (where he first encountered and adopted for himself Catholic spirituality and practice) and Balliol College, Oxford. He was elected to a Fellowship at Trinity College, Oxford in 1875 and ordained the following year. He initially served a curacy in and near Liverpool before returning to Oxford as Vice-Principal of Cuddesdon in 1880, then as first Principal of Pusey House in Oxford, which for six years he combined with a canonry at Westminster Abbey. In 1902 Gore was consecrated Bishop of Worcester, being translated first to Birmingham in 1905 as the first bishop of the new diocese, then to Oxford in 1911. He resigned in 1919 to devote himself to a life of preaching, lecturing and writing.

In 1892, while at Pusey House, Gore founded the Society (later the Community) of the Resurrection with the aim of adapting the religious life for men to the changed circumstances of the modern world. In 1898 the community moved from Oxford to Mirfield, near Huddersfield, which became its permanent home.

Gore was the author of numerous books, though perhaps the most influential and best remembered was *Lux Mundi*, which he edited in 1889. It reflected the views of the growing liberal wing of Anglo-Catholicism and was attacked by traditionalists whom he shocked by breaking with the more conservative views of the Oxford Movement. But this enforced demarcation allowed Gore to distance himself from the past and to give new direction to Anglo-Catholicism.

His achievement was to unite Anglo-Catholicism with a critical approach to the Scriptures and to give it a wider social conscience. Above all others Gore made Anglo-Catholicism 'respectable' and began the process by which a more eirenic and less extreme form of it became acceptable to a much wider constituency, capturing the middle ground of the Church of England and making it the normative expression of Anglicanism in the first half of the twentieth century.

On Gore's death in 1932, Hensley Henson, Bishop of Durham, and never one to bestow praise lightly, paid him this tribute:

> I judge him to have been the most considerable English churchman of his time, not the most learned, nor the most eloquent, but so learned, so eloquent, so versatile, and so energetic that he touched the life of his generation at more points, and more effectively, than any of his contemporaries.

Wulfstan, Bishop of Worcester, 1095

Wulfstan was born in Long Itchington in Warwickshire, and educated at the monasteries of Peterborough and Evesham. He became a Benedictine monk after refusing the offer of a richly endowed parish church on the occasion of his ordination. He settled in the small monastic community at Worcester Cathedral and in 1050 became prior.

In 1062 Wulfstan was consecrated Bishop of Worcester. He combined his roles as bishop and prior with great success, being passionate and vigilant in both. Thorough and systematic in his pastoral care, he is the first English bishop to be known to have made a complete visitation of his diocese.

Wulfstan was fully involved in the revitalization of monasticism in the second half of the eleventh century, building upon the work of Dunstan, Oswald and Ethelwold. As part of the second stage of that reform Wulfstan oversaw the introduction of laws and canons reforming the role and conduct of the clergy. He facilitated the relationships between the Church and the State. He was the first bishop to pay homage to William the Conqueror after the battle of Hastings, and he remained one of the few Saxons to keep his high office to the end of William's reign. In terms of administrative reform, Wulfstan increased the use and effectiveness of the archdeacons, particularly within large dioceses.

Wulfstan was influential in monastic reform. He encouraged a wider understanding of public penance, and brought up to date a full penitential system based on Frankish precedents. He also taught against the proliferation of pagan customs throughout the land.

Wulfstan was one of the most important church leaders of the eleventh century and the most renowned intellectual figure of the late Saxon Church. An energetic and powerful preacher, he was not only the mainstay of monastic reform but was also one of the most commanding figures of the monastic intellectual revival, having a great ability to clarify and explain the teaching of the Church. It was this ability to explain and challenge that saw abolition of the slave trade between Worcester diocese and Ireland (then under Viking rule), as Wulfstan persuaded the traders of Bristol of the sanctity of life and the human right to freedom.

According to tradition, Wulfstan died during his daily ritual of washing the feet of twelve of his parishioners.

20 January

Richard Rolle of Hampole, Spiritual Writer, 1349

Richard Rolle was born at Thornton-le-Dale in the North Riding of Yorkshire in 1305. The age in which he lived was one of change and worry with seemingly unfathomable reasons for the success or failure of many communities and businesses.

Richard started a degree at Oxford, but never completed it, choosing instead to live the solitary life, settling close to the Cistercian nuns at Hampole, his base for the rest of his life. It was here that he wrote his most famous works: *The Mending of Life*, probably in the 1320s, and *The Fire of Love*, written about 1343.

Three themes dominated Richard's spirituality. He challenged any equation of Christianity with power and wealth. He stressed the journey of the self rather than that of the community, and he focused upon the suffering Christ. These themes turned upside down the prevailing attitude of the day towards the Christian life.

Richard sought to encourage individuals to think of their personal journey towards God, rather than to see faith only as a communal activity. He stressed personal experience, and regarded his spiritual experience as a validation of his authority.

Richard saw no reason why an individual should not reach the highest level of spiritual life that can be attained on earth. He tried to communicate the incommunicable experience of God within himself to others. He produced some of the most passionate writings about prayer, but was so enwrapped in his own vision of God and quest for perfection that he was removed from those around him. As a consequence he struggled to apply the experience of God that he sought so vividly to his relationships with others, or to those within the Church whom he saw as defective or in error. His approach seems to be one so focused on heaven that earth is intolerable. However, his contribution both to mystic writings and to theology is undeniable, and his thirst for the tangible experience of the Holy Spirit cannot be doubted.

> O Holy Spirit, who breathes where you will, come into me and snatch me up to yourself. Fortify the nature you have created, with gifts so flowing with honey that, from intense joy in your sweetness, it may despise and reject all which is in this world, that it may accept (you giving them), spiritual gifts, and through melodious jubilation, it may entirely melt in holy love, reaching out for uncircumscribed Light.
>
> *Concerning the Love of God, Ch. 11*

Agnes, Child Martyr at Rome, 304

Known as the virgin martyr of Rome, Agnes has become one of the best known of the early Roman martyrs, despite uncertain information concerning her life. Early records state that she was 12 or 13 when she refused marriage in order to dedicate her life to Christ. She was martyred by being stabbed in the throat and was buried in the cemetery on the Via Nomentana in Rome in or around the year 304.

Agnes has been revered since the mid-fourth century as an example of faith under intense pressure, and of dedication to God. From the three accounts of her martyrdom it is known that she was either 12 or 13 when the Emperor Diocletian declared his persecution against the Christians. The Diocletian persecution of 303–4 was one of the most intense and well ordered attacks on the Church. Agnes openly declared herself a Christian and held to her faith and her virginity, despite being threatened with being sent into prostitution and ultimately to death. It is said that the ferocity of her martyrdom so shocked Roman society that she was one of the last martyrs of the Diocletian persecution.

Various hymns and works of art have been produced on the theme of Agnes' martyrdom and these illustrate the way in which she was venerated from a time very close to that of her death, although creative licence has added layers of myth to the kernels of truth that lie within her story. During the reign of Constantine, some 25 years after her death, a basilica was erected over her grave in the Via Nomentana in Rome and a relief of her is to be found on a marble slab that dates from the fourth century.

Although the later traditions embellish and at times fabricate her story, a few facts remain. Agnes was a young girl who died for her faith. She refused to trade her virginity for her life, and she died a martyr's death, alongside many others of the Early Church. She serves to remind us, not only of the cost of discipleship generally in the Early Church, but especially of the heroism and faith of children and families in many parts of the world today who continue to suffer persecution and even death for their faith.

22 January

Vincent of Saragossa, Deacon, first Martyr of Spain, 304

Vincent was another casualty of the Diocletian persecution of 303–4. The Emperor Diocletian issued a series of four edicts in two years, each designed to weaken and ultimately break the Church. His primary aim was to rid the Church of its leadership. As a deacon of Bishop Valarius of Saragossa, Vincent would have been in the group of people targeted at the outset of the persecution. Bishop Valarius suffered only imprisonment and exile, but Vincent was killed in January 304, between the third and fourth edicts.

A poem about Vincent, written by another Spaniard, Prudentius, has survived, and it is in this source that many of the details of the martyrdom of Vincent first appear. This legend of his martyrdom, written before the end of the fourth century, embellishes the story of his death, including great tortures, visions and heroic deeds. A word-play on his name allows for tales surrounding the defeat of demons. The legend tells how Vincent was arrested, imprisoned and weakened by starvation, then on his rejection of the command to sacrifice to the Emperor he was tortured to such an extent that he died of his injuries.

Whilst the legend of the martyrdom of Vincent has no direct historical evidence, it does fit with the general treatment of clergy throughout the Diocletian persecution. Clergy and other office holders within the Church were targeted by Diocletian on the basis that without leaders the people would simply dissipate.

Vincent is the first recorded martyr of Spain. Augustine, in a sermon commemorating his death, mentions that his death became known throughout the Empire.

Francis de Sales, Bishop of Geneva, Teacher of the Faith, 1622

Born into an aristocratic family at Thorens in Savoy in 1567 and educated in Paris and Padua, Francis turned from the law to the ordained ministry despite opposition from his family.

Francis was appointed Provost of Geneva, but he was based at Annecy, where the seat of the Geneva Diocese had been transferred after the city of Geneva had rejected Roman Catholicism and embraced the Reformed faith. So, one of Francis' major tasks was to attempt the conversion of the Genevans to the Roman Catholic faith. At the Pope's request he even went into the city of Geneva to interview Calvin's successor, Theodore Beza. In theological debate he gained a reputation for his courtesy, civility and good manners.

Though many of the inhabitants of the Chablais region returned to the Roman fold, most Genevans remained firm in the Reformed faith. But their respect for Francis was diminished neither by his different understanding of the Christian faith nor by his attempts to convince them of its rightness. One Calvinist minister in Geneva said of Francis, 'If we honoured any man as a saint, I know no one since the days of the apostles more worthy of it than this man.'

Despite his personal opposition, Francis was appointed coadjutor (assistant) bishop in 1599 and three years later when the diocesan bishop died he succeeded him as Bishop of Geneva. He was a model bishop. He revised and implemented catechetical instruction. He was conscientious in parish visitation, despite the mountainous nature of his diocese. His goodness, patience and mildness became proverbial. He demonstrated a practical love for the poor, and kept his own food plain, his dress and his household simple.

He wrote a number of books and treatises, one of he best known being *An Introduction to the Devout Life* (1609), a work intended to make the principles of Christian piety available for all. Everyone should strive to become pious, and 'it is an error, it is even a heresy', to hold that piety is incompatible with any state of life. It was a book later read and valued by John Wesley.

Francis died on a visit to Lyons in 1622. Crowds flocked to visit his remains, which the people of Lyons were anxious to keep in their city. The compromise reached was that his body was brought back to Annecy, but his heart was interred at Lyons.

28 January

Thomas Aquinas, Priest, Philosopher, Teacher of the Faith, 1274

Thomas, born in 1225, was the youngest son of the Count of Aquina. He was, by all accounts, a large man, who moved slowly and serenely through his daily tasks. He studied at Naples University and his fellow students christened him the 'dumb Ox'.

In 1224 Thomas joined the Order of Preachers, otherwise known as the Dominican Friars. At this time the Dominicans were spreading rapidly throughout Europe, and in particular focusing their work within the universities. The Dominicans were a relatively new order, and Thomas' family would have preferred him to join the more established Benedictine order, membership of which opened doors into influential positions in society. In response to his decision to join the Dominicans Thomas' family kidnapped him in an attempt to make him change his mind. Although they detained him for two years they were unsuccessful.

Thomas also studied at Paris and Cologne, returning to Paris to lecture in 1252. From that time on he taught in both Paris and Italy until he died in 1274. He wrote '*Summary against the Gentiles*' between 1252 and 1255, and in 1266 began his most famous work, *Summa Theologiae*, in which he considered key aspects and doctrines of Christianity.

A clear challenge which faced Thomas was whether to integrate or challenge the philosophy of Aristotle which had begun to enjoy a resurgence in the universities. Thomas chose to integrate the philosophy, and combined Aristotle's teaching with Catholic doctrine, basing his theological considerations on an Aristotelian framework. Unsurprisingly his views aroused passions and debate, and did not go unopposed. Indeed after his death some of his teachings were relegated or ignored, and it was not until recent centuries (especially since Vatican II) that he has become more widely appreciated.

Thomas is well known for his teaching on the Eucharist in which he defended the doctrine of the Real Presence of Christ. His understanding of Christ continuing the work of redemption through the sacraments was highly influential for the development of Catholic ecclesiology and doctrine.

On 6 December 1273 Thomas announced that he would write no more, and that all he had written was straw. The reasons for this are unclear. It may have been the result of either an immense spiritual experience, or simply a breakdown from overwork. A prayer attributed to Thomas reveals the motives and desires of this forward looking theologian:

Most loving Lord, grant me
a steadfast heart which no unworthy desire may drag downwards;
an unconquered heart which no hardship may wear out;
an upright heart which no worthless purpose may ensnare.
Impart to me also, O God,
the understanding to know you,
the diligence to seek you,
a way of life to please you,
and a faithfulness that may embrace you,
through Jesus Christ my Lord.
Amen.

Charles, King and Martyr, 1649

Born in Scotland in 1600, Charles moved to England at the age of three when his father, James VI of Scotland, succeeded Queen Elizabeth I. He was the first British monarch to be brought up in the Church of England and there is no doubt that his loyalty and attachment to the Church were entirely genuine on both an intellectual and spiritual plane. 'He was punctual and regular in his devotions, so that he was never known to enter upon his recreations or sports, though never so early in the morning, before he had been at public prayers.' No one can doubt Charles' personal faith or his devotion to a church which provided 'the middle way between the pomp of superstitious tyranny and the meanness of fantastick anarchy'.

Unfortunately there was more to it than that. His promotion of High Church practices in an overwhelmingly Calvinist (and increasingly Puritan) Church did not increase his popularity, nor did his use of harsh methods (in both Church and State) to enforce the royal will. And Charles was no statesman. Handicapped by his belief in the 'divine right of kings' he stood on his dignity, habitually failed to take the peaceful option, and showed in his public dealings that his word could not be relied upon. Even Archbishop Laud, who had more reason than most to be grateful to him, described Charles as 'a mild and gracious prince who knew not how to be, or be made, great'.

The deterioration and breakdown in relations between Crown and Parliament showed Charles at his worst and the tragedy of the Civil War, the fate of the Church of England (it should not be forgotten that Charles was still king when episcopacy was abolished in 1645) and Charles' personal fate were all largely (though, of course, not entirely) his own fault.

Perhaps sensing that he could do more good in death than he had ever done in life Charles resolved after receiving the death sentence to meet his end in a noble and fearless way and, as he told his daughter, to die 'for the laws and liberties of this land and for maintaining the true Protestant religion'. If his life and reign were largely a failure, he redeemed them both by the manner of his death in Whitehall on 30 January 1649. Paradoxically, his execution was a triumph which left an enduring legend, cemented the relationship between Church and State and gave the Church of England a martyr.

31 January

John Bosco, Priest, Founder of the Salesian Teaching Order, 1888

John Bosco was born to a peasant family near Castelnuovo, in Piedemont, northern Italy in 1815. John's early years were spent as a shepherd, but in 1835 he entered the seminary at Chieri and was ordained priest in 1841. With a remarkable gift for working among boys and young men, he was greatly concerned for the fate of youngsters brought up in the slums of cities like Turin, where he began his ministry in the poor Valdocco quarter, all drawn by a kindness they had never previously known. As well as church services he ran evening classes with the young in mind. Then he developed a boarding house (with his mother as housekeeper) and workshops teaching various trades. His 'Oratory' grew from 20 boys in early 1842 to 400 only four years later. As the work grew he founded a congregation to develop the work and, in 1859 the 'Pious Society of St Francis de Sales', commonly known as the Salesians, came into being. It was initially opposed by the municipal authorities, but they soon came to recognize the importance of the work that Bosco and the Salesians were doing.

Bosco was said to have had a vision as a child in which it was disclosed to him what his life's work would be, and the words 'Not with blows, but with charity and gentleness must you draw these friends to the path of virtue', remained with him throughout his life. Certainly he always sought to make learning an attractive proposition for those in his care and his teaching methods were remarkably progressive for the nineteenth century, even to the extent of encouraging play as a means of arousing curiosity and thus furthering education. He was also far ahead of his time in relation to punishment: 'As far as possible avoid punishing . . . try to gain love before inspiring fear'. Observance of rules was obtained by instilling a true sense of duty, by removing occasions for disobedience, and by allowing no effort towards virtue, how trivial it might be, to pass unappreciated. The teacher should be father, adviser and friend.

At the time of his death in Turin in 1888 there were 250 houses of the Salesian Society in all parts of the world, containing 130,000 children. By that date also the Salesians had provided the Roman Catholic Church with over 6,000 priests from among the boys they had cared for and educated.

Brigid, Abbess of Kildare, c.525

Brigid is held to have founded the first female monastery in Ireland, at Cill-Dare: the Church of the Oak (Kildare) in 470. The monastery became a 'double monastery' for both men and women, and at Kildare this would have reflected the higher social standing of the nuns. Brigid became abbess of the monastery.

The monastery and town of Kildare became an important ecclesiastical centre and in an attempt to heighten religious standing and authority subsequent leaders of the region enhanced the life of Brigid to absurd levels. Consequently, Brigid is a figure shrouded in mystery and legend, and impossible to trace with any certainty. Indeed some doubt her existence at all; others see her legend as a way of Christianizing the pagan goddess Brig.

Details of her life that can be gleaned with some certainty show that she was born into a peasant family in Dundalk, and became a nun at an early age. Legend states that her parents were baptized by Patrick.

Brigid was greatly honoured in Ireland, as a second Mary, from the sixth century onwards, and is second only to Patrick in terms of popularity and in the number of churches consecrated in her honour. Her cult spread rapidly throughout the Middle Ages, when many different versions of her 'life' were recorded, each including stories of miraculous events surrounding her and of her compassion.

Her legend is found throughout medieval Irish literature:

> It is she that helps everyone who is in danger:
> It is she that abateth the pestilences:
> It is she that quelleth the rage and storm of the sea.
> She is the Queen of the south:
> She is the Mary of the Gael.
>
> *Book of Lismore, c.1200*

Anskar, Archbishop of Hamburg, Missionary in Denmark and Sweden, 865

Anskar, originally from Amiens, was educated as a monk at Corbie (Picardy), before moving to Corvey in Westphalia (North West Germany). After a period of travel he eventually settled in Denmark where King Harold had recently become Christian. Under the authority of Harold, Anskar worked to evangelize the Danes. His efforts also took in the surrounding countries and he travelled to Sweden where he was responsible for building the first church, and to North Germany.

In 832 Anskar was appointed Bishop of Hamburg by Pope Gregory IV and in 848 was consecrated Archbishop of Bremen and Hamburg. By 854 he had returned to Denmark and was influential in the conversion of Erik, King of Jutland.

Anskar is an example of persistence in often discouraging circumstances. The areas in which he worked were heavily pagan and highly resistant to the gospel. His successes were infrequent, and often short lived. In 845 all the gains that he had made for the gospel in Scandinavia were lost as that region was attacked by northern invaders and pagan beliefs and practices were re-established. His greatest impact was in the north of Germany and Denmark, and these were the only areas that remained Christian after his death.

Throughout his ministry Anskar established schools and preached on the necessity to care for the poor. He was praised for his commitment to equality in society and worked hard to reduce the influence and practice of the slave trade. His personal devotional practice of saying prayers after reading a Psalm became widely imitated.

4 February

Gilbert of Sempringham, Founder of the Gilbertine Order, 1189

Gilbert was born at Sempringham (Lincolnshire). His father, Jocelin, was a wealthy Norman knight, his mother an Englishwoman of humble rank. Gilbert studied in France, eventually returning to England to work as a teacher near to his place of birth. His father, who had churches on his land, appointed him vicar, although he was not an ordained priest. However, Gilbert received the support of the Bishop of Lincoln and he became a member of the bishop's household. In 1123 the new Bishop of Lincoln ordained him priest.

Gilbert was offered the Archdeaconry of Lincoln, but he refused, saying that he knew no surer way to perdition. On the death of his father he returned to Sempringham and became Lord of the Manor. However, his newfound position in society did not change his austere lifestyle and he continued to give much of his income away.

It was at Sempringham that he renewed his acquaintance with a group of seven women, whom he knew from his earlier teaching career. They desired to live a life of devotion to God, but they were unable to form a monastery on their own. Gilbert presented the women with a 'rule of life' largely based on the Rule of St Benedict, and emphasized seclusion and solitude. Through the patronage of Gilbert the group received the support of the Bishop of Lincoln, and grew rapidly.

This growth required good government, and Gilbert applied to the Cistercians for oversight. Although his request was denied, the order grew rapidly and for two years he was continually founding new communities and houses. Thirteen houses were founded in Gilbert's life, four of which were for men only. There were approximately 1,500 members of his order at its height.

The Gilbertines were the only purely English monastic order and owed allegiance to no foreign superiors, unlike the Cluniacs and Cistercians. This brought them much support and financial assistance from the Crown. By the time of the Dissolution of the Monasteries in 1536 there were 26 communities throughout England.

Gilbert was a supporter of Thomas Becket, the Archbishop of Canterbury (see 29 December) and helped him escape from the king to the Continent after the Council at Northampton in 1164. Thomas, dressed as a Gilbertine monk, spent time in their houses before crossing the sea. Gilbert was summoned before the king to explain his actions, but obtained pardon and immunity for himself and his order.

The Martyrs of Japan, 1597

In 1854 the American naval Commodore Matthew Perry was received by the new Japanese government of the reforming Meiji dynasty which was beginning the process of opening up that previously closed land to Western trade and influence. Yet among the people of this overwhelmingly Shinto and Buddhist nation Perry was surprised to find a small number of persecuted Japanese Christians who had survived underground, without Bibles or clergy for centuries, and, though somewhat hazy in their understanding of Christian doctrine, had a firm faith in Jesus as Lord.

The Christian faith had been introduced into Japan three hundred years earlier by Jesuit and later by Franciscan missionaries who first arrived in Japan with the Portuguese in 1543. The Jesuit priest Francis Xavier (see 3 December) landed at Kagoshima in 1549. He studied the Japanese language for a year and then preached in many of the principal cities. By 1551, when he left Japan, he had established a vigorous Christian community and laid the foundation for the future Christian Church in Japan.

Initially the mission progressed: the first baptism was in 1563 and the first church was built in Kyoto in 1576, but the first decree banishing the propagation of Christianity followed in 1587. Nevertheless, for ten years Christian missionaries experienced a form of relative toleration and by the end of the sixteenth century there were probably about 300,000 baptized believers in Japan. But after the arrival of Spanish Franciscan and Dominican priests at the beginning of the 1590s quarrels broke out between the different orders and between Spanish and Portuguese nationals. On 5 February 1597, 6 Franciscan friars and 20 of their converts were executed at Nagasaki, becoming the first martyrs in Japan. They were tied to crosses in a parody of the crucifixion and speared to death. But in spite of local persecutions, the mission continued to expand. After a short interval of relative tolerance, many other Christians were arrested, imprisoned for life, or tortured and killed; in 1614 an effective edict of persecution was issued and by 1630 the Church was totally driven underground. A peasant uprising under Christian leadership in Kyushu in 1637/38 was suppressed and, as a result of it, the government closed the country to European traders as well as to Christian missionaries. Contact with the West was strictly controlled and persecution of Christians continued until Commodore Perry's arrival in 1854.

10 February

Scholastica, sister of Benedict, Abbess of Plombariola, c.543

Scholastica, whose name means 'learned woman', was the sister of Benedict, the founder of the Benedictine order. Gregory the Great tells us that Scholastica was consecrated to God from childhood, and that she established, and then led, an ascetic community that followed the Benedictine rule of life in Plombariola. The community was five miles away from the Benedictine community in Monte Cassino, which was led by her brother. We are also told by Gregory that it was Scholastica's practice to make an annual journey to a cottage just outside her brother's monastery at Monte Cassino where she would consult with him concerning spiritual matters and prayer.

Such scant evidence for her life has led to speculation about her existence at all. The first record of her life is found in the work of Gregory the Great (c.593), and is only brief. Gregory mentions the emotional last meeting between brother and sister, in which Benedict is prevented from returning to his monastery at nightfall by Scholastica praying for a storm to arise. Their last night together was then spent discussing heaven, before Benedict left the following morning. Scholastica died three days later, and Benedict is reported to have witnessed her soul rising to heaven in the form of a dove.

14 February

Cyril and Methodius, Missionaries to the Slavs, 869 and 885

Cyril and Methodius were brothers. They were born in Thessalonica (in 826 and 815 respectively) to a wealthy family.

Methodius, the elder brother, was initially governor in a Slav province of the Roman Empire, until he became a monk on Mount Olympus in Asia Minor.

Cyril, whose pre-monastic name was Constantine, studied in Constantinople and became a lecturer in philosophy and a librarian.

In 863 the Moravian ruler Rostislav requested some Christian teachers who could conduct services and teach in the Slavonic tongue for Moravia. Emperor Michael III sent Constantine and Methodius.

The Slavonic language had not yet been written down or recorded, and to help the Slavs teach and worship in their own language Constantine created an alphabet, which he called Glagothic and which eventually became the Cyrillic alphabet. The brothers used this written language to teach in Slavonic and they also translated much of the Liturgy and the Gospels to this form. Through their teaching the Slavonic language was widely spread and Constantine in particular became known as the 'Father of Slavonic Literature'. Slavonic eventually became the language of the Liturgy in the Russian Church.

During the brothers' time in Moravia missionaries from the German Church treated them with disdain and quickly grew to dislike the use of the new written Slavonic language in church services. They believed that the official languages of the Church should only be Hebrew, Latin and Greek. Constantine and Methodius were recalled to Rome to explain their actions and after examination by Adrian II were pronounced legitimate and orthodox, and consecrated as bishops. Constantine took monastic vows and the name of Cyril. Shortly after his consecration as bishop in 869, Cyril died and was buried in the Church of San Clemente in Rome.

Methodius returned to Moravia as Archbishop of the newly formed Archdiocese of Rastislav and Svatropluk. He was opposed by bishops from the German Church and due to their influence was imprisoned for two years. After his liberation Methodius continued to conduct church services in Slavonic. He was hounded by those who wanted to use only Latin in the Church and he was the subject of many false rumours and plots.

Both Cyril and Methodius are honoured and remembered as men who pioneered the use of the vernacular language in church services, and whose work had a great influence upon the emerging Church in ninth-century Russia.

14 February

Valentine, Martyr at Rome, c.269

The commemoration and celebration of Valentine has nothing to do with lovers, doves or Roman courting rituals. However, it has much to do with two separate people both called Valentine, two separate basilicas and a single road – the Flaminian Way.

Valentine of Terni was a bishop in the third century who was taken to Rome and martyred in 273. His remains were taken back to Terni for his burial. An eighth-century basilica named after him is found on the Flaminian Way, a road linking Rome and Terni.

Valentine of Rome was a priest who was also martyred in the middle of the third century but under the authority of Claudius II. His death occurred on the Flaminian Way. A basilica bearing his name is also found on this road. This basilica was completed by Pope Theodosius between 642 and 649.

The two stories have understandably become confused over time, and whereas some have even suggested that the two Valentines are in fact one person, one source even suggests that three individuals may have been conflated. There has been much speculation and misunderstanding surrounding these martyrs. Indeed, *Common Worship*'s choice of 'c.269' as the date of death is at best highly speculative since the Valentine commemorated today is most probably Valentine of Terni. The two events have become in effect one commemoration amidst confusion caused by the paucity of historical information.

Although few facts can be gleaned for either Valentine, it can be said that truth exists in both stories. Both Valentines serve as a reminder of the difficulty of living as a Christian in an era of persecution.

The present-day 'retail custom' of sending cards and flowers declaring love only clouds the commemoration and may owe its existence to John Donne (see 31 March). Donne wrote a marriage song for Princess Elizabeth, the daughter of James I who married Frederick V, Elector Palatine on St Valentine's Day in 1632. His marriage song merged the religious commemoration of Valentine with fertility symbolism. The spring mating rituals of birds and possibly the pagan Lupercalia festival also add flavour to the reasons behind the current celebration of the day.

15 February

Sigfrid, Bishop, Apostle of Sweden, 1045

Sigfrid was an Englishman who became known as the Apostle of Sweden.

Along with three of his nephews, Unaman, Sunaman and Vinaman, Sigfrid was sent to King Olaf of Norway by the English King Ethelred in 995. Olaf had converted to Christianity whilst living in England during a period of exile from Sweden and on his return had requested the help of the English king in his attempt to bring Christianity to his household and country. It was the intention of Ethelred that Sigfrid would not only work for the conversion of Norway, but of Sweden too.

On arriving in Sweden Sigfrid built a church at Vaxjo. He consecrated his nephews as bishops, and left to evangelize Sweden.

Whilst he was away, his nephews were murdered, and the church burnt to the ground. Those responsible for their deaths were caught, but when Sigfrid returned to Vaxjo he pleaded with the king that they should not be killed as punishment. King Olaf agreed to his request, and instead ordered that a large fine be paid. Sigfrid refused to accept any of this money, preferring to rebuild the church without it.

Sigfrid died in 1045 in Vaxjo after a ministry in Sweden, Norway and Denmark. Tradition has ascribed many stories of miracles to Sigfrid, some apparently used dubiously to frighten pagan tribes into accepting Christianity. The history of the spread of the gospel throughout Sweden, Norway and Denmark is difficult to ascertain with any degree of accuracy or impartiality. However, what is not in doubt is the efforts of Sigfrid to bring Christianity to a region in which governments and royalty were constantly changing and battles for supremacy were the norm.

15 February

Thomas Bray, Priest, Founder of the SPCK and the SPG, 1730

Born 1656 at Marton in Shropshire, Thomas Bray went from Oswestry Grammar School to All Souls College, Oxford, probably as a clerk or chorister – a recognized route for those from poor homes to gain a degree. He was ordained in 1681, quickly coming to the notice of influential patrons, and in 1690 was presented to the living of Sheldon, in Warwickshire.

By now a widower with two small children, he busied himself with a detailed teaching syllabus for the children and youth of his parish and in 1696 wrote and published a four-volume work on the Catechism. This filled a real need in the Church and brought Bray to the attention of Henry Compton, Bishop of London, who commissioned him to report on the condition of the Church in the colony of Maryland.

It was in investigating the needs of the colonial Church that Bray became aware of the chronic difficulty in accessing books which was restricting Christian teaching and making clergy reluctant to offer to serve in the colony. Consequently he hit upon the idea of providing both books and whole libraries for the benefit of the colonial clergy. This led to the foundation of the Society for Promoting Christian Knowledge in 1698, though SPCK quickly developed a dual focus both overseas and in Britain, as it sought 'to dispense, both at home and abroad, Bibles and tracts of religion; and in general to advance the honour of God and the good of mankind by promoting Christian knowledge'. The SPCK began commissioning tracts and pamphlets, something it has continued ever since, making it the third oldest publishing house still operating in England today. The Society's work in providing Welsh-language literature was a major contributory factor in kick-starting the evangelical revival of the eighteenth century.

In order to further the work overseas Bray and his associates also founded, in 1701, the Society for the Propagation of the Gospel (SPG). This was the Church of England's first overseas missionary society and had the twin objects of providing for the spiritual needs of Britons overseas and evangelizing those non-Christian races in territories subject to the Crown.

In 1708 Bray became Vicar of St Botolph, Aldgate, in the City of London, and until his death in 1730 continued to promote his vision of advancing Christianity through the power of the printed word.

Janani Luwum, Archbishop of Uganda, Martyr, 1977

Born into a poor Christian family at Acholi in 1922, Luwum spent his youth as a goatherd, but gave this up when the opportunity arose to train as a teacher at Boroboro. Undergoing a conversion experience in 1948, he left teaching to study for the ministry at the new Buwalasi Theological College. He was ordained in 1955 and served as a parish priest for three years. He studied further in England at the London College of Divinity, and returned to Buwalasi as Principal for two years. In 1969 he was consecrated Bishop of northern Uganda. Five years later he became Archbishop of Uganda, Rwanda, Burundi and Bogo-Zaire. But primatial authority was to bring him into open confrontation with an anti-Christian state bent on destroying the Church.

In 1971, three years before Luwum became archbishop, the government of Milton Obote had been overthrown by the Ugandan army under General Idi Amin. Amin initiated a policy of repression which soon escalated into a reign of terror. In an example of what would become known in the 1990s as 'ethnic cleansing', over 50,000 Asians were expelled from Uganda and troops from tribes hostile to Amin's own were summarily shot. Amin, a Muslim, sought to convert to Islam by force and terror a population with one of the largest percentages of Christians (about 70 per cent) in Africa.

Early in 1977, a small revolt in the army was put down with few fatalities. But the increasingly paranoid Amin determined to stamp out all traces of dissent. His men killed thousands, including the entire population of former President Obote's home village. One bishop, Festo Kivengere, addressing a congregation including many government officials, accused the government of abusing the authority that God had entrusted to it. Amin responded by ordering a night-time raid on the archbishop's home, on the pretext of searching for hidden weapons. Showing considerable bravery, Luwum visited Amin to deliver personally a note of protest from the bishops at the arbitrary killings and the disappearances of many, particularly Christians. He never returned from the presidential palace and was later found dead, together with two Christian cabinet ministers, the three having ostensibly died in a car crash. Few in Uganda or abroad doubted that he had been murdered on the dictator's orders.

23 February

Polycarp, Bishop of Smyrna, Martyr, c.155

When Polycarp was 86 years old, he was bound, slain by the sword, and his body burnt in the arena at Smyrna, in front of a crowd baying for his blood. He was one of the first Christian martyrs and, according to his own account, had been a believer since childhood. His words at his trial, when he was asked to swear against God, have echoed down through the centuries as a testimony of one man's obedience to Christ:

> For eighty-six years I have been his servant and he has never done
> me wrong; how can I blaspheme my King, who saved me?

Originally one of the disciples of John, Polycarp is a link between the apostles and the earliest Church Fathers. Accounts of his martyrdom were circulated from very soon after his death and give witness to the Early Church tradition of venerating martyrs and saints.

As one of the first bishops of Roman Asia, he tried to set a date for celebrating Easter with Anicetus, Bishop of Rome, but they failed to agree a compromise between their two traditions. The Church at Rome always celebrated Easter on a Sunday, but in Asia it was celebrated according to the Hebrew calendar, on whichever day of the week it fell. This had been a burning issue within the Early Church, and remained so for a long time. However, a mark of the esteem in which Polycarp was held can be seen in that he presided at the celebration of the Eucharist at Rome at the end of the discussions.

Polycarp is also remembered for the way in which he defended Christianity against early attacks, particularly by the Gnostics who sought to dilute the Church's understanding of the nature and person of Christ. Much of his writing is concerned with correcting heretical ideas of the Incarnation, particularly those of Marcion. On one occasion when Polycarp was asked if he recognized Marcion in a room, he replied 'Of course; I recognize the first born of Satan.'

Polycarp is remembered as an example of humility under persecution, and as a man who showed true Christlike character throughout his life. In his letters he exhorts the Church to pray for those that persecute them, and are in authority over them:

> Pray also for kings and powers and rulers, and for them that
> persecute you and hate you, and for the enemies of the cross,
> that your fruit may be manifest unto all, that you may be perfect in him.

27 February

George Herbert, Priest, Poet, 1633

Born at Montgomery in Wales in1593, George Herbert was educated at Westminster School and Trinity College, Cambridge. His original intention was to enter the Anglican ministry but this was overwhelmed by academic achievement and easy entry into the world of politics. He was elected a Fellow of Trinity and in 1618 he was appointed Reader in Rhetoric at Cambridge. Then in 1620 he was elected Public Orator of the university. In 1624 Herbert was elected to Parliament as MP for Montgomery. This brought him to the attention of King James I, who granted him an annual allowance and seemed likely to make him an ambassador. However, in 1625 the king died and Herbert, resolving to 'lose himself *in an humble way*' turned back from worldly ambition to his long-delayed vocation to ministry. Ordained deacon in 1626, he was priested four years later when he was presented to the living of Bemerton near Salisbury.

Though Herbert was suffering from tuberculosis and only lived for a further three years, he threw himself with vigour into the life of his parish, where he became known as 'Holy Mr. Herbert' because of his spiritual, pastoral and liturgical diligence. His book, *A Priest to the Temple, or the Country Parson,* was an attempt to share his insights of rural ministry with others. But privately he was a prolific writer of poetry and left his poems to his friend Nicholas Ferrar, to publish if he thought them suitable.

They appeared as *The Temple* in 1633. Herbert's poems, characterized by a precision of language and written as if to be read aloud, explore and celebrate the ways of God's love as he had discovered them from personal experience. Herbert was an unambiguously Christian and, some would say, a quintessentially Anglican poet. He wrote no secular verse and his poems are personal and intimate without being sickly, often revealing his own spiritual struggles and the strength and solace he found in the practical work of ministry.

Several of his poems, such as *Let all the world in every corner sing*, *Teach me, my God and King* and *King of glory, King of peace*, were later set to music and remain popular as hymns today. One example of his use of biblical themes in his poetry is *Redemption*:

> Having been tenant long to a rich Lord,
> Not thriving, I resolved to be bold,
> And make a suit unto him, to afford
> A new small-rented lease, and cancell th'old.
> In heaven at his manour I him sought
> They told me there, that he was lately gone
> About some land, which he had dearly bought

Long since on earth, to take possession.
I straight returned, and knowing his great birth
Sought him accordingly in great resorts;
In cities, theatres, gardens, parks, and courts:
At length I heard a ragged noise and mirth
Of theeves and murderers: there I him espied
Who straight, *Your suit is granted* said, & died.

1 March

David, Bishop of Menevia, Patron of Wales, c.601

Evidence concerning David (Dewi) dates from the late eleventh century and refers to his father being a chieftain from Ceredigion and his mother being St Non.

Facts concerning his life are few, but legends abound and it is virtually impossible to disentangle them. One of the few certain facts concerns his presence at the Synod of Brefi in 560, although the account of the eloquent speech he gave is in all probability fiction. The village of Llanddewi Brefi in Ceredigion still boasts the earth mound which was said to have miraculously risen beneath David's feet in order to make him more visible and audible as he denounced the Pelagian heresy. David became Patron Saint of Wales in the twelfth century. He was a representative of the Celtic Christian tradition, generally a non-hierarchical movement, with a distinct spirituality, whose bishops had freedom to roam across borders.

It is probable that the account of his life written by Bishop Rhygyfarch in the eleventh century was designed to support claims for the independence of Welsh bishops from the control of the Archbishop of Canterbury. According to this account of his life David was educated at Hen Vynyw (possibly modern Aberaeron) and studied under Paulinus. He founded up to ten monasteries which followed Egyptian monastic tradition involving a very rigorous regime. The monasteries were highly influential on both Welsh and Irish monasticism. David devoted himself to mercy and acts of charity, and was recorded as taking cold baths and eating only bread and water.

He became Bishop of Menevia – legend says that he was consecrated in Jerusalem while on pilgrimage – which later was re-named after him as St David's. He died in 601.

The commemoration of David is a reminder of the contribution of the Celtic tradition to the heritage of the Church, a tradition which has often been overshadowed by a historical bias to Rome, and a greater wealth of written material surviving from Canterbury.

Chad, Bishop of Lichfield, Missionary, 672

Chad was a pupil of Aidan (see 31 August), who had established Christianity within Northumbria during the reign of King Oswald (634–42). Chad spent some time at the monastery of Lindisfarne, where, along with his brother Cedd (see 26 October), he was taught by Aidan. He also spent some time in Ireland as part of his education.

In 664 he succeeded his brother as Abbot of Lastingham in the North York Moors. Later that same year King Oswy of Northumbria decided to consecrate Chad as his bishop. This was a somewhat irregular move, as the only reason for his consecration was Oswy's impatience. The designated Bishop of Northumbria, Wilfrid (see 12 October), had travelled to France to be consecrated but was an exceptionally long time returning. Eventually Oswy tired of the delay and consecrated Chad bishop in a ceremony under the authority of the Celtic bishops, rather than those of the newer Roman tradition.

On his eventual return to Northumbria, Wilfrid discovered that his original nominator (Oswy's deputy) had died, and that another bishop had been consecrated in his place. To his credit, Wilfrid made no attempt to regain his position, but when Archbishop Theodore (see 19 September) visited the region in 669 and remarked upon the irregularity of the situation Chad voluntarily gave up his position and returned to Lastingham. Impressed by the humility of Chad, Theodore made him Bishop of Mercia. He repeated the entire consecration ceremony, as he considered the first ceremony invalid because of the overwhelming presence of Celtic bishops.

Chad fixed his residence at Lichfield, and led the diocese for two years. He travelled widely and established a monastery at Barrow, Lincolnshire. He oversaw the formation of Lichfield as an ecclesiastical centre before his death from the plague in 672.

Perpetua, Felicity and their Companions, Martyrs at Carthage, 203

Perpetua, Felicity and their companions are witnesses to the passion and suffering of the early African Church. North Africa frequently suffered sustained and vicious persecution throughout the Early Church period. The persecution in 203 was instigated by Septimius Severus.

Perpetua was a lady of some wealth and Felicity was her slave. Along with their three male companions they were catechumens (those undergoing preparation for baptism) when they were arrested and placed under guard in a private house. Perpetua was 22, married, and had borne a child just months before she was arrested. Felicity gave birth whilst in prison.

The account of their martyrdom is notable for the fact that it concentrates upon the women in the group and the visions and ecstasy received by the martyrs. It is one of the most beautiful and interesting pieces of ancient literature. Most of the account is taken from Perpetua's own diary, making this the earliest known example of Christian writing by a woman. The story is then completed by an observer, most probably Tertullian. The account of their martyrdom quickly became an example to the wider Church, and for a time was held in equal honour with the Book of Acts.

At her hearing Perpetua refused to offer the sacrifice to the Emperor. Her diary says:

> Hilarianus the governor . . . said to me 'Have pity on your father's grey head; have pity on your infant son. Offer the sacrifice for the welfare of the emperors.'
>
> 'I will not' I retorted.
>
> 'Are you a Christian?' said Hilarianus.
>
> And I said 'Yes I am'.

Perpetua and Felicity were lauded not only because of their suffering, but because of the visions that were revealed to them whilst in prison, and the ecstasy and fortitude that was shown on the occasion of their death. Perpetua, after being mauled in the amphitheatre, was reported to have been so wrapped up in heavenly joy that she had no knowledge of being attacked by the beasts.

Those, including Perpetua and Felicity, who had survived the lions, were then put to death by the sword, with Perpetua being recorded as guiding the point of the gladiator's knife to her own throat.

Edward King, Bishop of Lincoln, 1910

Born in 1829, the son of a clergyman who later became Archdeacon of Rochester, Edward King had a private education before going up to Oriel College, Oxford in 1848.

Inevitably he was influenced by the then fashionable Tractarianism and also by Charles Marriott, Newman's successor as Vicar of St Mary's, who set an example of prayer, pastoral care and practical concern for the poor that was to greatly influence the young King who came to see the moral and pastoral aspects of ministry as higher gifts than the intellectual and doctrinal ones.

King was ordained in 1854 and became curate of Wheatley, an Oxfordshire village. Four years later he moved to Cuddesdon Theological College as chaplain and his personal qualities quickly commended themselves to Bishop Wilberforce of Oxford. Consequently, despite his lack of academic pretensions (he had only managed a pass degree at Oriel) he was appointed Principal of Cuddesdon in 1863 and then Regius Professor of Pastoral Theology at Oxford ten years later.

Although King was an unambiguous High Churchman, he was never a Ritualist – ceremonial matters took a backseat to pastoral care and his deeply spiritual and loving manner made friends of those who would otherwise have disagreed with him on purely theological and ecclesiological matters. In 1885, when he was appointed Bishop of Lincoln, his response was 'I shall try to be the bishop of the poor. If I can feel that, I think I shall be happy.' Indeed, his episcopate was a model of inspiring prayerful and pastoral concern taking him from regular parochial visitations to the death cells of Lincoln Prison.

King was an early exponent of the practice, subsequently adopted by most modern bishops, of fitting in with local tradition when visiting a parish, rather than simply imposing his own preferences. It was therefore doubly ironic that this most saintly and eirenic of bishops, who was loved by those of all shades of churchmanship in his diocese, should be prosecuted by the ultra-Protestant Church Association in 1888 through showing consideration for the local tradition at St Peter-at-Gowts in Lincoln. King accepted Archbishop Benson's 'Lincoln Judgement' in 1890 and, though it was largely in his favour, he carefully refrained thereafter from those liturgical practices where the ruling went against him.

Subsequently described by Archbishop Cosmo Lang as 'the most saintly of men and the most human of saints', King remained at Lincoln until his death in 1910.

8 March

Felix, Bishop, Apostle to the East Angles, 647

Felix originated from Burgundy, and it was there that he met, and converted, the exiled East Anglian Prince Sigeberht. When Sigeberht, now a Christian ruler, returned to East Anglia as king in 631 Felix followed.

Honorius, Archbishop of Canterbury consecrated Felix as Bishop of Dunwich and apostle to the East Anglians. Under the guidance and authority of the archbishop Felix spent 17 years preaching the gospel in Norfolk, Suffolk and Cambridge. He founded a monastery at Soham, and co-operated with the Irish monk Fursey who also founded a monastery in the region. Felix located the headquarters of his diocese in Dunwich on the Suffolk coast, and his reign brought peace to the region.

Evidence of his influence can still be seen in the name of the town of Felixstowe. Felix is an important witness to the influence of Gaul in the conversion of the Anglo-Saxons to Christianity. His relics are preserved at Ramsey Abbey as Dunwich has since been swallowed up by the sea.

8 March

Geoffrey Studdert Kennedy, Priest, Poet, 1929

Born in a Leeds vicarage in1883, Studdert Kennedy was educated at Leeds Grammar School and, in keeping with his Irish ancestry, took a degree at Trinity College, Dublin. He was ordained in 1908. After curacies at Rugby and Leeds he became Vicar of St Paul's, Worcester in 1914. In August that year Britain entered the Great War and, like many parish clergy, Studdert Kennedy volunteered for service as a military chaplain, serving in France from 1916 to 1919.

He became one of the best known of the Forces' chaplains, earning the nickname of 'Woodbine Willie' from the brand of cigarettes he distributed to the troops to whom he ministered (not so well known was the fact that he simultaneously distributed New Testaments). Noted for his bravery under fire, in 1917 he was awarded the Military Cross after entering 'no man's land' at Messines Ridge to comfort the injured. After the war he became chief missioner for the Industrial Christian Fellowship – a post which he combined with the living of the Wren church of St Edmund, Lombard Street in the City of London. Despite his indifferent health (he suffered from asthma from childhood) he wore himself out addressing meetings and leading missions across the country. He died, aged 45, in 1929.

Studdert Kennedy had the gift of communicating gospel truths to ordinary people who had little time for the Church as an institution. His unorthodox style of ministry and preaching alienated him from some traditional Anglicans, though not King George V, who made him a royal chaplain and made a point of hearing him preach every year.

In his later years he turned to writing and produced several volumes of poetry, usually written in dialect, in an attempt to bring spiritual matters down to earth and to bring before God the sufferings of his people. An example is *Indifference*:

> When Jesus came to Birmingham they simply passed him by,
> They never hurt a hair of him, they only let him die;
> For men had grown more tender, and they would not give him pain,
> They only just passed down the street, and left him in the rain.
> Still Jesus cried, 'Forgive them, for they know not what they do',
> And still it rained the wintry night that drenched him through and through;
> The crowds went home and left the streets without a soul to see,
> And Jesus crouched against a wall and cried for Calvary.

17 March

Patrick, Bishop, Missionary, Patron of Ireland, c.460

Patrick was born in Britain, in the region of Carlisle. The son of a deacon he was brought up a Christian although he was, at best, initially only nominal in his faith.

At the age of 16 he was kidnapped by pirates and forced to work as a shepherd in Ireland. During his captivity Patrick turned to God, eventually escaping his captors and returning to Britain. Details of his escape are sketchy, but it is known that he travelled 200 miles from his place of captivity to a seaport. The adventures and escapades of his journey home honed his reliance upon God, and when he finally returned to his family he felt that he should become a priest, and began a period of training that was to last for several years.

According to tradition, some years later in 431 Patrick, newly consecrated bishop, returned to Ireland. He devoted himself to evangelism, reconciliation amongst local chieftains, and the training of monks and nuns. He made frequent journeys throughout Ireland, and significantly influenced the island for Christ, laying the foundation for the Church for the years ahead.

At some point in his life Patrick was the subject of a vitriolic attack on his character. In response he wrote the *Confessions* – his personal account of his life. Patrick contrasted himself with learned and powerful men more concerned with political survival than in preaching the gospel. He is revealed as a man who experienced grace in a powerful way, and who chose to evangelize an unreached land in preference to Britain, whilst still remaining attached to his roots as a Romanized Celt, and thus to the Christians of Roman Gaul. Patrick is remembered as a man who trusted God against the odds.

I arise today
Through a mighty strength, the invocation of the Trinity,
Through belief in the threeness,
Through confession of the oneness
Of the Creator of Creation.

I arise today
Through God's strength to pilot me:
God's might to uphold me,
God's wisdom to guide me,
God's eye to look before me,
God's ear to hear me,
God's word to speak to me,
God's hand to guard me,
God's way to lie before me,
God's shield to protect me,
God's host to save me.

Lorica (or 'Breastplate')
attributed to Patrick, prob. c.8th century

18 March

Cyril, Bishop of Jerusalem, Teacher of the Faith, 386

A native of Jerusalem, Cyril was born in 315. Ordained priest in 348, he was soon consecrated as Bishop of Jerusalem in preference to Heraclius, his predecessor Maximus' designated successor. His period as bishop was turbulent and difficult. Cyril tried to establish his diocese's freedom from the control of Caesarea, and as a consequence found himself out of favour with the Bishop of Caesarea, Acacius. He was exiled three times, in 357, 360 and 367. In total he spent 16 years of his 35 years as bishop in exile.

Much of Cyril's exile was on account of his theological beliefs (which clashed with that of Acacius) and the lack of trust he showed in the ability of language to adequately convey doctrine. It has been said that he was probably always orthodox in thought, if not in language!

In the argument concerning the divinity of Christ, Cyril initially agreed with those who said that Christ was 'of a like nature' with God. He was suspicious of the influence of what he considered vague terminology in discussions about the presence of the divinity in Christ. Such disagreements in terminology led to misunderstandings and mistrust between Acacius of Caesarea and Cyril. Their relationship was fraught with theological rivalry and tension, and Acacius was instrumental in the councils that sent Cyril into exile. Cyril was ultimately reinstated to full episcopal duties in 378, and took part in the Second Ecumenical Council at Constantinople in 381.

Cyril was a teacher, and was in charge of teaching those in preparation for baptism at Jerusalem. Indeed, it may have been his desire to communicate the Christian faith effectively and accurately that led him into doctrinal controversy. Cyril was seeking precision, in an age where diverse opinion was the norm.

Cyril was not only active in theological debate and teaching. He was known as a protector of the poor, who willingly sold church property (property that had often been bequeathed by emperors and their families) and used the money gained to feed the poor. These actions were held against him on more than one occasion.

Many of Cyril's sermons and lectures have survived, and they reveal much about the life and teaching of the Early Church. He is remembered as a teacher of the Church, and as one who, although orthodox in thought, sought clarification of doctrine. He is an early example of those Christian leaders whose lot was often to be misunderstood because of the questions that he asked rather than the answers that he gave.

An excerpt from one of his lectures illustrates his teaching skill and his drive for precision:

> And why did He call the grace of the Spirit water? Because by water all things subsist; because water brings forth grass and living things; because the water of the showers comes down from heaven; because it comes down one in form, but works in many forms ... Thus also the Holy Spirit, being one, and of one nature, and indivisible, divides to each His grace, according as He will: and as the dry tree, after partaking of water, puts forth shoots, so also the soul in sin, when it has been through repentance made worthy of the Holy Spirit, brings forth clusters of righteousness.
>
> *Catechetical Lectures XVI*

Cuthbert, Bishop of Lindisfarne, Missionary, 687

Cuthbert was born about 635, either in Northumberland or the Scottish borders where he was a shepherd in his youth. In the year 651, while watching over his sheep, he is said to have had a vision, but for whatever reason he entered the religious life as a monk at Melrose Abbey. At Melrose Cuthbert soon became eminent for his holiness and learning and was greatly involved in mission work in Galloway. After ten years at Melrose a new monastery was founded at Ripon and Cuthbert was sent there to be the guest-master, but these were the years of disagreement between the Celtic and Roman traditions of Christianity (the date of Easter was one of the most contentious points at issue) and in 661, when Ripon adopted the Roman usage, Cuthbert and other monks who favoured the Celtic usage returned to Melrose. Shortly after his return he became prior.

In 664 the Synod of Whitby decided in favour of the Roman usage and committed the English Church to following the customs that had been introduced by Augustine. Cuthbert, who accepted the decision, was sent to be prior at Lindisfarne, in order that he might introduce the Roman customs into that house. This was a difficult matter which needed all his gentle tact and patience to carry out successfully, but he was able to minimize contention over the decision and the community remained united.

But Cuthbert felt a call to the solitary life and in 676, coveting a life of prayer and contemplation, he retired, with the abbot's permission, to a hermitage, first on the mainland (possibly near Howburn) then on Inner Farne, one of a small group of islands offshore from Bamburgh in Northumberland, where he gave himself up to a life of great austerity. Cuthbert was noted for the remarkable rapport he had with animals, both wild and domestic. Appropriately the island is today a bird sanctuary. In 684 he was elected Bishop of Hexham but refused to accept the post. The following year, however, he was he was elected Bishop of Lindisfarne, a post which he was eventually persuaded to accept. His brief episcopate of two years was marked with continuous missionary work and this almost certainly exhausted him. At Christmas, 686, foreseeing the approach of death, he resigned his see and returned to his cell on Inner Farne, where he died in 687.

Thomas Cranmer, Archbishop of Canterbury, Reformation Martyr, 1556

Born in Aslockton in Nottinghamshire, in1489, Cranmer was educated at Jesus College, Cambridge. He became a Fellow and was ordained in 1523, receiving his doctorate in divinity in 1526.

As a Cambridge don Cranmer came to the king's notice in 1529 when he was investigating ways forward in the matter of the proposed royal divorce. His rise was rapid. He was appointed Archdeacon of Taunton, made a royal chaplain, and given a post in the household of Sir Thomas Boleyn, father of Anne. In 1530 Cranmer accompanied Boleyn on an embassy to Rome and in1532 he himself became ambassador to the court of the Emperor Charles V. His divergence from traditional orthodoxy was already apparent by his marriage to a niece of the Lutheran theologian Osiander despite the rule of clerical celibacy.

Returning to England to become Archbishop of Canterbury, he was in a dangerous position. Henry VIII was fickle and capricious and Cranmer was fortunate to survive where many did not. Yet Henry seemed to have a genuine affection for his honest but hesitant archbishop, even if he did (apparently in jest) describe him as the 'greatest heretic in Kent' in 1543. Four years later Henry died with Cranmer at his bedside and during the brief reign of Edward VI the archbishop now had an opportunity to put into practice his reform of the English Church.

He edited the *Homilies* (1547) and wrote those on salvation, good works, faith, and the reading of Scripture. He compiled the two Prayer Books of 1549 and 1552, and wrote the original 42 Articles of Religion (1552). But the young king's death brought Cranmer's phase of the English Reformation to a premature end. He was imprisoned first in the Tower then in the Bocardo prison in Oxford. Under great physical and mental pressure he several times recanted of his deviations from Roman doctrine. But at the last he re-found his courage and repudiated all his recantations before he was burned at the stake on 21 March 1556.

In later years it would become apparent that the seed Cranmer had sown had taken deep root and his 1552 Prayer Book (as amended in 1559 and 1662) clearly demonstrated his gift for both rhythmical fluency and memorable phrase. It was to become a lasting treasure of the English language and Cranmer's principle of liturgical worship in contemporary English has become a defining element of the Anglican Church.

Walter Hilton of Thurgarton, Augustinian Canon, Mystic, 1396

Born in 1343, Walter was Canon of the Augustinian Priory of Thurgarton, near Nottingham. He studied law at Cambridge, practising both canon law and civil law, before becoming a priest. His writings on mysticism were highly valued in the Middle Ages, although much neglected after the Reformation.

Walter placed his mystical writings within ascetic theology, and saw mysticism as an essential journey for the soul. He presented to his readers the eternal truth of the gospel and the purifying work of the Holy Spirit, but he did so in a way which sought to bring clarity, not confusion.

His *Ladder of Perfection* was the first work of mystical theology in the English language. His efforts to bring mystical theology into everyday English (as opposed to Latin) often led to misunderstandings and confusion. The resulting uncertainty and ambiguity would have been frustrating for him, and Walter frequently attempted to clarify his pronouncements. Walter also wrote for ordinary people who lived 'in the world' but who wanted to dedicate their lives to God. In *The Mixed Life* Walter encouraged the contemplation of the passion of Christ, but recognized the difficulty of such devotion within a busy lifestyle. He suggested limiting time spent both in the contemplation of Christ, and in work, so that the soul may be eager for more of both.

The idea of progress in the spiritual life was a classic ascetic theme, taken by Walter and brought to an everyday level throughout his writings. Walter was not an academic removed from the real world by his books and thought. He wrote for anyone who sought to progress in the spiritual life. Though his world was one of suffering, disease, poverty and corruption his desire was a cleansing of the soul and an experience of grace for all who genuinely desired to move towards God. He stressed the role of the Church, the liturgy and particularly the Eucharist in the journey of the soul. In his writings can be seen a blend of both precision and love, reflecting his twin experiences as lawyer and pastor.

> In like manner, it is said that God is fire. That is to say, God is not elementary fire, that heats and burns a body, but God is love and charity. For as fire wastes all bodily things, that can be wasted, even so the love of God burns and wastes all sin out of the soul and makes it clean, as fire cleans all manner of metals.
>
> *Ladder of Perfection, Bk II part III, Ch. III*

> When a soul is purified by the love of God, illumined by wisdom, and stabilized by the might of God, then the eye of the soul is opened to see spiritual things, as virtues and angels and holy souls, and heavenly things. Then, because it is clean, the soul is able to feel the touching, the speaking of good angels.
>
> *The Angels' Song*

24 March

Oscar Romero, Archbishop of San Salvador, Martyr, 1980

Born in Cuidad Barrios in El Salvador in 1917, Oscar Romero was ordained to the Roman Catholic priesthood in Rome in 1942 before returning home the following year. As a parish priest in the diocese of San Miguel Romero gained a reputation as a hard worker in the traditional priestly mould with a taste for asceticism and a particular devotion to the Blessed Virgin Mary (his birthday was the Feast of the Assumption). Perhaps not surprisingly, after gaining considerable parochial experience he began, in 1967, to rise in the church hierarchy becoming Secretary to the Episcopal Conference of El Salvador. In due course he became Auxiliary Bishop of San Salvador and later Bishop of Santiago de Maria. Much influenced by the conservative Opus Dei movement, he was a staunch opponent of the increasingly popular school of liberation theology.

It was an irony that in an age of liberation theology, Romero was appointed Archbishop of San Salvador in 1977 precisely because of his conservative and traditionalist views and his personal devotion to the papacy. But like Thomas Becket seven hundred years earlier (see 29 December), Romero's new responsibilities made him look afresh at relations between Church and State. He began to see that social unrest and poverty were the result of government repression and the Church was not exempt from the spiral of violence in Salvadorian society. Several priests were murdered and the expulsion of a number of (allegedly Marxist) Jesuits forced Romero to speak out. Right-wing Latin American governments were accustomed to being criticized by parish priests who ministered to the poor and were influenced by liberation theology. But to be criticized by the nation's archbishop was a very different matter.

A convert to liberation theology, Romero condemned violence and championed the right of the poor to economic and social justice. He even went so far as to issue a pastoral letter from the Salvadorian bishops endorsing proportionate counter-violence to the oppressive policies of the right-wing regime. Nevertheless he sought to act as mediator between the rival groups and was nominated for the Nobel Peace Prize.

His achievement was to maintain a balance between extremist groups, receiving death threats from both left- and right-wing paramilitary groups and it was perhaps only a matter of time before he was murdered as he was celebrating Mass on 24 March 1980.

Harriet Monsell, Founder of the Community of St John the Baptist, 1883

Harriet O'Brien was born in 1811 at Dromoland, County Clare, the daughter of an Irish baronet. In 1839 she married Charles Monsell and accompanied him to Oxford where he studied for ordination. Inevitably, both were influenced by the spirituality and practice of the Oxford Movement. They returned to Ireland when Charles became Prebendary of Aghadoe near Limerick. But he was found to be suffering from tuberculosis and the couple spent four years in the warm climate of Naples before Charles died in 1851. Before the funeral service Harriet knelt by her husband's coffin and dedicated herself to God's service, a dedication she renewed each subsequent year on 30 January.

But how best to serve God was the problem. Opportunities for women were very limited in 1851. Returning to England she was put in touch with Canon T. T. Carter, Rector of Clewer near Windsor. He had founded a 'house of mercy' for former prostitutes, single mothers and other vulnerable women in his parish and was now in need of someone to take charge. Initially on a temporary basis Harriet offered her help but soon she knew clearly that this was the work to which God was calling her. On Ascension Day 1851 Carter admitted her as a 'Sister of Mercy'. But there was no community until two other women joined her the following year and the secular staff of the house of mercy withdrew, leaving the sisters in sole charge.

Consequently, on St Andrew's Day 1852 the Community of St John the Baptist came into being when Harriet was professed as a Religious in the presence of Bishop Samuel Wilberforce of Oxford and admitted as the first Mother Superior of the order. With Carter as Warden and Harriet as Mother Superior, the work of the order expanded to include orphanages and hospitals, with foundations being established in India and America by the 1880s. The sisters cared for orphans, ran schools and hospitals, and opened mission houses in parishes. The Community of St John the Baptist was a model Victorian Anglican sisterhood, and Harriet a perfect Mother Superior who, it was said, possessed 'strength of character, firmness of faith, an infectious sense of humour, a gift for listening, and a magnetism which none could resist'. Eventually in 1875, she retired as Superior through ill-health, moving to a small hermitage in Folkestone, where she died on Easter Sunday 1883.

31 March

John Donne, Priest, Poet, 1631

John Donne was born into a Roman Catholic family in London in 1572. His father, an ironmonger, died when Donne was four. After periods of study at both Oxford and Cambridge, he came down without a degree and began the study of law at Lincoln's Inn in 1592. About two years later he relinquished the Roman Catholic faith and conformed to the Church of England, possibly in order to qualify for a career in government service. But whatever his motives Donne took his new-found Anglican faith seriously.

In 1596, he joined the naval expedition led by the Earl of Essex against Cadiz in Spain. On his return to England in 1598 he was appointed private secretary to Sir Thomas Egerton, Lord Keeper of the Seal and in 1601 he secretly married Egerton's 16 year-old niece, Anne More. This lost him his job and earned him a short period of imprisonment. But in a few short years he had turned from a debauched and sceptical youth into both a faithful husband and a man of faith. During the next few years Donne made a meagre living as a lawyer. A book he wrote in 1610, encouraging Roman Catholics to take the Oath of Allegiance to the king, brought Donne to the notice of James I who may have suggested that he consider a career in the Church. Certainly, he was appointed as a royal chaplain a few months after his ordination in 1615.

Donne continued to write poetry, but most of it remained unpublished until 1633. In 1617 his wife died, and, in his bereavement, Donne turned fully to his vocation as an ordained minister. From 1621 until his death he was Dean of St Paul's, and with a growing reputation as a preacher, drew large crowds to hear him, both at the Cathedral and at Paul's Cross, the nearby outdoor pulpit.

Largely forgotten by the century after his death, Donne's reputation was restored in the 1920s when Ezra Pound and T. S. Eliot openly acknowledged their literary debt to him. Today, Donne is recognized as one of the greatest of the seventeenth-century 'Metaphysical' poets, many of whom, like George Herbert (see 27 February), were influenced by his work. Unlike George Herbert, however, Donne wrote both sacred and secular poetry. And his main themes of human love and divine love remain ever relevant, as demonstrated in this extract from *Holy Sonnet*:

> Batter my heart three-personed God; for, you
> As yet but knock, breathe, shine and seek to mend;
> . . .
> But I am betrothed unto your enemy,
> Divorce me, untie or break that knot again,
> Take me to you, imprison me, for I
> Except you'enthrall me, shall never be free,
> Nor ever chaste, except you ravish me.

1 April

Frederick Denison Maurice, Priest, Teacher of the Faith, 1872

Born at Normanstone near Lowestoft in 1805, F. D. Maurice was the son of a Unitarian minister. He studied civil law at Cambridge, but in 1827 refused to subscribe to the Thirty-Nine Articles in order to receive his degree. Four years later, however, at the age of 26, a personal crisis, perhaps linked with the terminal illness of his sister, brought home to him his need for a 'personal deliverer' and he was baptized into the Church of England. Yet it was not a text-book evangelical conversion, for his was always a faith with more questions than answers, one that challenged rather than reassured. Yet for Maurice, Christ was clearly present in the questioning and in the striving for certainty.

After a period at Exeter College, Oxford, Maurice was ordained in 1834 to a curacy at Bubbenhall in Warwickshire. Then in 1836 he moved to London as chaplain of Guy's Hospital. Here he gave lectures on moral philosophy and he published his major work, *The Kingdom of Christ*, a discussion of the causes and cures of divisions within the Christian Church. Already he was much concerned with the role of the Church in the social issues that were coming to the fore in nineteenth-century Britain. In 1840 Maurice was elected Professor of English Literature and History at King's College, London, and in 1846 he added the chair of Theology. But trouble came with the publication of his book *Theological Essays* in 1853 in which he attacked the popular understanding of hell as endless punishment. Consequently his orthodoxy was regarded as suspect in some quarters. Maurice put truth before personal advantage and vigorously defended himself. Nevertheless King's College dismissed him from both his professorships.

Maurice was much involved (with John Ludlow and Charles Kingsley) in the foundation of, and the various projects sponsored by, the Christian Socialist Movement, which emerged following the final eclipse of Chartism in 1848. It sought to reform both individuals and society by applying Christian principles to social relationships. One of their projects was the Working Men's College, of which Maurice became the first head.

It has been noted by historians that socialism and trade unionism in England have frequently had Christians in leadership roles and have thus avoided the anti-Christian flavour that has often been apparent in European socialism and trade unionism. But whether the credit for this lies with Maurice or with Methodism is more difficult to determine.

Maurice served as Professor of Moral Theology at Cambridge from 1866 until his death in 1872.

9 April

Dietrich Bonhoeffer, Lutheran Pastor, Martyr, 1945

Bonhoeffer was born at Breslau in Silesia (now the Polish city of Wroclaw) in 1906. The family moved to Berlin in 1912 when his father became Professor of Psychiatry and Neurology at Berlin University. He received his theological education at the universities of Tübingen and Berlin and was greatly influenced by the work of Karl Barth. After serving (1928–9) as an assistant pastor in a German-speaking congregation in Barcelona, and a further year of study at Union Theological Seminary in New York, he became a lecturer in theology in Berlin in 1931.

An outspoken opponent of Adolf Hitler and the Nazis, Bonhoeffer joined the Confessing Church, which had formed in opposition to the infiltration and takeover of the German Lutheran Church by Nazi sympathizers. They sought to be the authentic voice of the gospel in Germany and to oppose attempts to force anti-Semitism on Church and society. Leaving Berlin in protest, he spent two years (1933–5) as pastor of German-speaking congregations in London. While in England he became friendly with Bishop George Bell of Chichester.

Returning to Germany in 1935, Bonhoeffer became director of the Confessing Church seminary at Finkenwald in Pomerania. But this institution quickly incurred the wrath of the Nazi authorities, who closed it down in 1937. Bonhoeffer was in America when war broke out in 1939, but returned to Germany, explaining, 'I shall have no right to participate in the reconstruction of Christian life in Germany after the war if I do not share the trials of this time with my people.' He became involved with the underground anti-Nazi opposition, no small step for a Lutheran accustomed to believe in the God-given nature of the Church–State relationship. In 1942 he attempted to put the German underground in touch with the British government via Bishop Bell. But the net was closing in and he was arrested in April 1943 and imprisoned at Tegel prison in Berlin. The involvement of many of his contacts in the July 1944 plot to kill Hitler may well have sealed his fate, and he was moved several times, finally to Flossenberg concentration camp close to the Czech border.

It was as American troops were approaching the camp in April 1945 that Bonhoeffer was hanged. His writings, and especially his *Letters and Papers from Prison* have been an inspiration to many who have sought to make sense out of persecution and needless suffering.

On New Year's Day 1945 he wrote a poem which included the following verse:

> Should it be ours to drain the cup of grieving
> even to the dregs of pain at thy command,
> we will not falter, thankfully receiving
> all that is given by thy loving hand.

William Law, Priest, Spiritual Writer, 1761

William Law was born at King's Cliffe, Northamptonshire in 1686 and educated at Emmanuel College, Cambridge. He was ordained deacon and became a Fellow of the college in 1711. With the accession to the throne of the Hanoverian George I in 1714 Law refused to take the Oath of Allegiance and so lost his Fellowship. He allied himself with the Nonjurors (who had split from the Church of England in 1689 for refusing to take the Oath of Allegiance to William and Mary) and was eventually ordained priest in 1728. In1727 he became a private tutor for ten years and then retired to his native King's Cliffe. Here he involved himself in the work of schools and almshouses and other charitable works, living in great simplicity as an expression of his faith until his death in 1761.

Law's greatest contribution to English spirituality was by his writing, the titles of his books giving an indication of his concerns: *Christian Perfection*, *The Spirit of Love*, *The Spirit of Prayer*, and *A Serious Call to a Devout and Holy Life*. This last book, published in 1728, quickly became a spiritual classic and is still in print today. Again, the title summarizes the contents: God calls Christians to complete obedience to him in a Christ-centred life.

The immediate influence of the book was considerable and it profoundly influenced many – among them John Wesley, Charles Wesley (see 24 May), George Whitefield, Henry Venn (see 1 July) – who were to be leaders of the evangelical revival. Indeed, John Wesley published extracts from the book in 1744, introducing it to a wider audience. *A Serious Call* is reckoned to have had more influence than any English post-Reformation spiritual work other than *Pilgrim's Progress*:

> If we are to love our enemies, we must make our common life a visible exercise and demonstration of that love. If content and thankfulness, if the patient bearing of evil be duties to God, they are the duties of every day, and every circumstance of our life. If we are to be wise and holy as the new-born sons of God, we can no otherwise be so, but by renouncing everything that is foolish and vain in every part of our common life. If we are to be in Christ new creatures, we must show that we are so, by having new ways of living in the world. If we are to follow Christ, it must be our common way of spending every day.

William of Ockham, Friar, Philosopher, Teacher of the Faith, 1347

William was born at Ockham, near Woking in Surrey in 1285. He entered the Franciscan order, and initially studied and taught at Oxford.

With society becoming more cash-based and the feudal system disintegrating and eroding, William was part of a society that saw little of value in the past, and saw the present as having an authority of its own. This negative approach to the past was to lead him into difficulty with papal authority, whilst his recognition of the role of the present led to him stretching the thought and understanding of both Church and society. He has been called the 'first protestant' for his continual protest against corruption and over-complication of the rules of faith, and for his rejection of a form of authority that gained legitimacy from the past.

William never progressed beyond the 'inceptor' (beginner) level of the Franciscan order, probably because the Chancellor of Oxford University accused him of heresy in 1323. This heresy involved a questioning of the authority of the Pope. The accusations led to William being examined by a papal commission which eventually censured 51 propositions from his works, but did not formally discipline him.

In 1327 a dispute occurred concerning Franciscan poverty. Some Franciscans (known as the Spiritual Franciscans) were seeking to follow the way of absolute poverty as demanded by Francis' rule. This ideal was condemned by Pope John XXII as a heresy. William was summoned to the papal court at Avignon and asked to investigate the matter. He concluded that it was Pope John XXII who had taken a heretical position. As a consequence of his conclusions William was forced to flee from the court, to Bavaria, where he stayed until 1347. Whilst in Bavaria, William wrote several works arguing against the Pope's position on Franciscan poverty. He was never fully reconciled to the Church and he died in Bavaria in 1347.

William was a critical theologian, and an independent thinker, who stretched boundaries and introduced new concepts whilst holding onto the spiritual traditions of the Franciscan order. His thought greatly affected university teaching for a considerable time. His concept of 'Ockham's Razor', that is, the elimination of all hypotheses that are not absolutely essential (or that the simplest explanation is the best) was important for the development of a theory of justification that emphasized the individual person, rather than humankind as a whole. William was undoubtedly the most influential theologian of the fourteenth century.

George Augustus Selwyn, first Bishop of New Zealand, 1878

George Augustus Selwyn was born in Hampshire and educated at Eton and St John's College, Cambridge. He became a Fellow of the college and was ordained in 1833. He served as curacy at Windsor while a private tutor at Eton. In 1841 he was consecrated Bishop of New Zealand and took up his duties the following year. He studied the Maori language on his long sea voyage, and was able to preach in it on his arrival. In fact Selwyn never saw himself as a colonial bishop and in the ten-year war between the Maoris and the European colonists, he managed to keep the confidence of both sides, making sure that the principle of full participation by Maori Christians in church government was affirmed at the New Zealand Church's first general synod in 1859.

Selwyn laid the foundations of the Church, not only in New Zealand, but throughout the islands of Melanesia. The New Zealand diocese extended from latitude 47 degrees South to latitude 36 degrees *North* (a clerical error in the Letters Patent). But Selwyn made no complaint and cheerfully accepted responsibility for the vast Pacific regions of the Melanesian and Polynesian islands as well as New Zealand. From 1848 he visited the islands, first on HMS *Dido*, later on the mission ship *Southern Cross*, from which this fearless exponent of muscular Christianity often swam ashore and made personal contact with the islanders.

A convinced Tractarian, Selwyn experienced difficulties in his relations with the Church Missionary Society in New Zealand. His understanding of episcopacy and mission led him to favour an alternative strategy, that rather than voluntary agencies missions should be an enterprise of the whole Church in its corporate capacity, led by bishops. This model came into increasing use by High Church missions as the century progressed. In 1852 Selwyn had noted in his diary that 'the careful superintendence of this multitude of islands will require the services of a missionary bishop, able and willing to devote himself to this work'. Thus, in 1854, he founded the Melanesian Mission and recruited John Coleridge Patteson to lead it. By 1861 the diocese was ready for division with Selwyn relinquishing authority in Melanesia to Patteson as the new missionary bishop.

In 1867, Selwyn was persuaded to become Bishop of Lichfield. It was with some reluctance that he returned to England the following year, and served at Lichfield until his death on 11 April 1878. Selwyn College was founded in his memory at Cambridge in 1881.

16 April

Isabella Gilmore, Deaconess, 1923

Born in 1842, Isabella was the sister of William Morris, and was brought up in a privileged home on the edge of Epping Forest. In 1860 she married a naval officer, Lt Arthur Gilmore. In 1882 Arthur died suddenly and Isabella, though in no financial need, found herself without a clear purpose in life. Her strong sense of duty led her towards the newly established nursing profession and she entered Guy's Hospital in London in order to train as a nurse.

Unexpectedly, in 1886 she was approached by Bishop Thorold of Rochester to pioneer deaconess work in South London. After much initial reluctance she agreed and together they planned for an order of deaconesses along the same lines as the ordained ministry. Isabella was ordained deaconess in 1887 and took charge of the newly-founded Diocesan Deaconess Institution, first at Park Hill in Clapham then in more spacious premises appropriately named 'The Sisters' (later renamed 'Gilmore House' in her memory) on the North Side of Clapham Common. She later provided out of her own pocket for the building and furnishing of a chapel by Philip Webb.

She served for 19 years as head of the Rochester deaconesses, earning a reputation as a both a strict disciplinarian and a tireless worker with the poor. William Morris said of his sister, 'I preach socialism, you practise it'.

Isabella described the kind of deaconesses she was looking for:

> I want first and foremost women whom the spirit of God has entered into, whose one desire is to live a Christ-like life, not for themselves, not for their own reward, but for the coming of his Kingdom.

While she had nothing against the growth of sisterhoods in the Church of England she was convinced that the deaconess order was entirely different and that the two concepts should not be mixed. She keenly advocated what she called her 'Rochester lines' of deaconess service with no community vows in addition to those taken at ordination (this pattern contrasted with the deaconess sisterhoods of Elizabeth Ferard in North London – see 18 July) and this served to emphasize the ministerial role which she saw as essential to the order of deaconesses. Isabella herself retired in 1906 and moved to Reigate. Here she kept in personal touch with her former trainees all over the world, and had the satisfaction of seeing the deaconess order become an integral part of Anglican ministry. She died at Parkstone at the age of 80.

19 April

Alphege, Archbishop of Canterbury, Martyr, 1012

Alphege was a monk from the monastic community at Deerhurst, and for some years was a hermit near Glastonbury. He became Abbot of Bath before succeeding Ethelwold as Bishop of Winchester in 984. During this time he was known for both his frugal lifestyle and his generosity to others.

The early part of the tenth century was the second major period of Viking raids against England. In 954 King Ethelred the Unready sent Alphege as a peace envoy to the Danes. (Unready does not mean that Ethelred was always unprepared, but rather that he would not accept 'rede' or counsel from his advisers.) This was a mission that was initially successful for both State and Church, bringing peace. In 1006, Alphege became Archbishop of Canterbury.

However, in later years Danish invasions increased, and the south of England was largely overrun by the Vikings. In 1012 Canterbury was surrounded and captured by Vikings who were aided by the treachery of Archdeacon Elfmaer. Alphege was imprisoned and a ransom was demanded for him from his citizens. The sum required was far greater than anything the tenants of the Canterbury estates were able to pay. Alphege, known as a man of justice and charity, refused to allow himself to be ransomed for such a vast sum of money. Infuriated, and in a drunken frenzy, the Danes murdered him, cutting his body to pieces with an axe. As news of his death spread Alphege came to be thought of as a national hero. According to tradition the parish church of St Alfege (sic) in Greenwich was built on the site of his martyrdom.

Alphege is remembered as a martyr because he gave his life standing up for Christian justice. He sought the good of others over that of himself, and forbade others to suffer in order to save him.

21 April

Anselm, Abbot of Le Bec, Archbishop of Canterbury, Teacher of the Faith, 1109

Anselm was an Italian-born Norman monk, who became one of the most important thinkers and writers of the medieval Christian Church.

He was born in Aosta in the far north of Italy in 1033, and, after the death of his mother, suffered at the hands of his father. He left home in 1056 on a journey that led him from Italy to Burgundy and eventually to the monastery of Le Bec in Normandy. The prior of the monastery was Lanfranc (see 28 May), one of the foremost Christian thinkers of the time. Anselm studied under him for ten years, paying great attention to the work of Augustine. Anselm eventually succeeded Lanfranc as prior when he was appointed Archbishop of Canterbury in 1070. Anselm became Abbot of Le Bec in 1078.

After Lanfranc's death Anselm succeeded him once again, becoming Archbishop of Canterbury in 1093. Anselm only reluctantly agreed to take up the position, such was his attachment to the monastery at Le Bec, and such was his distrust of the English King William Rufus. This was with good reason, as William had blocked Anselm's appointment for four years after the death of Lanfranc. Theirs was an ambiguous relationship, and Anselm and William clashed on several matters over the years, most notably over papal authority and jurisdiction. Anselm was unwavering in his support of the Pope, and this was to lead to his exile to Italy in 1097 until the death of the king in 1100, and then again in 1103 under King Henry I. Only papal intervention brought peace and the resulting compromise left the Crown with the responsibility for the selection of bishops, and the Church with responsibility for investiture with the symbols of authority.

Anselm contributed much that was original to Christian thought, especially in the areas of philosophy and spirituality. He made an original contribution to the debate on the nature of the Atonement in *Cur Deus Homo* (*Why God became Man*). His proposal of the 'perfect satisfaction' of God through the cross has been, and still is, extremely significant in the development of Christian thought. His argument for the existence of God (the ontological argument) is still influential. Anselm's original spirituality was evident in his 'Prayers and Meditations' which introduced a new style of devotional literature in which a meditation upon a saint relates both to Christ and to the individual praying.

His writings combine personal and spiritual experience with theological argument. Anselm is honest and clearly wrestles with doubt and anxiety in his work. He left to the world a spirituality in which the painful reality of humanity was balanced by the intense hope of the crucifixion and the self-sacrifice of God. Anselm reveals an intense self-knowledge, and a real awareness of the eternal within the Christian faith.

> O Lord our God,
> grant us grace to desire You with our whole heart;
> that, so desiring, we may seek,
> and, seeking, find You;
> and so finding You, may love You;
> and loving You, may hate those sins
> from which You have redeemed us.
>
> *A Prayer of St Anselm*

23 April

George, Martyr, Patron of England, c.304

George is remembered as a martyr; the details of his life have been lost in time, although fifth-century records attest his existence, and the beginning of his commemoration. In all probability George was a soldier, and a victim of the Diocletian persecutions in Lydda, in Palestine. The known facts of his life state that George, an officer in the Roman Army, 'gave his goods to the poor, and openly confessed Christianity before the court'.

Diocletian was responsible for the most devastating and sustained persecution of the Early Church, from 303 to 304. Only his abdication prevented more permanent damage being sustained by the Church, and many unknown Christians, like George, would have given their lives for the sake of the gospel, and would have been remembered with gratitude from that time onwards.

The more popular stories of the life and death of George can be traced back to the eighth century. The slaying of the dragon is not connected with his name until the twelfth century, and it may be that the origin of this story is the Greek myth of Perseus slaying a sea monster. George's story was included in the 'Golden Legend' (1260), which became a popular source of 'history', and received widespread attention in the Middle Ages.

His popularity as a saint of national identity grew with the Crusades, and he became the patron saint of soldiers. Richard I called upon him for protection before the third Crusade in 1187, and a red cross on a white background became the 'uniform' of his crusaders and, in time, England's national flag. George was personified as the ideal knight. He was made patron of England in preference to Edward the Confessor by Edward II in 1347. Shakespeare added to the reputation of George in 1623, when he 're-created' Henry V's speech before the battle of Agincourt (1415) in which St George is invoked as a powerful ally of king and nation:

> Follow your spirit; and upon this charge,
> Cry, 'God for Harry, England and Saint George!'
>
> *Henry V, Act III, Scene i*

Mellitus, Bishop of London, first Bishop at St Paul's, 624

Mellitus, born of a noble family, was first a monk, and then abbot of a monastic community at Rome. He led the second group of monks sent by Pope Gregory the Great to evangelize Britain in 601. This group was sent to support the work of Augustine of Canterbury, who had been given the responsibility for the mission to the Anglo-Saxons earlier in 597. Mellitus was consecrated by Augustine in 604/5 as the first Bishop of the East Saxons and was based in London.

After an inauspicious start, Augustine's and Mellitus' missionary activity was modified by Gregory the Great. He instructed Mellitus to use the old Saxon temples as places of Christian worship. He was only to cleanse the temples and to remove the Saxon idols, not completely destroy them. As a result the Saxon temples became Christian places of worship, and old Saxon feast days were re-directed towards Christian celebrations. Bede reports that the Pope declared 'If the people are allowed some worldly pleasures ... they will more readily come to desire the joys of the Spirit'. This instruction to Mellitus radically altered missionary endeavour throughout the Saxon regions, and had a profound effect on the spread of the gospel.

At the end of the sixth century Britain was a collection of independent Anglo-Saxon kingdoms – the Heptarchy. The southern parts of Britain were receptive to the particular form of Christianity spread by the Church of Rome. The rest of the country was more responsive to Celtic Christian influence. In spite of their similarities, political emphasis and difficult relationships led to division. Two key areas of Britain, Kent and East Anglia, proved to be a stronghold for the Roman interpretation of Christianity, yet it was with these areas that Mellitus was to encounter difficulty.

In 604 Mellitus was involved in a dispute with new kings of both Kent and the East Saxons who once enthroned ceased practising Roman Christianity and reverted to paganism instead. However, they both still demanded that Mellitus perform the Eucharist for them. This was unacceptable to Mellitus, and he refused. Accordingly he was banished from their kingdoms and he fled to Gaul in 616. He returned in 619 and in the same year became the third Archbishop of Canterbury.

A staunch follower of Roman Christianity, Mellitus attempted to secure the dominance of this interpretation of the faith in southern Britain, and stood against syncretism in the face of great pressure.

27 April

Christina Rossetti, Poet, 1894

Christina Rossetti, the youngest member of a remarkable artistic Anglo-Italian family, was born in London in 1830. A devout Anglican from an evangelical background, Christina and her sister became greatly influenced by the Tractarians and her sister Maria eventually entered the sisterhood of All Saints', Margaret Street.

Some of Christina's earliest work, written under the pseudonym 'Ellen Alleyne', was published in *The Germ,* the organ of the pre-Raphaelite Brotherhood. Her poetry reflected her Christian faith and also a pervading sense of melancholy, both strong facets of her character. She also wrote fantasy poems and pieces for children, for example her 1862 work, *Goblin Market*. But this can also be interpreted as a religious allegory with themes of temptation, sin and redemption clearly apparent.

She gave up the prospect of marriage for religious reasons. She broke off her engagement to James Collinson in 1850 when he became a Roman Catholic and in 1866 she turned down a proposal from James Bagot Cayley. Not surprisingly the themes of renunciation of earthly love and the habitual Victorian concern with death are also recurring themes, particularly in her later poetry. Her poetry is recognized by critics as having a high degree of technical perfection and encompasses a wide range of styles and forms. Two Christmas carols, *In the bleak mid-winter* and *Love came down at Christmas*, remain popular today and are in many hymn books. At one point she was considered as a possible successor to Tennyson as Poet Laureate.

When her father's failing health and eyesight forced him into retirement in 1853, Christina and her mother attempted to support the family by starting their own school, but it was a short-lived venture. Her brother Dante's breakdown in 1872 and death ten years later affected her deeply. She herself suffered from chronic ill-health in later life and became something of a recluse. She developed cancer in 1891 and died three years later. Shortly before her death she published the poem 'None other Lamb', later put to music as a hymn:

> None other Lamb; none other name,
> None other hope in heaven or earth or sea,
> None other hiding-place from guilt and shame,
> None beside Thee.
>
> My faith burns low, my hope burns low,
> Only my heart's desire cries out in me,
> By the deep thunder of its want and woe,
> Cries out to Thee.
>
> Lord, Thou art life, though I be dead,
> Love's fire Thou art, however cold I be:
> Nor heaven have I, nor place to lay my head,
> Nor Home, but Thee.

Peter Chanel, Missionary in the South Pacific, Martyr, 1841

Born of humble parentage at Cuet in the Ain department of France in 1802, Peter Chanel was ordained priest in the Roman Catholic Church in 1827. Routine parish ministry occupied him for some years, but his imagination was fired by reading the letters of missionaries in far-away lands and in due course he himself offered for missionary service, joining the Society of Mary (the Marists) in 1831. In 1836 he embarked for the South Pacific.

He was assigned by his bishop to the island of Futuna, in the New Hebrides (today Vanuatu) and landed in 1837, the first Christian missionary to set foot there. In common with many Pacific islands cannibalism and endemic inter-tribal warfare had reduced its population to a few thousand by the time Chanel landed there.

Despite the difficulties of mission work among such savagery, Chanel laboured faithfully amid the greatest hardships, learning the native language, attending the sick, baptizing the dying and gathering around him a small band of Christian converts and a larger group who were being taught the rudiments of the Christian faith. European missionaries were always vulnerable in such situations but Niuliki, the chief, initially gave Chanel his support and even declared him 'taboo', so that he was not harmed; but his attitude changed when he saw the decline of tribal religion and, what was even worse, the conversion of his son and daughter.

With the chief's apparent agreement, a plot against Chanel was put into practice by Musumusu the Prime Minister. At dawn on 28 April, 1841 the mission compound was attacked and after a number of the converts who were caught unawares were wounded, Chanel's hut was attacked and he was battered to death, his head being split by a blow from an adze.

But as so often, before and since, the blood of the martyrs proved to be the seed of the Church and two Marist missionaries resumed Chanel's work the following year with remarkable results. At the same time Chanel's remains were exhumed and taken back to France. Chanel was beatified by Pope Leo XIII in 1889 and is revered in the Roman Catholic Church as the proto-martyr of Oceania, though in fact his death took place some eighteen months after the martyrdom of John Williams of the London Missionary Society at Dillon's Bay on the nearby island of Erromanga.

29 April

Catherine of Siena, Teacher of the Faith, 1380

Born at Siena in Italy in 1347 Catherine was the 23rd of 25 children. From an early age she was known to want to lead a life of prayer and penance, despite opposition from her parents and family. She refused marriage, and instead opted for a life of solitude. She joined the Dominican order as a Tertiary (lay volunteer) at the age of 16. She lived in solitude for three years, until she felt a call to leave her seclusion and care for the poor.

As Catherine became involved for caring for the sick, a diverse group of followers, both men and women, clerical and lay, gathered around her. This group soon became known for their desire for reform of the Church, their call for a life of total devotion to God, and their focus upon the crucified Christ. Unsurprisingly this group attracted criticism as well as praise wherever they went.

Catherine was a great correspondent, but had to dictate all her letters as she never learned to write herself. She wrote a 'Dialogue' in which explained her beliefs and expounded the sense of devotion to the crucified Christ that so ordered her life. This work was dictated to others when she was in a state of prayer and ecstasy.

Eventually, as her calls for reform went unheeded, Catherine became more and more involved in the political life of the Church. She acted as a peacemaker between Church and State when relationships deteriorated. The schism of 1378, when rival popes were elected after the death of Gregory XI, saw Catherine attempting to intervene and bring clarity to the situation. She supported Urban as the genuine Pope, although she was not unafraid to challenge him on his more extreme and unbending attitudes to the Avignon papacy.

She died, of a stroke in 1380, before the papal split was resolved. Her devotion to Christ is evident throughout her 'Dialogue':

> The soul begins to lose fear, knowing that fear alone is not sufficient to give eternal life. And so the soul proceeds, with love, to know itself and God's goodness within, and begins to take hope in God's mercy in which the heart feels joy. Sorrow for grief, mingled with the joy of hope in mercy, causes the eye to weep, and these tears issue from the very fountain of the heart.
>
> *The 'Dialogue' of St Catherine of Siena*

30 April

Pandita Mary Ramabai, Translator of the Scriptures, 1922

Born into a high-caste Indian family in South Kanara in 1858, Ramabai was taught Sanskrit by her father, an expert on the language. But she lost both her parents during a pilgrimage to South India in 1874 and had to fend for herself, travelling with her bother to sacred Hindu shrines, where she recited Sanskrit poetry to the crowds. She ended up in Calcutta and it was there that she was accorded the then novel title of Pandita ('mistress of learning'), so unusual in Indian culture was an educated woman with such linguistic skills.

She challenged traditional Indian culture by making calls for female emancipation and by marrying a man of a lower caste. But her marriage was short-lived and she was left a widow with no status and with a small child to care for. This experience gave her an insight into the sufferings of Hindu women and widows less privileged than herself.

In Bengal she encountered Christian believers and finding that Hinduism, with its expectation of resigned suffering was no help to her, studied the Bible and Christianity. At the same time she opened welfare and education centres and campaigned to improve the political situation of widows and women in general. Invited to England by Anglican nuns – the Wantage Sisters – for further education, she and her daughter were baptized there.

Returning to India she continued her work, extending it to unmarried mothers and young girls. She was criticized by Hindus for denying her roots and by Christians because conversion of the people she worked with was not a major priority. She had no time for denominational in-fighting and based her faith on the Jesus of the Bible and sought to express it in an authentically Indian way.

In 1891 she experienced an evangelical conversion and added evangelism to her social work. Her main sphere of work was the administration of the Mukti Institution which she had founded at Kedgaon near Poona (Pune). Opening as a small school, it quickly developed into a much larger institution where lower-caste women, widows and orphans found care and support. This demonstration of practical Christianity resulted in many of the women becoming Christians.

But Ramabai never turned entirely away from her scholarly upbringing and, in addition to her work amongst women in need, she lectured widely on social issues and translated the Bible into the Marathi, the language of educated Hindus. She died in 1922.

Athanasius, Bishop of Alexandria, Teacher of the Faith, 373

Athanasius was born and educated in Alexandria, a city of cultural diversity and academic excellence. He became a Christian in his youth, whilst undergoing a classical education. He became secretary to Alexander, bishop of the diocese, with whom he attended the First Ecumenical Council at Nicaea in 325. He somewhat controversially succeeded Alexander as bishop in 328.

Controversy and conflict surrounded Athanasius throughout his life. This controversy mainly concerned the Arian movement which taught that Christ was not fully God. Athanasius was an avowed anti-Arianist, and leader of the defence of Nicene orthodoxy, arguing vehemently in favour of the full divinity of Christ. This allegiance to the Nicene cause meant that Athanasius spent much of his time in exile, as different Arian sympathizers, emperors and bishops campaigned against him. He was exiled four times, by four different emperors. Initially deposed in 335, he returned to Alexandria on the death of the Emperor Constantine in 337, but was exiled again in 339, this time to Rome. He was restored in 346, but exiled for the third time in 356, returning to the city in 362. His fourth and briefest exile occurred in 365–6, when the pagan Emperor Julian tried to eradicate Christianity from the Empire. Athanasius greeted the news of Julian's enthronement, and his own impending exile, with the words 'It is only a little cloud. It will soon pass.' Julian died in battle in 366, and Athanasius returned to the city of his birth, where he remained for the rest of his life.

As Bishop of Alexandria he was the Church's greatest and most vociferous opponent of Arianism, and a staunch defender of the Christian faith as proclaimed at Nicaea. He never ceased teaching the deity of Christ. From 361 Athanasius sought to clarify the various theological terms that were used within the debate. He also argued for the deity of the Holy Spirit. He was greatly supported by monks and was partly responsible for the spread of monasticism to the Western Church, through his biography St Antony (see 17 January).

Athanasius is remembered chiefly as a theologian and defender of the faith. He was concerned to protect the deity of Christ, stressing that the Incarnation was a saving act, as deity joined humanity, and that Christ's life was as much a part of his sacrifice as was his death upon the cross.

8 May

Julian of Norwich, Spiritual Writer, c.1417

Julian was born in 1342 and her life is something of a mystery. It has been argued that she had been married and widowed before becoming a recluse. What is known for certain is that at the age of 30 Julian fell ill, and just when she thought she had reached the point of death her pain vanished and she received 16 visitations. Julian wrote these down in what came to be known as the 'short text', before meditating on them and producing her 'long text' 20 years later.

Julian focuses upon spirituality and creation. She stresses that all things have their being through the love of God. She believes that we were loved from eternity. The high point of her spirituality is the cross and she shows a desire to enter into the sufferings of Christ. She is convinced that humanity was separated from God by sin, and is redeemed and reunited with God through Christ.

Julian places stress upon Christ as mother, as divine wisdom, but she does so with a distinctly Trinitarian understanding. One of the notable features of Julian is that her theology determines her experience, rather than the other way round. Thus seeing Christ's suffering allows Julian to see the meaning of this life generally, and of her own suffering especially. For Julian the image of God as mother speaks more powerfully than anything else of the outgoing love of the Trinity for creation.

Julian was writing at the point in history when theology and spirituality were being slowly but surely prised apart. Her vision of God is formed out of both an intellectual approach and a response of love. Her writings have influenced many throughout the centuries, and are the result of reflection on the questions of life in the light of an immediate spiritual experience.

> Thus I saw and understood that our faith is our light in the night;
> which light is God, our endless day.
>
> *Julian, Long Text 83*

> When the soul is tempest tossed, troubled and cut off by worries, then is the time to pray, so as to make the soul willing and responsive towards God. But there is no kind of prayer that can make God more responsive to the soul, for God is always constant in love. And so I saw that, whenever we feel the need to pray, our good Lord follows us, helping our desire.
>
> *Showing 14*

Caroline Chisholm, Social Reformer, 1877

Better known in Australia than in Britain (for over 20 years her portrait was on the Australian five dollar note) Caroline Jones was born in Northamptonshire in 1808 into a family with a strong tradition of charitable works. In 1830 she was received into the Roman Catholic Church in order to marry Captain Archibald Chisholm, an officer with the East India Company, and after the wedding she accompanied him to Madras in India. Her interest in the welfare of women soon became apparent and she founded a school for daughters of European soldiers.

In 1838 her husband was granted sick leave, which they spent in New South Wales, and Caroline remained there when he went back to active service. Sydney at this time still had the flavour of a convict town – outside the sheltered middle class suburbs it was still a brutalized, male-dominated society – and Caroline was horrified with the condition of many women who had to resort to prostitution or begging in order to support themselves and their families. The problem was aggravated by unrestricted immigration, but with no facilities to receive the immigrants when they arrived in Sydney and to arrange jobs and homes for them, poverty and destitution were the lot of many.

In 1835, after much lobbying, Caroline persuaded the governor to allow her to use a disused barracks as a women's home. Here she worked to settle the thousands of unemployed immigrants, especially women. She met incoming ships, offering the women and girls shelter; she then arranged transport to inland areas, often escorting the women herself to help them find work. Caroline also ran schemes to place men and their families on the land. It is calculated that during her six years in Sydney, some 11,000 immigrants passed through her hands. Her report on this work, *Female Immigration* (1842), was the first publication by a woman in Australia.

On her husband's retirement, in 1845, Caroline returned to England where she promoted her work, raised money and support, and opened an emigration office in London. In 1854 she went back to Australia, where her welfare initiatives included providing shelters for workers going out to the goldfields. She also lectured on land reform and later opened a girls' school in Sydney. In 1857 she developed health problems and in 1866 she and her family returned to England where she died the following year.

19 May

Dunstan, Archbishop of Canterbury, Restorer of Monastic Life, 988

Dunstan was born in Somerset in 909 into a family who had royal connections. Along with Oswald and Ethelwold he was one of the chief architects of a monastic revival in the Church in the tenth century. Ravaged by Viking raids and the destruction of the monasteries, the Anglo-Saxon monastic community was further weakened by the loss of many monks who travelled abroad to spread the gospel. The English throne was similarly weakened by a combination of young kings and short reigns. The result was instability and insecurity throughout the country.

A serious youth, happier in books than in sport, and proficient in skills as diverse as music and metalwork, Dunstan spent his early years at Glastonbury, where he learned not only scholarship, but Irish spirituality too. After completing his education, Dunstan joined the court of King Athelstan, but in 935 was expelled for studying 'vain poetry, pagan writings and magic'. He returned to Glastonbury and lived as a hermit, before becoming a monk.

In 940 Dunstan was the subject of intrigue and rumour, and was close to banishment before a hunting accident suffered by the then King Edmund led to his being appointed as Abbot of Glastonbury. For the next 15 years Dunstan focused upon rebuilding the monastic community there, and he established the Rule of St Benedict as the mainstay of community life.

In 955 Eadwig was proclaimed king and ruled England for less than four years, during which time he sent Dunstan into exile. The precise reasons for this are lost in history, although rumour suggests that it was to do with Dunstan reproving the young king for 'over-exuberance' at his coronation feast. Eventually England North of the Thames rejected Eadwig and followed his brother, Edgar, who appointed Dunstan Bishop of Worcester in 957. In 959 Edgar, at the age of 16, became sole king of England, and appointed Dunstan as Bishop of London. A year later, in a highly irregular move, Edgar disregarded the election of Brihtric as Archbishop of Canterbury, and installed Dunstan instead. The papacy, in a weak condition, was in no position to protest and Dunstan was allowed to remain in post. Edgar also appointed Oswald and Ethelwold to influential positions, revitalizing the Church in general.

The stability brought to the throne by Edgar, and the reforming zeal of Dunstan, allowed not only the re-establishment of old monastic customs, but also the introduction of new foundations. The king and Dunstan together carried out a significant reform of both Church and State until the king's death in 975. The succession was disputed between Edgar's two sons, Edward and Ethelred. In 978 Dunstan enthroned Ethelred, before moving into retirement. The ceremony he devised on that occasion is said to have formed the basis for subsequent coronation rites.

Alcuin of York, Deacon, Abbot of Tours, 804

Alcuin was born of noble parentage about 735, probably in or near York. He was educated at York Cathedral School by Aelbert, a former pupil of Bede. Alcuin, a highly able pupil, soon attracted the special attention of Aelbert, who took his pupil on several visits to the Continent. When, in 767, Aelbert became Archbishop of York, Alcuin, who had been ordained deacon, succeeded him as master of the school, work he continued for the next 15 years, attracting numerous students and enriching the already valuable library. In common with many effective teachers, it was Alcuin's gift to be able to inspire those he taught with his own enthusiasm for learning. Not surprisingly, the school attracted talented students from far and wide. Returning from a visit to Rome in 781, he met Charlemagne, then King of the Franks, who persuaded Alcuin to relocate to his court in Aachen as master of the palace school, in effect his minister of education.

Alcuin was responsible for the process of establishing a primary school in every town and village and, because the clergy would be the teachers, in ensuring higher standards of literacy and education amongst both parish priests and ordinands. He established scriptoria for the copying and preservation of ancient manuscripts, thus preserving the writings of many classical authors that might otherwise have been lost. He is also credited with inventing cursive script ('joined-up writing') as an aid to speedier copying.

To Alcuin belongs much of the credit for the revision and organization of the Latin liturgy, the preservation of many of the ancient prayers, and the development of plainchant. He wrote nine biblical commentaries and was responsible for a revision of the Latin Bible, the Vulgate. He was a foremost opponent of the Adoptionist heresy and an advocate of the doctrine of the joint procession of the Holy Spirit from the Father and the Son, though the widespread acceptance of this doctrine by the Western Church only hastened the split with the East.

In 796, when Alcuin was over 60 and anxious to retire from public life Charlemagne appointed him Abbot of St Martin's at Tours (at some point in his busy life he had probably entered the Benedictine order). Here, in his declining years, he built up a model monastic school as he had previously done at York and Aachen. He died in May 804.

Helena, Protector of the Holy Places, 330

Born at Drepanum in Bithynia, Helena rose from humble origins to become the concubine of Emperor Constantius Chlorus. Helena bore Constantius a son in 274, named Constantine. Helena was banished by Constantius in 292 when he ended their relationship so that he could marry Theodora, the step-daughter of Augustus Maximian as part of his political ambitions. Helena returned to Rome in honour in 306 when her son Constantine became sole ruler of the Roman Empire. She was made 'most noble woman' and honoured throughout the Empire.

Helena became a Christian in 312, and fully embraced the Christian life. She became renowned as one who lived modestly and gave charitably, a protector of religious buildings and as a woman who sought out relics of the Christian faith. Her most famous 'achievement' was the recovery of the supposed cross of Christ, an event attested to by Ambrose, and recorded in fifth-century church histories. She was held in special honour by the Church as the mother of the Emperor who legalized the Christian faith.

Helena almost certainly visited the Holy Land on a pilgrimage, where she worked amongst the orphans and the poor. She became known for her gifts to churches and convents, and for erecting shrines in significant places detailing the life of Christ. It is from this period of her life that the story of the discovery of the cross of Christ is thought to have originated.

In the eleventh century Geoffrey of Monmouth gave rise to the false claim that Helena was of British origin, and many churches, and some towns, were named after her. This was due to confusion between Helena, mother of Constantine, and Helena Luyddog, a British noblewoman, who lived at the end of the fourth century.

John and Charles Wesley, Evangelists, Hymn Writers, 1791 and 1788

John Wesley (1703–91)

Born at Epworth Rectory in Lincolnshire in 1703, John Wesley was educated at Charterhouse School and Christ Church, Oxford. Ordained into the Anglican ministry, he acted for a time as his father's curate. In 1729 he went into residence at Oxford as Fellow of Lincoln College. There he joined his brother Charles and George Whitefield in the Holy Club, a group of students who met together for private worship and good works, including visiting prisons and comforting the sick. Their strict and methodical religious practices earned them the nickname 'methodists' from their fellow students.

In 1735 Wesley went to Georgia with the Society for the Propagation of the Gospel, but his personal faith was far from sure at this time. On board ship he met some German Moravians, whose simple faith and fearlessness in the face of Atlantic storms greatly impressed him. On his return to England in 1738, he sought them out and, while attending one of their meetings in Aldersgate Street, London, on 24 May 1738, he had a profound spiritual experience, often referred to as his 'conversion'. He famously recorded in his Journal:

> About a quarter before nine while [the speaker] was describing the change which God works in the heart through faith in Christ, I felt my heart strangely warmed. I felt I did trust in Christ, Christ alone for my salvation; and an assurance was given me that he had taken away my sins even mine, and saved me from the law of sin and death.

In March 1739 he was persuaded by George Whitefield to begin outdoor preaching and the following month founded the first Methodist society in London. Methodism was initially intended to be an add-on for Anglicans who had experienced conversion and Wesley expected them to attend worship and the sacraments at their parish church. But as time went on Methodism began to develop its own structures with classes for pastoral care, authorized lay preachers to address the societies and, from 1744, an annual Conference.

An indefatigable preacher and organizer, Wesley travelled around 5,000 miles a year on horseback, sometimes delivering up to five sermons a day. Huge numbers came to hear him and the response varied from tearful repentance to violent attack. Rejecting Whitefield's moderate Calvinism, he rejoiced to be known as an 'Arminian', emphasizing that salvation was available for all through Christ. He also stressed the doctrine of assurance: 'every man can be saved and every man can *know* that he is saved'. He died on 2 March 1791, and was buried at City Road Chapel, London.

Charles Wesley (1707–88)

John's younger brother by four years, Charles Wesley was educated at Westminster School and Christ Church, Oxford. While at Oxford he was a founder member of the Holy Club. Ordained in 1735, later that year he went to Georgia with his brother John as secretary to the colonial governor James Oglethorpe. But ill health forced him to relinquish the post and he returned to England the following year. Caught up in the growing evangelical revival, Charles had a conversion experience on Whit Sunday, 21 May 1738, three days before his brother.

Charles subsequently was closely associated with the Wesleyan movement and travelled extensively as a preacher. In 1749 he married Sally Gwynne, the daughter of a Welsh magistrate and, unlike his brother, for whom marriage was much more of a trial than a joy, he enjoyed a happy family life in Bristol, where he ministered to the Methodist Society at the New Room. From 1771 he lived in London.

The two Wesleys differed on certain doctrinal matters, Charles always being the more conservative of the two. In addition, Charles strongly opposed steps that might lead to separation from the Church of England and thus disapproved of John's unilateral ordinations of Methodist ministers for North America and Scotland from 1784 and from 1788, the year of Charles' death, for England also. Charles greatly regretted this innovation that could only cause greater discord between Methodism and the Church of England, but suggested that his brother's judgement might have been sounder if he had been younger: ''Twas age that made the breach, not he'.

But Charles Wesley's greatest work was his poetry and hymn writing. It was he who ensured that Methodism would be noted for its congregational singing and he left a incomparable legacy of nearly 7,000 hymns, far more than any other hymn writer, before or since, and many of them are still regularly sung. Among the most widely known are *And can it be?*, *Hark! the herald angels sing*, and *Love divine, all loves excelling*. Yet Charles has not been without his critics who have claimed that early Methodist worship encouraged emotionalism, dwelt unhealthily upon sin and that some of his lyrics had unnecessarily erotic imagery. Nevertheless Charles Wesley remains probably one of the greatest Christian poets and certainly the greatest hymn writer of all time. A day or two after his conversion Charles wrote the hymn *Christ the friend of sinners*, with the first verse:

> Where shall my wandering soul begin?
> How shall I all to heaven aspire?
> A slave redeemed from death and sin,
> A brand plucked from eternal fire,
> How shall I equal triumphs raise,
> Or sing my great Deliverer's praise?

The Venerable Bede, Monk at Jarrow, Scholar, Historian, 735

Born around 673, Bede was sent as a seven-year-old to Wearmouth monastery and later transferred to the new foundation at Jarrow, where he spent the remainder of his life, probably never travelling further than Lindisfarne to the north and York to the south. In about 692 he was ordained deacon at a relatively early age and priested when he was about 30.

His own words are often quoted: 'I have devoted my energies to a study of the Scriptures, observing monastic discipline, and singing the daily services in church; study, teaching, and writing have always been my delight.' In many ways his was a quiet and uneventful life but he spent it fruitfully as a scholar. He was the first person to write scholarly works in the English language, although unfortunately only fragments of his English writings have survived. He translated the Gospel of John into Old English, completing the work on the very day of his death. He also wrote extensively in Latin. He wrote commentaries on the Pentateuch and other portions of Holy Scripture.

But it is not as a theologian but as a historian that Bede is best remembered. His magisterial *Ecclesiastical History of the English People* was completed in 731 and remains in print today. It is one of the most importance sources for early English history. Fortunately for later historians, Bede was scrupulous in use of sources, which are clearly identified, as well as showing an attitude well in advance of his time in distinguishing clearly between fact, hearsay and legend. In a credulous age Bede showed a healthy caution in not believing all that he was told was true. The book is a history of Britain up to 729. Beginning with the Celtic peoples who were converted to Christianity during the first three centuries of the Christian era, Bede moves on to the invasion by the Anglo-Saxon pagans in the fifth and sixth centuries, and their subsequent conversion by Celtic missionaries from the north and west, and Roman missionaries from the south and east. He is believed to have been the first historian to date events from the birth of Christ and the earliest known writer to cast doubt on the accuracy of the Julian calendar.

Bede was a shrewd observer of the life of the Anglo-Saxon Church and suggested (to the Bishop of York) that episcopal visitation, confirmation and more frequent communion were appropriate remedies for the Church's ills.

Aldhelm, Bishop of Sherborne, 709

Aldhelm was born in 640, and educated at Malmesbury, an Irish monastic community in Wiltshire, and then in Canterbury. He later became Abbot of the Malmesbury community. A man of high standing who was a close relation to Ine the King of Wessex, Aldhelm took a prominent part in the reforms of Archbishop Theodore (see 20 September) particularly in the area of administration, which prior to Theodore was a weakness of the Church.

Aldhelm was a man of intense learning and scholarship who rivaled Bede in ability. He was also eccentric and unconventional. His letters are almost impenetrable due to the overuse of simile, metaphor and alliteration. He also created a collection of one hundred riddles on biblical themes.

Although his letters were difficult to understand, Adhelm had a desire to communicate the message of the gospel effectively. In an attempt to teach the gospel to the illiterate of his diocese, he wrote hymns which were accompanied by the playing of the harp. Adhelm would also intersperse his preaching with clowning and songs, and realized the value of entertainment in communicating a message. His aim was to 'win men's ears, and then their souls'.

In 705 Aldhelm became the first Bishop of Sherborne, and continued to rule the monastery at Malmesbury introducing the Benedictine Rule into the community. He founded churches at Sherborne, Wareham and Corfe and several monasteries, including those at Frome and Bradford-on-Avon.

The last riddle in *Aldhelm's 100 Riddles* (answer: Creation) illustrates his linguistic skill:

> I am greater than this world, smaller than a tick, brighter than the moon, swifter than the sun. The seas, the ocean floods, are all in my embrace, and this expanse of earth, the green plains: I reach to their foundations. I stoop below hell, I mount above the heavens, the glorious homeland, and extend abroad over the angel's abode. I fill the earth, the aged world, and the ocean streams, amply with my own self. Say what I am called.

Augustine, first Archbishop of Canterbury, 605

Augustine's date of birth and origins are unknown. What is known is that he was prior of the monastery of St Andrew at Rome in 596 when he was instructed by Pope Gregory the Great to lead a group of 40 monks to England to preach to the heathen English. (Bede recounted the story of Gregory being intrigued by the sight of fair-haired boys in the slave market at Rome and conceiving the idea of a mission to their homeland.) Though Augustine famously turned back to Rome while the mission party was passing through Gaul, this was not so much cold feet on his part as a desire by the highly conscientious Augustine to inform the Pope of the mission party's corporate reticence and to ask his advice. Returning with a papal letter of encouragement, Augustine led the monks on to England, landing at Thanet in Kent in 597.

After some initial wariness, Augustine was well received by King Ethelbert of Kent, whose wife, Bertha, had been brought up in the Christian faith and, indeed, had a Frankish bishop, Luidhard, as her chaplain (though neither, it seems, had used their influence in any form of mission). Augustine was allowed the use of the old Roman church of St Martin in Canterbury as his base and here he and his companions established the daily rhythm of the Benedictine Rule. Whether it was the personal influence of the new arrivals or because their presence had emboldened the queen and her chaplain is not known, but very soon afterwards King Ethelbert asked to be instructed in the faith and prepared for baptism.

The king's conversion naturally gave a great impetus to the spread of Christianity and though Bede was careful to state that compulsion was not used there can have been few in Kent who could not see that Christianity was the faith of the future. An indication of this was that on Christmas Day, 597, Augustine is said to have baptized more than ten thousand people near the mouth of the Medway. Shortly afterwards he crossed over to Gaul and was consecrated bishop by Virgilius, the Metropolitan of Arles.

Ethelbert sponsored a meeting with the existing Celtic bishops in the West of Britain. The conference took place in Malmesbury in 603, but Augustine badly mishandled it, appearing imperious and arrogant. It took another sixty years before an accommodation was reached at the Synod of Whitby. Nevertheless Augustine is revered by Anglicans as the first of a line of over one hundred archbishops, whose enthronement takes place in 'St Augustine's chair' in Canterbury Cathedral. From his day to the present, there has been an unbroken succession of archbishops of Canterbury.

26 May

John Calvin, Reformer, 1564

Born at Noyon in Picardy, north-east France in 1509, Calvin studied law at Orléans, Bourges and Paris. He grew to appreciate the humanistic and reforming movements, and he undertook studies in the Greek Bible. He underwent a conversion experience in his mid twenties: 'God subdued and brought my heart to docility. It was more hardened against such matters than was to be expected in such a young man.' He renounced Roman Catholicism and left Paris with the intention of travelling to Strasbourg to study with the reformer Martin Bucer. But war made a lengthy journey via Geneva necessary and there the reformer Guillaume Farel prevailed upon Calvin to stay and work with him.

Thus began a love–hate relationship between Calvin and the people of Geneva. Indeed for three years (1538–41) Calvin sought refuge in Strasbourg after the Genevan citizens refused to swear loyalty to a Protestant statement of belief. While in Strasbourg, Calvin married Idelette de Bure, a widow. John Knox, who was hardly unbiased, described Geneva as 'the most perfect school of Christ that ever was on the earth since the days of the Apostles'. Knox, like many others, experienced Geneva as a welcoming centre for Protestant refugees. Though Calvin was never entirely successful in his attempts to enforce the Church's moral discipline on the people, he sought to improve the life of the city's citizens in many ways. He supported good hospitals, a proper sewage system, special care for the poor and infirm, and the introduction of new industries.

Calvin's writings, however, have proven to be his most lasting contribution to the Church, in particular his massive yet easily readable work of Protestant systematic theology, *The Institutes of the Christian Religion*. The first edition was produced in 1536 and constantly enlarged until the final edition of 1559. Calvin stressed the sovereignty of God, the nature of election and predestination, the sins of pride and disobedience, the authority of Scripture, and the nature of the Christian life. His theology was greatly influenced by Augustine. Calvin tried to steer a middle course between an exclusive emphasis on divine providence and an exclusive emphasis on human responsibility. His influence was felt widely elsewhere in Europe, including England and Scotland.

Calvin's health was never robust (he was a chronic asthmatic) and he became very frail after an attack of fever in 1558. He died on 26 May 1564 and, at his request, was buried in an unmarked grave in Geneva.

Philip Neri, Founder of the Oratorians, Spiritual Guide, 1595

Philip Neri was born in Florence in 1515, the son of a notary. After school he served as an apprentice in a family business. In 1533 he left his work and went to Rome, initially to study and later to teach theology and philosophy. When he considered that he had learned enough he sold his books and gave the money to the poor. He devoted himself to prayer, often in the catacomb of St Sebastian, where in 1544 he experienced an ecstasy of divine love so great that his heart was said to have been miraculously enlarged.

From 1538 he began to work amongst the men of the city and in 1548 founded the Confraternity of the Most Holy Trinity, a lay brotherhood devoted to aiding pilgrims, convalescents and the poor. He was ordained in 1551 and soon moved to the community at San Girolamo in Rome. He became a much sought after confessor and spiritual guide with evident gifts of discernment. His informal meetings and services with vernacular hymns and prayers became so popular that a special room – an 'oratory' – was built over the church in order to accommodate the growing number of people who wished to attend this unusual and popular form of worship. The oratory became the centre of Philip's activities, which included programmes of sacred music. Other young clergy were attracted to this work and in 1575 the Congregation of the Oratory was formed – a congregation of secular priests living in community without vows, and those with private means being required to support themselves.

His ministry was to the people and primarily to the men of Rome – to the extent that he became known as the 'Apostle of Rome' and was regarded by many as virtually a living saint. His private life was ascetic in the extreme, though he did not make a display of this and tried to prevent it from becoming widely known. So great a devotee of Philip Neri and his work was Pope Gregory XIII, that Neri had the greatest difficulty in refusing a cardinal's hat in 1559.

Noted for his gentleness and cheerfulness, Philip Neri taught that the Christian faith was a joy as well as a duty. It was one where lay people as well as the clergy had a vital role to play and where experimental forms of worship had an important place. It is perhaps hardly surprising that a modern Reformation historian describes Neri as 'the most attractive of the Counter-Reformation saints'. He died in Rome on 26 May 1595.

Lanfranc, Prior of Le Bec, Archbishop of Canterbury, Scholar, 1089

Lanfranc was born in Pavia in Northern Italy in about 1005. He studied and then practised law in Pavia before moving to France in 1035, where he became a pupil of Berengar of Tours. He taught in Avranches before, in 1042, he entered the newly founded Benedictine abbey of Le Bec, near Rouen. Only three years later he became its prior and was then able to open a school there, which rapidly became famous, and attracted scholars from many parts of Europe, several of whom later rose to high rank, especially the future Pope, Alexander II, and Anselm (see 21 April), who was to succeed Lanfranc both as Prior of Le Bec and as Archbishop of Canterbury.

While at Le Bec, Lanfranc met Duke William of Normandy, and though he initially opposed William's marriage to his cousin Matilda of Flanders, he later withdrew his objections and was reconciled with William. William was clearly aware of Lanfranc's abilities and when, in 1063, he founded St Stephen's Abbey at Caen he appointed Lanfranc as its first abbot. Three years later William invaded England (it is generally supposed that it was Lanfranc who arranged for a papal blessing for the expedition) and, after his victory at Hastings, was crowned king. In 1070 Archbishop Stigand was deposed and Lanfranc (who had been elected Archbishop of Rouen in 1067, but had declined the post) was summoned to England to replace him at Canterbury. William had seen Lanfranc's outstanding administrative skills at Le Bec and wanted to make use of them in England.

Lanfranc repaid him as an energetic and vigorous archbishop who oversaw the reform (some would say the Normanization) of the English Church. The changes he instituted included: enforcing clerical celibacy, reforming cathedral chapters, rationalizing a number of dioceses, insisting on the subordination of York to Canterbury, drawing a clear legal and jurisdictional distinction between matters civil and ecclesiastical, rebuilding Canterbury Cathedral and re-establishing a library there after its destruction by fire in 1067. He also supported William's policy of replacing Anglo-Saxon bishops with Normans.

During the Conqueror's frequent absences in Normandy, Lanfranc generally acted as regent and demonstrated his military ability in suppressing a rising against William in 1074. Theologically he wrote on Paul's Epistles and was involved in the debates concerning the nature of the divine presence in the Eucharist.

After William's death Lanfranc crowned William Rufus. Rufus increasingly disregarded the boundaries between Church and State when it was to his political and financial advantage, but before matters could come to a head Lanfranc died in 1089.

Josephine Butler, Social Reformer, 1906

Josephine Grey was born in 1828 to an old Northumberland family (her father was cousin to Earl Grey, Prime Minister 1830–34). In 1852 she married the Revd George Butler, a writer on education and later a Canon of Winchester. After the birth of four children in five years the couple moved from Oxford to Cheltenham, then again to Liverpool in 1866 when George became head of Liverpool College. It was in the busy seaport city that Josephine first encountered the problem of prostitution. Instead of adopting the normal Victorian attitude of ignoring the problem, with her husband's support Josephine opened her home as a refuge for prostitutes, quickly becoming aware that they were the victims rather than the enemies of society, and began to campaign on their behalf.

In Victorian England it was deemed unseemly for a lady to be aware of such matters let alone to hold opinions and air them in public. Josephine thus encountered much opposition to her work. But her strong dislike of injustice perpetrated by the strong on the weak was underpinned by her faith – she was a devout Anglican and even found time to write a biography of Catherine of Siena.

A particular injustice was the Contagious Diseases Acts, passed by Parliament in the 1860s in order to protect military and naval personnel from sexually transmitted diseases. The Acts criminalized the prostitutes rather than their clients and imposed police surveillance, arrest on suspicion, and compulsory medical examination of women suspected of being prostitutes. Inevitably, there were cases of 'respectable' women who were in the wrong place at the wrong time being forcibly subjected to a painful and degrading medical examination with no right of appeal. Josephine objected strongly on the grounds that women were being denied their constitutional rights. She won the support of other influential women such as Florence Nightingale and Harriet Martineau, and after a prolonged campaign succeeded in influencing Parliament to repeal the Acts in 1886.

Josephine also campaigned against the white slave traffic and, despite the flamboyant involvement of the press, stuck to the real issues and succeeded in getting legislation on the statute book which, among other things, raised the legal age of consent in Britain from 13 to 16. She wrote a number of books promoting education and equality for women and was involved in putting pressure on Cambridge University to improve educational opportunities for women. This eventually led to the foundation of Newnham College. She died in 1906.

Joan of Arc, Visionary, 1431

Joan was born in a peasant family at Domrémy in the Champagne region of France, probably in 1412, towards the end of the Hundred Years' War between France and England. Uneducated but highly intelligent, she was a pious and virtuous child and in 1425 experienced the first of her supernatural visions, which she described as a blaze of light with an accompanying voice. In due course she was able to identify Michael the Archangel, along with Catherine of Alexandria and Margaret of Antioch (who were, perhaps significantly, two early virgin martyrs). To Joan, they revealed a mission to save France.

King Charles VII of France (the Dauphin in Shakespeare's *Henry V*) had been obliged to delay his coronation in order to fight the English. In 1429 Joan managed to meet Charles who became convinced of her *bona fides*. He allowed her to lead the French army to Orléans where, clad in a suit of white armour, she raised the siege by the English army. After a further campaign in the Loire Valley, she persuaded Charles to proceed to Reims for his coronation, which took place with Joan at his side.

Once he had been crowned the king lost interest in the war but Joan carried on nevertheless. So it was that, without adequate military support, she failed to recapture Paris from the English, and in 1430 she was taken prisoner and eventually put on trial. In the 15 sessions of her trial for sorcery and heresy the 19-year-old Joan made a robust defence against her accusers. But, inevitably, she was convicted and burned at the stake in Rouen on 30 May 1431.

Charles had made no effort to ransom or rescue her, but now cynically sought to rehabilitate Joan's reputation (no doubt for personal advantage) pressuring the church courts for a review of the verdict against her. Joan's condemnation was finally annulled by a papal commission in 1456. In 1920 she was canonized and is now regarded as the second patron saint of France.

But why should the Church of England commemorate Joan? Neither for her military prowess, nor even because her visions were necessarily authentic, but because, being persuaded of the will of God for her life, she responded in faith and obedience. Joan's experience also provides a salutary reminder of the fate of the idealists and the innocent who get in the way of power politics and the 'national interest'.

Apolo Kivebulaya, Priest, Evangelist in Central Africa, 1933

The CMS Nyanza mission first brought Christianity to Uganda in 1877 and in 1894 Uganda became a British Protectorate. As a result of a request for Christian missionaries by the chief of Boga, in the far west of Uganda, two Ugandan teachers were sent in 1896 and made some converts. But their firm stand against sorcery, polygamy and drunkenness offended the chief, and he deprived them of food forcing them to leave.

Later that same year a second attempt was made to take the gospel to Boga by a recently converted soldier, Apolo Kivebulaya. After his baptism he had declared a willingness to serve as a catechist in western Uganda, so he was sent out to Boga later in the same year. There he grew his own food, and so could not be forced out by having the market closed against him. Not surprisingly his opposition to sorcery, polygamy, and other practices aroused strenuous opposition and when the chief's sister died in an accident Apolo was blamed. A mob seized him, beat him and then turned him over to the British colonial authorities for trial. He spent several months in jail awaiting trial, and became greatly discouraged until he had an experience of the presence of Christ, and his faith was strengthened. The charges were eventually dropped, and he returned to Boga, where his preaching and the example of his life resulted in many conversions, including the chief who had opposed him so bitterly. He was ordained deacon in 1900 and priest in 1903.

An international boundary commission in 1907/8 realigned the border, with Boga being transferred to the Belgian Congo. But Apolo remained in Boga for what proved to be a life-long ministry. His 'big flat feet with spread-out toes enabled him to walk everywhere. He never wore shoes.' But in his later years he was persuaded to acquire a bicycle and it is said that he chose a women's model which was easier to ride in a flowing robe. He trained up those with leadership gifts, so that when he died in 1933, the Boga Church continued to flourish. However, it remained a small and isolated Christian community. Not until 1972 did Boga become a separate diocese with its own bishop. Today it is one of the six dioceses of the Anglican Church in the Congo.

Justin, Martyr at Rome, c.165

Justin was born in Palestine but was a Greek by education and upbringing. He was a philosopher, who, after studying the teachings of the Stoics, Pythagoreans and Platonists, turned finally to Christianity. He is thought of as the first Christian philosopher, teaching at Ephesus and then in Rome, where he opened a Christian school. Justin engaged in debates with both Jews and pagans, often wearing his philosopher's cloak. Justin's understanding of the Christian faith was that it did not involve a rejection of the philosophical disciplines, rather he gathered all his previous learning and used it in both defending and explaining the gospel. He saw Christianity as 'the only sure and worthy philosophy'. Three of his writings have survived: in his two Apologies, addressed to successive Roman emperors, he sought to explain Christian worship in order to reveal its innocence, and his *Dialogue with Trypho* he sought to demonstrate that the Christian Eucharist superseded Jewish sacrifices.

Thus through Justin we learn much about early Christian worship. He was particularly faced with the challenge of explaining Christianity in a time of much misunderstanding. He dealt with charges of immorality at the eucharistic feast, and charges that Christians were guilty of sedition and atheism against the Empire's own gods. However, Justin's main aim was apologetic: he would seek to explain the Christian faith and doctrine in a manner that was accessible to all, although he was particularly responsive to the Greeks. In an age of superstition and myth Justin clarified Christian teaching on the devil and demons, and emphasized the liberating power of God at work through the Holy Spirit.

Justin argued that Christianity was the true philosophy, the culmination of all previous philosophies, which only contained partial truth. He was the first Christian writer after Paul to grasp the universal nature of the gospel. He was martyred, by being beheaded, in the reign of Marcus Aurelius, to whom he confessed his faith after refusing to offer a sacrifice to the gods.

> God has announced in advance that he has joy in all the sacrifices offered in the name of Jesus that are made in accordance with the precepts of Christ, that is, in the Meal of Thanksgiving of the bread and cup, which is celebrated by Christians in all places throughout the earth.
>
> *Dialogue with Trypho 117.1*

The Martyrs of Uganda, 1885–7 and 1977

The martyrdoms of James Hannington (see 29 October) in 1885 and Janani Luwum (see 17 February) in 1977 were both part of a wider series of persecutions in which much larger numbers of Ugandan Christians were martyred.

In 1885 the first indigenous Ugandan martyr was the Roman Catholic Joseph Mkasa Balikuddembe, who was beheaded after having rebuked the Kabaka (king), Mwanga, for his debauchery and protested against the murder of Bishop Hannington. Initially, the Christian faith had been preached only to the immediate members of the court, by order of King Mutesa. His successor, Mwanga, became increasingly angry as he realized that the first converts put loyalty to Christ above their traditional loyalty to the king. The Christian pages in his court undoubtedly passed state secrets to the missionaries and fed Mwanga's paranoia, allowing him to view native Christians, especially those at court, as a treacherous fifth column, and this view was compounded by their refusal to submit to his perverted sexual practices.

On 3 June 1886, a group of 32 men and boys, 22 Roman Catholic and 10 Anglican, were burned at the stake at Namugongo for their refusal to renounce Christianity. Most of them were young pages in Mwanga's household. But the Namugongo martyrdoms produced a result entirely opposite to Mwanga's intentions. The example of these martyrs, who walked to their deaths singing hymns and praying for their enemies, so inspired many of the bystanders that they began to seek instruction from the remaining Christians. The dynamic of Christian growth in Uganda was transformed. Within a few years the original handful of converts had multiplied many times and spread far beyond the court. The blood of the martyrs was indeed the seed of the Ugandan Church. The martyrs had left the indelible impression that Christianity was truly African, not simply a European religion. Most of the missionary work was carried out by Africans rather than by white missionaries, and Christianity spread steadily. Uganda now has the largest percentage of professed Christians of any nation in Africa.

But the Ugandan Church had a further tribulation to endure 90 years later. The overthrow of Milton Obote's government in 1971 by the Ugandan army under the Muslim Idi Amin led to renewed persecution of Christians in the 1970s by Amin's military dictatorship. Janani Luwum, Anglican Archbishop of Uganda, was only one among the thousands of new martyrs, both Anglican and Roman Catholic.

4 June

Petroc, Abbot of Padstow, 6th century

Petroc, the foremost Cornish saint, is said to have been the son of a chieftain in South Wales. He rejected the call to rule the clan after his father's death, opting instead to travel to Ireland to study. Eventually leaving Ireland he travelled to Cornwall. Once in Cornwall, Petroc founded a monastery at Lanwethinoc (Padstow). He remained for 30 years, only leaving to undertaking a pilgrimage to Rome.

One unsubstantiated legend tells that as he approached the monastery on his return it began to rain, whereupon Petroc confidently predicted it would soon stop. However the rain continued for three days and Petroc returned to Rome as penance for presuming to predict God's actions.

He founded a second monastery at Petherick (Nanceventon) where he also built a mill and a chapel. Once this monastery was established Petroc moved to Bodmin Moor and began to live a solitary life. By the eleventh century the Augustinian monastery built on the site of Petroc's cell had become a place of popular pilgrimage.

Like many early saints, an account of his life was written centuries after his death (eleventh century), and it is often difficult to distinguish between fact and embellishment. Petroc was referred to as the 'captain of Cornish saints' and the large number of place names and church dedications in Devon and Cornwall (and to a lesser extent in Wales) testify to his place in the pantheon of Celtic saints. He is also honoured in Brittany as St Perreux.

In 1177 his relics were stolen and taken to Brittany where they were housed in the abbey of Saint-Méen. Their return was only secured by the personal intervention of King Henry II.

5 June

Boniface (Wynfrith) of Crediton,
Bishop, Apostle of Germany, Martyr, 754

Wynfrith was born in 675 at Crediton in what was then Wessex. He only took the name 'Boniface' much later in life. He entered the monastic life at Exeter, later moving to Nursling near Southampton, eventually working in the community as a teacher. Here he specialized in biblical exposition and compiled the first Latin grammar written in England.

In 718, and by then in his forties, Wynfrith left both Wessex and England, never to return. Abandoning a ecclesiastical career in England he started to work among the pagan tribes of Frisia (Holland and Northern Germany). Initially this exercise bore little fruit, and hostility from the governing class there forced him to flee. In 719 he was offered the post of abbot back at Nursling, but refused to return. Three journeys to Rome eventually saw him commissioned by Gregory II to preach to the unconverted in Bavaria and Hesse, and from 722 he received the Pope's complete support for his work, being consecrated missionary bishop. Boniface returned to Frisia, and encouraged by further directions and communications from Rome saw more success in his work.

Boniface committed his life to the work of the Church in Frisia. He was fearless, famously felling a sacred oak dedicated to the worship of Thor. The lack of retribution inflicted upon him by Thor caused many to convert to Christianity.

Boniface also established monasteries and in 741 made a joint commitment with the Frankish King Pepin to reform corrupt clergy, and introduced regional councils to give accountability. He worked hard at relationships between the Church and the State, and was said to have been the most influential Englishman in the history of Europe. In around 747 he was made Archbishop of Mainz, however, after only five years as Archbishop Boniface resigned his position, and returned to Frisia, to continue his mission. Although in his eighties he continued to strive for the spreading of the gospel and the purity of the Church. He was martyred at Dokkum in 754 in an attack by a group of pagan bandits.

Boniface was a man of iron will, who, although at times became discouraged, always pressed ahead with his given task. Not only was he responsible for the conversion of many, he was also responsible for the organization and the installation of effective leadership within the Church throughout Europe.

In the mid twelfth century Hildegard of Bingen eulogized Boniface in song:

> O Boniface
> the living light saw you
> like a wise man
> who returned to their source
> the pure waters flowing from God
> when you watered the greenness of the flowers.
> So you are the friend of the living God
> and the true crystal shining
> in the benevolence of the straight way
> where you ran wisely.

Hildegard of Bingen: Antiphon 73, 'On Boniface'

Ini Kopuria, Founder of the Melanesian Brotherhood, 1945

Ini Kopuria was born about 1900 near Maravovo on Guadalcanal in the Solomon Islands. Part of his schooling was at Norfolk Island where the Melanesian Mission, in a manner observed since the days of Bishop Patteson (see 20 September), gathered together and educated promising pupils with a view to their future usefulness to the mission. An independent young man, with a streak of originality, Ini rejected the route planned for him into teaching and opted for a more adventurous life in the Native Armed Constabulary of the Solomon Islands Protectorate. While recovering in hospital from a leg injury in 1924 Ini had an intense conversion experience. It was out of this that came his proposal to form a brotherhood of young men who would take the Christian faith to the heathen villages on Guadalcanal, where he had worked as a policeman. 'I have visited all the villages as a police sergeant and they all know me: why not go to them now as a missionary?'

Bishop Steward was sympathetic and helped Ini to draw up a Rule and formally constitute the Brotherhood. Ini took his vows in October 1925 and the following year six others joined him. The Brotherhood was essentially evangelistic, their aim being 'to declare the way of Jesus Christ among the heathen, not to minister to those who have already received the law'.

It was a uniquely Melanesian institution. The brothers took vows of poverty, chastity and obedience, not for life but on an annual basis (later extended to five years). They worked in pairs and were organized in 'households' of up to of twelve, each led by an 'Elder Brother'. The bishop was 'Father' of the Brotherhood and Ini was Head Brother. Numbers soon increased from the initial seven to 128 by 1935. The Brotherhood aimed to live the gospel in a direct and simple way, following Christ's example of prayer, mission and service. But European clergy were not always impressed and there was a tendency to treat the brothers as a convenient supply of labour for odd jobs. As far as he could Ini resisted both this misuse of the brothers and also the racist assumptions of Melanesian inferiority held by some Europeans.

In 1940 Ini relinquished the office of Head Brother and, after being released from his vow of celibacy, he married and worked as a village deacon until his death in 1945.

Thomas Ken, Bishop of Bath and Wells, Nonjuror, Hymn Writer, 1711

Thomas Ken was born in Hertfordshire in 1637 and reared by his half-sister Anne and her husband, the well-known angler Izaak Walton. Educated at Winchester and Hart Hall, Oxford, he was ordained and became Fellow of New College in 1657. After working in several parishes he became a tutor at Winchester in 1672. It was probably here that he wrote the two hymns for which he largely remembered: the morning hymn, *Awake my soul*, and the evening hymn, *Glory to thee my God this night*.

In 1679 he went to The Hague as chaplain to Princess Mary, niece of King Charles II of England and wife of the Dutch Prince William of Orange. Ken publicly rebuked William for his treatment of his wife, which may well account for his return to England after only a year. Upon his return he was made personal chaplain to King Charles. When the king requested that Ken provide lodging for his current mistress, Nell Gwynn, as the chaplain's residence was conveniently close to the palace, Ken sent the king a bold refusal, complaining that he was the royal chaplain and not the royal pimp. Charles admired his honesty and bluntness, and made him Bishop of Bath and Wells in 1685. Some authorities have suggested that, when Charles died the same year, he asked for Ken's ministrations on his deathbed.

The next king, James II, was a Roman Catholic, and caused political turmoil by his heavy-handed attempts to favour Roman Catholics. He issued a decree – the Declaration of Indulgence – which attempted to override the legal restrictions on Catholics. The declaration was required to be read in churches, but seven bishops, among them Thomas Ken, refused, and were imprisoned in the Tower of London. But James was forced to release the bishops and to flee abroad. Parliament declared the throne vacant and then offered it jointly to the king's daughter Mary and her husband William of Orange.

But nine bishops – among them Ken – and some 300–400 clergy refused to take the oath to William and Mary on the grounds that their oath to King James was still valid. Known collectively as the Nonjurors, they were all deprived of their livings. In his enforced retirement Ken lived a celibate, ascetic life, initially working as a private tutor.

A man who repeatedly put principle before personal comfort, Ken refused an offer of reinstatement at Bath and Wells in 1703. He died in 1711.

Columba, Abbot of Iona, Missionary, 597

Columba, otherwise known as Colum Cille, which means 'Dove of the Church', was born at Gartan in Donegal in 521. He was a descendant of the pagan High King Niall, and a member of the prominent clan of Ui Neill. Columba was educated in Irish monasteries by some of the leading figures of his day, including Finian of Clonard and Finian of Moville, as would befit a member of the royal line. He was one of a group of privileged clergy who dominated the Irish Church.

Columba founded two monasteries in Ireland, at Derry (546) and Durrow (556), before he relocated to Iona, off the west coast of Scotland, with twelve companions. Iona was given to him for a monastery by the ruler of the Irish Dalriada. Columba reputedly went into exile on the island, as a result of his part in the battle of Culdrebene (about 563) – a monastic disagreement which turned violent. Columba lived the rest of his life in Scotland, returning to Ireland only for short periods of time, usually for an official occasion.

From Iona Columba visited Bridei, King of the Picts and according to Bede converted him. In 574 Columba anointed Aeda'n mac Gabrian as King of the Scots of Dalriada, and a year later attended a convention of the kings at Druim Cett in Ireland. Columba obviously retained his influence in certain circles, despite his choice of the monastic life. At Druim Cett, Columba argued for the preservation of the Bards of Ireland, and sought clarification from the Irish king on the role of the Irish in Scotland.

From Iona, Columba was perfectly placed to evangelize both the Picts, and the kingdom of Da'l Riata in north-east Ireland. It has been traditional to see Columba as the Apostle of Scotland, and to credit him for the conversion of numerous Picts. In reality however, Columba was more of a figurehead for the Irish in Scotland, and others who came after him evangelized the Picts, no doubt building upon his foundations.

Columba did establish at least two churches in Inverness, but spent much of his energy setting up the monastery at Iona and training its members. When the influence of Iona in Scotland and Northumbria is considered, Columba's efforts can be said to have been a wise investment.

> At once, when the stars were made, lights of the firmament,
> the angels praised for His wonderful creating
> the Lord of this immense mass, the craftsman of the Heavens.
> With a praiseworthy proclamation, fitting and unchanging,
> in excellent symphony they gave thanks to the Lord
> not out of any endowment of nature, but out of love and choice.
>
> *Altus prosator verse F, attrib. Columba*

Ephrem of Syria, Deacon, Hymn Writer, Teacher of the Faith, 373

Ephrem, born in Nisibis (in modern Turkey), was one of the most prolific and gifted hymn writers in the history of Christianity. Over five hundred of his hymns survive, which were arranged after his death into 'hymn cycles'. He also wrote many biblical commentaries. He was baptized in 324, and joined the cathedral school, of which he later became the Head. It was whilst he was head of this school that he wrote most of his hymns.

Ephrem recognized the value of sung theology after encountering Gnostic songs in his native Nisibis. He saw the value of combining music and biblical exegesis to encourage the adoption of 'orthodox' doctrine. Originally written for the female choir at his church in Nisibis, Ephrem's hymns soon spread throughout the Roman Empire. Several of his hymns were written to counter specific heretical teachings, whilst others expound the beauty of the Mother of God, and the sacrifice of the life of Christ. His poetry had a great influence upon the development of hymn writing in both Syriac and Greek.

Ephrem emphasized the need to see God in all that is around the believer. Everything is capable of directing the eye of faith to God, and to engage the heart in worship. However, Ephrem was not so wrapped up in theological wonderment that he could not relate to the world around him. He encountered great hardship when his home town of Nisibis was captured by the Turks, and he is recorded as an old man struggling to distribute food to the hungry in the midst of famine.

> Each, according to the level of his own measure, can tell of you;
> in my boldness I approach the lowest step.
> Your birth is sealed up within the silence –
> what mouth then dares to meditate upon it?
>
> Your nature is single, but there are many ways of explaining it;
> our descriptions may be exalted, or in moderate terms, or lowly.
> Make me worthy of the lowest part, that I may gather up, as crumbs,
> the gleanings from your wisdom's table.
>
> Any elevated account of You is hidden with the Father;
> at your lesser riches the angels stand amazed,
> While a small trickle of words describing you
> provides a flood of homilies for mortals below.
>
> *Ephrem: A Hymn on the Eucharist*

Richard Baxter, Puritan Divine, 1691

Richard Baxter was born at Rowton in Shropshire in 1615 and educated at Donnington Free School in nearby Wroxeter. He was ordained deacon by the Bishop of Worcester in 1638. He was successively master of a school in Dudley, and curate first of Bridgnorth then of Kidderminster until civil war broke out in 1642. Though he served as a chaplain in the Parliamentary army for five years Baxter was always a moderate. He sought to curb the excesses of the Parliamentary troops and opposed both the execution of the king and Cromwell's assumption of power.

Baxter returned to Kidderminster as vicar in 1647. His ministry among the 'ignorant, rude and revelling people' of the town was remarkable. In addition to his preaching ministry Baxter set about implementing a policy of systematic parochial catechizing. So successful was this practice that five galleries were built in the parish church in order to accommodate the much larger number of churchgoers. *The Reformed Pastor*, published in1656, was Baxter's own account of this ministry ('Reformed' in this context meant not Calvinistic in doctrine but renewed in practice) and the book was both read and warmly recommended by the leaders of the evangelical revival of the following century.

Baxter was among those who invited Charles II to return in 1660 and his reward was to be offered the bishopric of Hereford. But, still questioning the nature and necessity of episcopacy after what he had seen of it in the years leading up to the Civil War, he declined and thus effectively ended his career in the Anglican ministry. At the 1661 Savoy Conference Baxter presented the 'Exceptions' – proposed changes to the Book of Common Prayer from a Puritan standpoint, most of which were rejected. But once again he appeared as the voice of moderation, producing a reformed eucharistic liturgy that satisfied neither Puritans nor Laudians.

Following the 1662 Act of Uniformity, Baxter lived privately in and around London. He suffered a great deal of petty persecution and was twice imprisoned. His second imprisonment, when he was 70, was for 21 months at the hands of the notorious Judge Jeffreys, for alleged sedition in his *Paraphrase of the New Testament* (1685). An advocate of moderation, toleration and fellowship across denominational divides he recognized that 'God breaketh not all men's hearts alike' and welcomed the Toleration Act of 1689. He died in London in 1691.

Evelyn Underhill, Spiritual Writer, 1941

Evelyn Underhill was born in Wolverhampton in 1875, the daughter of a barrister. After an education at home, supplemented by three years at a private school in Folkestone, she attended King's College, London. In 1907 she married a childhood friend, Hubert Stuart Moore. In the same year Evelyn underwent a conversion to the Christian faith, though she joined no particular Church. Her inclination was towards Rome but the condemnation of modern theological developments by Pope Pius X served to keep her at arm's length from a formal commitment to that Church. It was 1921 before she returned to the Church of England in which she had been baptized.

As a non-denominational Christian, who had recently undergone conversion, Evelyn turned to a study of the largely neglected mystics and published her first important book, *Mysticism,* in 1911. Through this she made the acquaintance of Baron Friedrich von Hügel, who became her teacher and spiritual director. Evelyn introduced the mystics to a wider audience and helped to establish the respectability of mystical spirituality in the Church of England. She taught that the life of contemplative prayer is not just for monks and nuns, but for any Christian who is willing to undertake it.

In 1924, after her return to the Anglican fold, she also began to conduct retreats, a service for which she was in great demand, as she also was for spiritual direction. It was said that her 'love of souls coupled with the determination to help them to grow at God's pace and not at their own or hers, won her the love and trust of all who went to her for help'. She was also a speaker, broadcaster and writer in the church press. For some years she was the theological editor of *The Spectator*. Among her many published works were *Practical Mysticism* (1914), and *Worship* (1936).

Evelyn had worked for naval intelligence during the First World War, but her views changed and as the Second World War approached she embraced pacifism. Just a few weeks before her death at Hampstead in June 1941, and during the worst of the blitz, she wrote to a friend:

> Yes – I am still a pacifist though I agree with you about the increasing difficulty of it. But I feel more and more sure that Christianity and war are incompatible, and that nothing worth having can be achieved by 'casting out Satan by Satan'.

Richard, Bishop of Chichester, 1253

Born in what is today Droitwich, Richard was the son of a farmer. He abandoned the agricultural life to pursue an academic career at Oxford. After his initial studies in that city, Richard studied at Paris and Bologna, and became an expert in canon law. In 1235 he returned to Oxford and was made Chancellor of the University. He also became Chancellor of Canterbury, being appointed by Edmund Rich, Archbishop of Canterbury. He went into voluntary exile with Edmund in protest at royal and papal interference and he was present when Edmund died, at Pontigny, on a journey to Rome to meet with the Pope in 1240. With Edmund, Richard was prepared to stand against royalty and secular powers in the battle for church authority. He was also prepared to stand up to clergy in the battle for reform.

While in exile Richard trained for the priesthood with the Dominicans at Orleans. After his ordination Richard returned to England as a parish priest at Charing and Deal in Kent. He was reappointed Chancellor of Canterbury by the new archbishop, Boniface.

Soon after, in 1244, Richard was elected Bishop of Chichester in opposition to the king's candidate for the see. He was forced to seek consecration abroad, being consecrated by Pope Innocent IV at Lyons the following year. The king backed down after the threat of excommunication and Richard was duly enthroned as Bishop of Chichester in 1245.

He was a legislator, and quickly introduced new instructions for his diocese. He emphasized that Mass should be celebrated with dignity, and that priests were not to be paid for the administration of the sacraments. He greatly improved the standard of clerical life. Richard's preaching recruited many soldiers for the Crusades, but he did not travel with them beyond Dover, where he became ill and died in 1253.

Richard was an excellent model of a diocesan bishop, accessible, generous and yet fair in his dealings with those in need of correction. Richard's prayer has remained in wide use in the centuries since his death:

> Thanks be to Thee,
> My Lord Jesus Christ
> for all the benefits thou hast given me,
> for all the pains and insults which thou hast borne for me.
> O most merciful redeemer,
> friend and brother,
> may I know thee more dearly
> and follow thee more nearly
> day by day.

Joseph Butler, Bishop of Durham, Philosopher, 1752

Butler was born at Wantage in Berkshire in 1692, the son of a Presbyterian draper. He was educated at the Dissenting academy in Tewkesbury, and was probably intending to enter the Presbyterian ministry. But his Dissenting background would have barred him from a university degree in England, and in 1714 he joined the Church of England in order to enter Oriel College, Oxford, where he read law and divinity. Ordained into the Anglican ministry in 1718, from 1718 to 1726 he was preacher at the Rolls Chapel in Chancery Lane, London. In 1726 he published a number of his sermons which brought him to public notice. In the same year he became incumbent of Stanhope in County Durham.

It was at Stanhope that Butler wrote his most famous work, *The Analogy of Religion*, published in 1736. Using empirical argument, Butler stressed fact in support of religion. He pointed to the order found in nature as a parallel to the order found in revelation, suggesting God as the author of both. The *Analogy* is said to have influenced many later writers, particularly David Hume and John Henry Newman. Although Butler did not specifically attack it, the *Analogy* went a long way to discrediting the popular eighteenth-century philosophy of Deism which denied revealed truth and relegated God to the level of an aloof supreme being, who took no personal interest in his creation.

In 1736 Butler was appointed Clerk of the Closet, in effect the personal chaplain to Queen Caroline, wife of King George II, and he was in constant attendance on her during her final illness until her death the following year. He was rewarded by being made Bishop of Bristol in 1738.

Bristol was one of the centres of the growing Methodist movement, but in common with other eighteenth-century bishops Butler had a distaste for religious 'enthusiasm', once famously telling John Wesley that 'the pretending to extraordinary revelations and gifts of the Holy Ghost is a horrid thing – a very horrid thing!'. Bristol was then the poorest diocese in England and in 1750 Butler was translated to the more important and much wealthier diocese of Durham, where he died in 1752. Butler's name had become so respected that a persistent but apocryphal rumour began (which can still be found in some sources) that he declined an offer to become Archbishop of Canterbury in 1747.

But his influence remained profound: a century later in 1860 Gladstone commented, 'I never take a step in life without thinking how Butler would have advised me.'

Samuel and Henrietta Barnett, Social Reformers, 1913 and 1936

Born into a Bristol manufacturing family in 1844, Samuel Barnett was educated at Wadham College, Oxford. In 1867 he was ordained to a curacy at St Mary's, Bryanston Square in Marylebone where he met, and in 1873 married, Henrietta Rowland (born 1851), the daughter of a wealthy London businessman. With a deep practical faith of her own Henrietta was working with the housing reformer Octavia Hill (see 13 August). Later in 1873 the Barnetts moved to London's East End when Samuel became Vicar of St Jude's, Whitechapel. They were both deeply affected by the squalid conditions in which their parishioners lived and became much involved in promoting social reform both locally and on the national stage. Active Christian Socialists, they sought to ensure that social reform was based on Christian principles and that Christians were actively involved in social reform. In 1885 they jointly wrote *Practicable Socialism.*

Samuel was unafraid to experiment in worship and educational practice and even to borrow ideas from urban Nonconformity in order to bring the gospel to those who would not normally attend church services. He lobbied for the Artisans' Dwellings Act of 1875. He served on the Whitechapel Board of Guardians and was one of the first in England to propose universal pension provision. Henrietta was also involved in various projects of her own, mainly involving education and the welfare of children. She was also a founder of Whitechapel Art Gallery.

Perhaps their best-known legacy is that of Toynbee Hall, the first of the 'university settlements', based on the principle that those with money and education should live and work among the poor. Samuel was its first Warden, from 1884 to 1896. After a visit in 1884, Georges Clémenceau, later Prime Minster of France, remarked that Samuel Barnett was one of the 'three really great men' he had met in England.

In 1906 Samuel was appointed a canon (and later sub-dean) of Westminster and the couple moved to leafy Hampstead. The contrast with Whitechapel inspired Henrietta to create a model suburb in which decent housing, open spaces and recreational amenities would be available to people of modest income. This was the origin of Hampstead Garden Suburb, which developed after 1907. When completed the development featured special housing for the old and disabled, modern schools and new churches. After Samuel's death at Hove in 1913 Henrietta continued her work and became a Dame of the British Empire in 1924. She died in 1936.

Bernard Mizeki, Apostle of the MaShona, Martyr, 1896

Bernard Mizeki was born in Mozambique in about 1861. When he was twelve or a little older, he left his home and went to Cape Town, South Africa, where for the next ten years he worked as a labourer, living in the slums of Cape Town but, unlike many migrant workers, rising above the squalor of his surroundings. After his day's work, he attended night classes at an Anglican school run by the Cowley Fathers. So he became a Christian and was baptized in 1886. Besides the fundamentals of European schooling, he showed a rare aptitude for language study, mastering at least ten languages. In time these skills would be a valuable asset in the work of translating the Scriptures and prayer books and hymn books into African languages.

After graduating from the school, he accompanied Bishop Knight-Bruce to Mashonaland, in Southern Rhodesia (now Zimbabwe), to work as a lay catechist. In 1891 he was sent to Nhowe, and there he built a mission complex. He grew crops, studied the local language, observed the daily office and cultivated friendships with the villagers. In due course he opened a school for the children, which further endeared him to the local people.

Eventually he moved the mission complex on to a nearby plateau, next to a grove of trees sacred to the ancestral spirits of the Mashona. Although he had first obtained the chief's permission, he angered the local religious leaders when he cut some of the trees down and carved crosses into others. But this clear assertion of the authority of Christ did not hinder the mission's work and over the next five years (1891–6), the mission at Nhowe experienced many conversions.

In 1896 there was a native uprising against the rule of Cecil Rhodes' British South Africa Company, which administered Southern Rhodesia. Missionaries, regarded as agents of the colonial power, were especially vulnerable. Bernard was advised to flee but refused to desert his converts or his post. On 18 June 1896, he was speared to death outside his hut. His wife and a mission worker went for help and, when some distance away, claimed to have seen a blinding light on the hillside where Bernard had been lying, and heard a rushing sound, as though of many wings. Certainly, when they returned there was no sign of the body. The site of Bernard's martyrdom has since become a popular place of pilgrimage.

19 June

Sundar Singh of India, Sadhu (holy man), Evangelist, Teacher of the Faith, 1929

Sundar Singh was born in 1889 into a wealthy landowning Sikh family in Rampur, North Punjab. The death of his mother when he was 14 unhinged him. He abused the missionaries at the mission school he attended, burnt a Bible and resolved to commit suicide on a railway line. However, he experienced a vision of Christ and was converted. Expelled by his family for this act of treachery to their faith he was taken in by a nearby Christian community and the following year, 1905, was baptized in the Anglican church at Simla.

The following year he set out on the roads of India wearing a yellow robe and turban. The yellow robe was the recognized dress of a Hindu sadhu, a solitary holy man. Proud of his Sikh ancestry, he never wore European dress, preferring to present the Christian faith 'in an Eastern bowl rather than a European vessel'. He had a special burden for the land of Tibet and in 1908 at the age of 19, he crossed its frontiers for the first time. Most years until 1923 he made a journey there and he disappeared on his final journey in 1929.

In 1909 Sundar Singh began training for the ordained ministry at the Anglican college in Lahore. As the course drew to an end, the Principal informed him that he must now discard his sadhu's robe and wear 'respectable' European clerical dress; use formal Anglican worship; sing English hymns; and never preach outside his parish without permission. Knowing he was not called to a ministry with such constraints he left with great sadness to pursue his itinerant ministry as a sadhu. He was now not a member of any denomination, and did not try to begin one of his own, though he shared fellowship with Christians of all kinds.

It is said that he recognized the flaw in European mission to India while on a train. A high-caste Hindu – a Brahmin – had collapsed in the heat but refused water from the Anglo-Indian stationmaster. He could only accept it in his own drinking vessel. When that was brought he drank, and revived. So India would not accept the gospel of Jesus offered in Western guise. That was why many listeners responded to him in his Indian sadhu's robe. He made it clear that Christianity was not an imported, alien, foreign religion but indigenous to Indian needs, aspirations and faith.

22 June

Alban, first Martyr of Britain, c.250

Records of Christians living in Britain have been found as early as the second century, and in 314 three 'British' bishops attended a council in Arles.

Alban, held to be the first British martyr, has traditionally been regarded as having being martyred in the Diocletian persecution of 303. But his death is more likely to have occurred in the reign of either Septimius Severus c.209, or Decius c.250.

Alban was a Romano-British pagan living in Verulamium, known today as St Albans, Hertfordshire. He met a fugitive priest and gave him shelter in his home. Alban was so struck by the way of life and the commitment of the priest that in time he was converted to the faith. When soldiers came searching for the fugitive Alban disguised himself in the priest's cloak and was arrested and condemned to death. The priest was subsequently arrested and stoned to death some days later.

Holmhurst Hill, where Alban's martyrdom is traditionally located, became the site first of a shrine and then of a church dedicated to his memory. By the Middle Ages this church had grown into the Abbey of St Albans and is now the cathedral of the diocese which bears his name.

Bede, writing in the early eighth century, recorded the torture and trial of Alban. He mentions the crowds at his execution, a spring of water rising up at his feet at the top of a hill, and the miraculous conversion of the appointed executioner. Bede also records that his executioner was unable to see the death of Alban, as the instant he beheaded him his own eyes fell out.

> Saint Alban suffered on the twenty-second day of June near the city of Verulamium . . . Here, when the peace of Christian times was restored, a beautiful Church worthy of his martyrdom was built, where sick folk are healed and frequent miracles take place to this day.
>
> *Bede: Ecclesiatical History 1.7*

Etheldreda, Abbess of Ely, c.678

Etheldreda, sometimes referred to as Audrey, was the daughter of Anna, a Christian King of the East Angles.

Etheldreda was married at a young age to Tondberht, an earldorman of South Gyrwas, but having taken a vow of chastity she kept her virginity. Tondberht died three years into their marriage and Etheldreda withdrew to live on the Isle of Ely. She stayed there for five years until in 660, at the request of her family, she married Egfrith, the 15-year-old son of King Oswy of Northumbria.

Once again Etheldreda refused to consummate her marriage, initially securing the agreement of her husband. However, after twelve years of unconsummated marriage Egfrith admitted failure in his lengthy campaign for marital normality and gave Etheldreda permission to become a nun. Egfrith's final attempt at instigating a full marital relationship was an attempt to bribe Bishop Wilfrid of York (see 12 October) to release her from her vow of chastity. The bishop refused and Egfrith gave up. The marriage was annulled and Etheldreda moved into the monastery at Coldingham in 672.

A year later Etheldreda founded a 'double monastery' for both men and women at Ely in the Fens. This was no ordinary monastic community, having been formed out of much family wealth. Etheldreda lived a relatively ascetic life there until her death from the plague in 678. The present Ely Cathedral occupies the site of Etheldreda's monastery.

Ethelreda became one of the most popular female Anglo-Saxon saints partly because of the legend which surrounded her body. Seventeen years after her death her body was said to be incorrupt and her grave-clothes fresh. Many churches were dedicated in her honour and Bede wrote a long hymn in her praise.

Cyril, Bishop of Alexandria, Teacher of the Faith, 444

Cyril was the nephew of the powerful Bishop of Alexandria. Alexandria was a culturally diverse city steeped in tradition and when Cyril succeeded his uncle as bishop it was the second city of the Roman Empire.

Cyril was a distinctive and able theologian believed by some to have been the most distinguished theologian of the Alexandrian theological tradition. He systematized earlier theology on the person of Christ and the doctrine of the Trinity. He wrote eloquently and precisely, and preached persuasively. He is regarded as a defender of orthodoxy and remembered as the guiding force behind the Third Ecumenical Council at Ephesus in 431. However, he was also arrogant, intransigent, outspoken and harsh in relations both with pagans outside of the Church and with heretics within it. These tendencies were to be a source of both strength and of conflict in Cyril's life and ministry.

Cyril's major theological argument was with Nestorius, Bishop of Constantinople. Nestorius thought that there were two distinct persons in Christ: God and humanity, joined only by a loose union of wills. In Cyril's view this invalidated the Incarnation. He preferred to speak of a single nature in Christ, resulting from the union of divinity and humanity.

Rivalry between Alexandria and Constantinople was intense. The rising power and influence of Constantinople was threatening to eclipse the position of Alexandria, and this tension intensified the argument between Cyril and Nestorius. Cyril was a vicious opponent, politically astute and uncompromising. The motivation for his attacks on Nestorius was a concern for the doctrine of salvation. Nestorius, in turn, was known to have desired to be orthodox and affirm the unity of Christ, but to have been unable to fully commit to this position while retaining his own integrity.

The dispute between the two was harsh, loud and lengthy, and the theological argument was often eclipsed by the clash of personalities, politics and civic rivalries. Although ultimately victorious, Cyril himself was accused of being imprecise in his theology and after his death some of his pronouncements were a source of contention.

> For Scripture says not that the Word united himself to the person of a man, but that he was made flesh. That means nothing else than that he partook of flesh and blood like us. He made our body his own, not ceasing to be God.
>
> *Letter 4*

Cyril established the term *theotokos* (God-bearer) as a title for Mary the mother of Jesus, and maintained the doctrine of the Incarnation for the future of the Church. It is for this that he is commemorated rather than for his political manoeuverings. He is a reminder that even when the stakes are high the furnace of debate is not the best place to judge one another.

Irenaeus, Bishop of Lyons, Teacher of the Faith, c.200

As a young boy in Smyrna (on the Aegean coast of Asia Minor) Irenaeus had listened to Polycarp, who in turn had known the apostle John. He studied at Rome before becoming a priest in Lyons, a large trading city in the Rhône valley which was growing in strategic importance in the West.

Irenaeus was aware of the heritage of the Christian faith, and of the need to affirm the tradition of Christianity in the face of opposition from emerging philosophical systems. He stood against heresy and incorrect interpretations of the gospel, particularly by the Gnostics, a faith movement that stressed secret knowledge and creation myths.

In 177 Irenaeus was sent to deliver letters to the Church in Rome. On his return a year later he discovered that Christians in the city of Lyons had been persecuted, and many, including the bishop, had died. Irenaeus, who was renowned as a peacemaker, was appointed as the next bishop.

In his writing and his debating Irenaeus sought to expose the inadequacies and discrepancies within Gnostic thought and he challenged Gnostic claims to secret gospel traditions. He put great emphasis upon the apostolic succession and the continuation of the teaching given to him by the Church Fathers. The Scriptures did not have any credence amongst opponents to Christianity. Irenaeus united two separate defences of the gospel by appealing both to Scripture and tradition and greatly strengthened the case for Christianity. He affirmed the Christian belief in God, and emphasized the unity of the Father and the Son in the work of salvation.

Irenaeus' defence of Christianity against the threat from Gnosticism was largely successful. Because of his appeal to both the tradition of the Church and to the 'Fathers of the Church' he is known as the first Catholic theologian.

Irenaeus instigated the 'Rule of Faith', a short credal statement summarizing the message of the gospel, as a weapon against heresy:

> The whole church believes in one God the Father Almighty, maker of heaven and earth and the seas and all that is therein, and in one Christ Jesus the Son of God, who was made flesh for our salvation, and in the Holy Spirit, who through the prophets preached the dispensations and the comings and the virgin birth and the passion, and the rising from the dead and the assumption into heaven in his flesh of our beloved Lord Jesus Christ.
>
> *Irenaeus: Rule of Faith*

Henry, John and Henry Venn the younger, Priests, Evangelical Divines, 1797, 1813 and 1873

It is said that there were Venns in Holy Orders from the end of the sixteenth century to the beginning of the twentieth. In the eighteenth and nineteenth centuries three successive generations of this family provided remarkable Anglican clergy.

Henry Venn (1724–97)

Born at Barnes, Surrey, in 1724 Venn was ordained in 1749 and elected as Fellow of Queens' College, Cambridge. Influenced by the writings of William Law (see 10 April), he took his ordination with great seriousness, embarking on a disciplined spiritual life and giving up the pleasure of playing cricket. After several short curacies he became curate at Clapham near London in 1754 where he became involved in the evangelical revival.

But to the surprise of many in 1759 he left London to become vicar of the growing Yorkshire mill town of Huddersfield. Here he wrote his spiritual classic, *The Complete Duty of Man*. In this reply to the anonymous but influential devotional guide, *The Whole Duty of Man*, Venn stressed a total trust in Christ alone as the basis for salvation.

Two clear inferences can be drawn from Venn's twelve-year ministry in Huddersfield. First is his endorsement of the parochial system at a time when it was being by-passed or ignored by Wesley, Whitefield and other evangelical leaders. Venn demonstrated that the parish could be an effective vehicle for mission and evangelism in an ongoing pastoral context of nurture and discipleship. In one three-year period, for example, there were estimated to have been 900 conversions in Huddersfield. Secondly, Venn provides a warning against overwork and 'burn-out'. Quite simply, in his twelve years of ministry in Huddersfield he wore himself out and was compelled to spend the remainder of his ministry in a much lower gear. The 5.00 am rising, the ceaseless round of preaching and teaching around his large and growing industrial parish, his willingness to travel long distances to preach at the request of other evangelical clergy, and the death of his wife in 1767 leaving him with five young children, all took their toll. Not all evangelical clergy of the eighteenth century had the constitution of a John Wesley.

Suffering a breakdown of his health and the apparent symptoms of approaching consumption, the 49-year-old Venn reluctantly left Huddersfield for the small country parish of Yelling near Huntingdon in 1771. Happily, he survived for a further 26 years, but he was never the same as in his glory days in Huddersfield, exercising a much more low-key ministry in a quiet rural backwater. His last six months were lived at Clapham with his son John. He died there in 1797 and is buried in St Paul's Church.

John Venn (1759–1813)

John Venn was born in 1759 at Clapham where his father was curate. A reticent personality, suffering poor health throughout his life, he was refused entry to Trinity College, Cambridge because of his 'Methodist' parentage, and went instead to Sidney Sussex. At Cambridge he was influenced, and overawed, by his contemporary Charles Simeon (see 13 November). Ordained in 1782, he became Rector of Little Dunham in Norfolk where, as the first resident clergyman in 75 years, he began the process of reorganizing and modernizing the parish.

In 1792, thanks to Simeon's influence, he returned to his birthplace as rector. Here he made a deliberately cautious start, winning the confidence of his parishioners before making the many changes (afternoon lectures, Sunday schools, regular ministration of the sacraments, confirmation classes, work among the poor, etc.) that turned Clapham into a model evangelical parish. Among those who worshipped in Venn's congregation were William Wilberforce (see 30 July), Henry Thornton, Thomas Clarkson, Zachary Macaulay and a number of others – the 'Saints' or the 'Clapham Sect', who were the leaders of the anti-slavery movement. Indeed, the year before Venn came to Clapham, Wilberforce had introduced his first abolition bill in Parliament. Becoming their rector, Venn in many ways also became the chaplain of the anti-slavery movement.

As his confidence grew his ministry widened. He led the London branch of the Eclectic Society, founded by John Newton to provide fellowship and a forum for discussion for evangelical clergy. In 1802 he was also involved in founding a new Christian publication, the *Christian Observer.*

But it was the founding of the Church Missionary Society that was perhaps Venn's greatest achievement. Considering the existing SPCK and SPG (see 15 February) too exclusive and the newly-founded interdenominational London Missionary Society not Anglican enough, Venn – with the support of the Eclectics and the Clapham Sect – became first chairman of what was initially named the Society for Missions to Africa and the East in 1799. But the new society was slow in taking root and in some ways reflected Venn's own cautious attitude. It took several years before any missionaries were sent out and then they were mainly German Lutherans. It was under the leadership of his son Henry that John Venn's vision for the CMS as a voluntary society at the heart of the Church of England, both paid for and staffed by ordinary Anglicans, eventually came to fruition.

Henry Venn (1796–1873)

Born at Clapham Rectory in 1796, the younger Henry Venn was to become probably the greatest missionary strategist of the nineteenth century. Influenced by Charles Simeon (see 13 November) at Cambridge, Venn moved to a curacy at St Dunstan's in Fleet Street and an incumbency at Drypool in Hull, before becoming Vicar of St John's, Holloway in 1834.

In 1822 Venn accepted an invitation to join the committee of the Church Missionary Society. In 1837 this interest in mission was rewarded by the offer of the See of Madras, which he declined and in 1841 he became 'Honorary Clerical Secretary' of the CMS, a post which he retained for 31 years. For the first five years he combined it with parish work but in 1846 he resigned his living in order to devote himself full-time to mission work.

Venn developed a clear strategy for the CMS, drawing clear distinctions between 'mission' and 'Church', and between the roles of missionary and pastor. In his view the mission was not itself the Church but was there to create an indigenous Church and should, at the right time, withdraw (the 'Euthanasia' of the mission) in order to ensure that that Church would be truly indigenous and not an alien institution. To Venn the great object of a mission was:

> the raising up of a Native Church – self-supporting, self-governing, self-extending. The Mission is the scaffolding; the Native Church is the edifice. The removal of the scaffolding is the proof that the building is completed.

Venn aimed to develop 'native pastors' initially under European superintendence and prepare the way 'eventually to leave the work in their hands'. He pursued a policy of advancing indigenous clergy into office and was largely responsible for Samuel Ajayi Crowther's appointment as the first black bishop in the Anglican Communion in 1864.

Venn's attitudes were progressive and far-sighted: he recognized the reality of cultural distinctiveness, and he was tolerant and supportive towards indigenous Christians, warning missionaries of judging them by European standards. On the practical level Venn engaged in networking, lobbying and organizing worldwide prayer for specific objects. He had an incredible appetite for hard work, maintaining a personal correspondence, by hand, with all CMS missionaries. It is estimated that he wrote 6,000 letters.

Venn took CMS from being a somewhat marginal body reliant on hiring German and Swiss missionaries to being the largest and most effective body in Britain for the delivery of overseas mission.

Thomas More, Scholar, and John Fisher, Bishop of Rochester, Reformation Martyrs, 1535

Thomas More (1478–1535)

The accounts of Thomas More's happy home life at Chelsea, recorded after his death by his son-in-law Will Roper, the growth in More's popularity following his canonization by Pope Pius XI in 1935 and Robert Bolt's 1960 play *A Man for All Seasons*, with its widely popular film version, have left a delightful but anachronistic picture of an enlightened twentieth-century family man trapped in the political bear garden that was Tudor England.

The real Thomas More was born in London in 1478, the son of a judge, and educated at Oxford and Lincoln's Inn. Called to the Bar in 1501, elected to Parliament in 1504 and appointed under-sheriff of London in 1510, the young More was left a widower with four small children. He subsequently married Alice Middleton, a widow, to provide his children with a mother. An articulate Renaissance humanist, More's best known work was *Utopia* (1516), a satirical account of life on the fictitious island of Utopia where conditions there are contrasted favourably with those of contemporary English society. Encountering the growing force of the Reformation, More had no sympathy with either the Reformers or their beliefs. He endorsed the burning of heretics and conducted an acrimonious pamphlet war with William Tyndale.

More came to the attention of Henry VIII and the two men became friends, the king greatly valuing More's company, conversation and advice. More's rise in the royal favour was indicated by his becoming a member of the Privy Council in 1518 and being knighted in 1521. Two years later he became Speaker of the House of Commons and in 1529 Lord Chancellor, the first layman to hold the post. His fortunes changed, however, when he refused to support Henry's divorce from Catherine of Aragon, his religious principles making him unwilling to support any defiance of the Pope. He resigned from the Chancellorship in 1532 and withdrew from public life at great personal financial cost.

But a private life did not exempt More from the requirements of the 1534 Act of Succession and he refused to take the accompanying oath since it would have involved a rejection of papal authority. After a trial at Westminster Hall, More was condemned to death and was beheaded on Tower Hill on 6 July 1535, declaring himself on the scaffold to be 'the King's good servant, but God's first'.

John Fisher (1469–1535)

John Fisher is often coupled with Thomas More in the dedications of Roman Catholic churches and schools, and the two share feast days (albeit different ones) in both Roman and Anglican communions. Fisher was born in Beverley in Yorkshire in 1469, the son of a merchant. He was educated at Michaelhouse, Cambridge, where he was elected Fellow in 1491 and became Vicar of Northallerton in Yorkshire. He returned to Cambridge in 1496 as Master of Michaelhouse. An able scholar, he rose rapidly in the academic world, becoming Vice-Chancellor of the University in 1501 and Chancellor in 1504.

Fisher served as personal chaplain to a powerful and influential patron – Lady Margaret Beaufort, the mother of King Henry VII. Her backing enabled him to exert a progressive influence at Cambridge, promoting humanism and bringing the Dutch scholar Erasmus to Cambridge to teach divinity and Greek. In 1502 Fisher became the first Lady Margaret Professor of Divinity at Cambridge and in 1504 he became Bishop of Rochester. As a preacher his reputation was so great that in 1509, when both Henry VII and Lady Margaret died, Fisher preached at both their funerals.

Fisher's progressive views only extended so far, however, and though he had denounced abuses in the English Church, he strongly opposed the European Reformation, preaching and writing against it, especially the doctrines of Martin Luther. When Henry VIII proposed to divorce Catherine of Aragon, Fisher objected, not surprisingly perhaps, since he was the queen's confessor. In May 1532, the same month as More resigned the Lord Chancellorship, Fisher publicly preached against the divorce. But with the divorce accomplished and Henry re-married to Anne Boleyn, Fisher lost any influence he may have had. Along with Thomas More he refused to take the oath of the Act of Succession (which gave Anne Boleyn's offspring precedence over Catherine of Aragon's) and was imprisoned in the Tower of London.

In May 1535, Pope Paul III's award of a cardinal's hat to Fisher may have been intended as a comfort to the imprisoned bishop, but in practice it appeared in England as a provocative act and unwarranted interference in the English judicial system by the Pope. It thus even further undermined Fisher's cause. One month later, the new cardinal was brought to trial, accused of the treasonous act of refusing to accept Henry VIII as head of the Church. He was beheaded on 22 June 1535, two weeks before More. Like More, Fisher was prepared to pay the ultimate price for his beliefs rather than submit to an authority which, however high, seemed to him to contradict, or even usurp, divine authority.

Benedict of Nursia, Abbot of Monte Cassino, Father of Western Monasticism, c.550

Benedict was born in the region of Nursia, some 70 miles from Rome. He studied in the city, but found the hedonistic lifestyle of his companions overbearing, and withdrew to live as a hermit at Subiaco. As news of his life spread, he was joined by others, who formed an embryonic monastic community around him. Such were the numbers that joined him, that he eventually found himself directing twelve communities in the region of the Aniene Valley.

Rivalry and jealousy from local clergy eventually forced Benedict away from the area to Monte Cassino. He spent the last 17 years of his life establishing a monastery there, and during this time he wrote his 'Rule of life' for monks.

The Rule of St Benedict drew on ascetic tradition, including the 'Life of Antony', and the 'Rule of the Master'. Benedict's 'Rule' is not a list of instructions on how to live as a monk, but rather guidance offered in humility by a person of long experience in the Christian life. Benedict places great stress upon the role of the abbot in any monastic community, emphasizing the incarnational element of such a leadership position. He stresses the importance of this role, and also highlights the required behaviour and attitudes of the one responsible for the whole community. Obedience to superiors is an essential element of Benedictine spirituality, as obeying the abbot's directives and advice frees the other monks within the community to fully engage with, and worship, God. Benedict stressed that the motive for all obedience is not fear, but love, ultimately, the love of God. Humility before others, and God, is paramount. His 'Rule' was clearly subordinate to Scripture, and Benedict had a strong belief in the necessity of orthodox practice.

Benedict taught that the spiritual side of a person could not be divorced from any other part. For him, the whole of life is spiritual, because God calls the whole person and the whole person is to respond to God. The Rule spread quickly throughout the West, and it is for this that he has become known as the 'Father of Western Monasticism'.

> If we do not venture to approach men who are in power, except with humility and reverence, when we wish to ask a favour, how must we beseech the Lord God of all things with all humility and purity of devotion. And let us be assured that it is not in many words, but in the purity of heart and tears of compunction that we are heard.
>
> *Rule of St Benedict, Ch. XX*

John Keble, Priest, Tractarian, Poet, 1866

In later years John Henry Newman declared that it was the sermon on 'National Apostasy', which John Keble preached at the opening of the Oxford Assizes on 14 July 1833 that marked the real beginning of what came to be known as the Oxford Movement.

Born into a clergy family in 1792, John Keble proved an able scholar at Oxford and at the age of 19 he was elected Fellow of Oriel College. Ordained deacon in 1815 he initially worked as a tutor at Oriel but resigned in 1823 in favour of parish work, acting as his father's curate in Gloucestershire. It was in this period of his life that he composed the poems which were published as *The Christian Year*. Its popularity was shown by going through almost fifty editions during Keble's lifetime and many of the poems were transformed into hymns. The best known, *New every morning* and *Blest are the pure in heart*, remain a staple of many modern hymn books. His work was recognized by his election as Professor of Poetry at Oxford in 1831.

Keble's natural conservatism found an echo with many in the 1830s who were unnerved by the reforms being carried out in both Church and State by the reforming Whig government. Keble used the opportunity of the 1833 Assize Sermon to protest against the Church being subordinate to a Parliament that was no longer exclusively Anglican. His views struck a chord in clerical circles in deeply conservative Oxford. Although Keble wrote nine of the Tracts for the Times and engaged in written debate, he was essentially a scholarly parish priest who preferred to eschew both controversy and limelight. In 1836 he returned to parish life at Hursley, near Winchester.

He sought to revive sacramental confession in the Church not just to quieten consciences but as an aid to more effective pastoral work, considering that, 'we go on working in the dark . . . until the rule of systematic confession is revived in our church'. Naturally he was much sought after as a confessor and spiritual director. When, in 1846, Dr Pusey (see 16 September) made his first sacramental confession, it was to Keble: 'I cannot doubt but that through your ministry and the power of the keys, I have received the grace of God, as I know not that I ever did before.'

He died in 1866 and four years later Keble College was founded at Oxford as his memorial.

Only, O Lord, in thy dear love
Fit us for perfect rest above;
And help us, this and every day,
To live more nearly as we pray.

Swithun, Bishop of Winchester, c.862

Swithun was Bishop of Winchester from 852 until his death in 862. Little is known of his life that can be traced with historical certainty.

Swithun was born in Wessex, an area that was in the process of becoming the most influential of the Anglo-Saxon kingdoms, and educated at Winchester Minster. He was chosen to become chaplain to Egbert, King of Wessex, and then was given the responsibility for the education of Egbert's son Ethelwulf.

He was subsequently appointed as Bishop of Winchester by King Ethelwulf when he was enthroned in 852. During the period of his office the kingdom of Wessex grew in reputation and influence throughout the land, despite Viking attacks. The post of Bishop of Winchester grew in importance and influence during the time of Ethelwulf's reign.

Later legends give Swithun a reputation for compassion and evangelism, but it is his intellectual ability and learning for which he was first remembered.

On his death he was buried in a humble grave outside of the walls of the minster at his own request, and in 971, some 90 years later, his body was moved to a shrine within the cathedral. His commemoration in popular culture seems to date from this period rather than from his life. The translation of his remains was the occasion for a dramatic rainfall, which was taken to be a sign of his spiritual power. Miraculous events were also held to have occurred during the re-interment, and this added to the legends surrounding him. The belief that the weather on St Swithun's Day will hold for the following 40 days remains a popular legend today.

Bonaventure, Friar, Bishop, Teacher of the Faith, 1274

The son of a physician, Bonaventure was born at Bagnoreggio, near Orvieto in Italy. He was known throughout his life for his gentleness, compassion and his availability to those in need. He became a Franciscan in 1243, and was sent to Paris to continue his studies. In 1248 Bonaventure was given a licence to teach, and in 1253 he was appointed head of the Franciscan school in Paris.

A notable theologian, and a contemporary of Thomas Aquinas, Bonaventure emphasized the importance of a rational approach to the mysteries of the faith. In contrast to Aquinas he asserted that the creation of the world could be demonstrated by human reason, and he denied the doctrine of the immaculate conception of the Blessed Virgin Mary.

Bonaventure was a great mystical theologian. He stressed simplicity of life and the importance of detachment from both riches and the rich. He emphasized that all human wisdom was folly when compared with the mystical illumination which God gives to the faithful Christian.

In 1257, when he was 36, he was elected Minister-General of the Franciscan order. He worked to reform the movement, stressed the need to study, and allowed the possession of books and buildings for this purpose. He disapproved of the teaching of absolute poverty. He extended the practice of working in universities. Bonaventure laid emphasis on the Franciscan order as completing and aiding the work of the diocesan clergy, rather than competing against it. In 1263 his biography of St Francis was given official approval by the Franciscan order.

Bonaventure combined the highest intellectual attainments with personal simplicity and humility. In 1265 he was offered the Archbishopric of York but turned it down. In 1273 he was ordered by the Pope to accept the post of Cardinal-Bishop of Albano. The story is told that when his cardinal's hat was brought from Rome Bonaventure continued washing the dishes and instructed the papal legate to hang the hat in a tree since his hands were still wet and greasy from the dishes.

The last acts of his life were focused on the possible reunion of the Western and Eastern Churches. Preliminary agreement was reached, and Bonaventure presided at the Mass of reconciliation. But he died shortly afterwards, and so did not see Constantinople reject the terms of the reunion.

> All [these] sciences have certain and infallible rules, like rays of light shining downupon our mind from the eternal law. And thus our mind, illumined and flooded by such brilliance, unless it is blind, can be led through itself to contemplate that Eternal light. The radiation and contemplation of this light lifts up the wise in wonder; and on the contrary it leads to confusion the fools who do not believe so that they may understand.
>
> *The Soul's Journey into God, Ch. III*

Osmund, Bishop of Salisbury, 1099

The history of Osmund's early life is lost in time, and he is first known through his appointment as Chancellor of England in 1072. He is said to have arrived in England with William the Conqueror. Life histories of Osmund before 1072 do exist, but they are largely unreliable and chronologically impossible.

Osmund was made Bishop of Salisbury in 1078. This diocese included Dorset, Wiltshire and Berkshire. The headquarters of the diocese was Old Sarum, a fortress rather than a city, placed on a high hill, surrounded by massive walls. He completed the cathedral of 'Old Sarum', consecrating it on 5 April 1092. Five days later the roof was destroyed in a thunderstorm.

Osmund instigated cathedral reform and improved administration. He initiated a 'cathedral chapter' with its own constitution. The positions of dean, precentor, chancellor and treasurer were created and each had their duties exactly defined. Thirty-two cathedral canons were also created to be advisers to the bishop, also carrying out missionary work and other duties. These and other regulations that he produced for Salisbury came to be adopted by many other cathedral bodies and were extremely influential within the development of the Church in England.

Osmund's position as bishop did not prevent him from taking up further roles within the royal court. He was involved in the preparation and evaluation of the Domesday survey, and he was at the court when the Domesday Book was presented to King William in 1086.

At one time Osmund disagreed with Archbishop Anselm in a dispute concerning investitures and in 1095 at the Council of Rockingham he favoured the king over the archbishop. However he reputedly asked for forgiveness from the archbishop, and later sided with him against the king in a subsequent Church–State dispute.

For a time Osmund was believed to have produced the Sarum Liturgy, but this has since been shown not to be the case as the liturgy did not coming into full form until the time of Richard le Poore (1198–1228). His love of learning and books led to the creation of a sizeable library for himself and his canons at Salisbury. By enforcing cathedral reform Osmund instigated a style of governance that spread quickly throughout the south of the country. Also crucial to his theology and position was the idea of the cathedral as the 'mother church' of a diocese.

Elizabeth Ferard, first Deaconess of the Church of England, Founder of the Community of St Andrew, 1883

The 2004/5 edition of *Crockford's Clerical Directory* has less than a page and a half devoted to the 55 remaining members of the order of deaconesses. Yet from 1861 until 1986, when women were first ordained to the diaconate in the Church of England, the role of deaconess was the highest clerical role to which they could be admitted.

The Lutherans had been the first denomination to revive the order of deaconesses, a deaconess institution being founded at Kaiserwerth by Pastor T. Fliedner in 1836. In 1858 the recently revived Convocation of Canterbury discussed a revival of the order in England.

Elizabeth Catherine Ferard was descended from an old Huguenot family and had been awaiting an appropriate opportunity to serve God in the Church of England. After the death of her mother in 1858 she went to Germany to stay for several months in the Kaiserwerth institution. She worked in the orphan house, learned nursing skills and commented, 'I again heard of the continual spreading of the Deaconess work in every direction except in England, and more than ever wished we could have something of the kind in England, where the materials for it are so abundant, could we but found a Deaconess House on the right principles without falling on the stumbling block of Romanism.'

Returning to England, Elizabeth was to demonstrate that she had the singleness of purpose and strength of mind to put her vision into practice. She initially worked for a short time with the Community of All Hallows at Ditchingham in Suffolk. Then, in 1861, she took the step of faith and offered herself to begin the deaconess order in England. She and two other like-minded women began the Community of St Andrew at a house in Burton Crescent, King's Cross under a common rule of life dedicated to worship and to works of mercy. On St Andrew's Day 1861 the Community merged (though kept its own identity) with the new Deaconesses' Institution and the following July Bishop Tait of London admitted Elizabeth as the first deaconess in the Church of England. The new order began to flourish as more dioceses began to admit women to the order, though some disliked the concept of sisterhoods and preferred the parochial model pioneered by Isabella Gilmore (see 16 April) in Rochester diocese. The growth of the work in London resulted in a move from King's Cross to larger premises in Westbourne Park. The same year Elizabeth's health failed and she resigned her leadership role. But she lived for a further ten years, dying on Easter Sunday 1883.

Gregory, Bishop of Nyssa, and his sister Macrina, Deaconess, Teachers of the Faith, c.394 and c.379

Gregory of Nyssa

Gregory was both a speculative theologian, and a mystic. Along with his brother Basil and Gregory of Nazianzus (see 2 January) he is known as one of the three 'Cappadocian Fathers' whose thought developed and influenced the doctrines of the Holy Spirit and of the Trinity in the fourth century.

Born in 335, Gregory initially trained as a rhetorician, and endured a painful marriage before entering the monastic community that had been founded by his brother. While the rest of Gregory's family embraced the ascetic life wholeheartedly, Gregory was less enamoured of it, and although a member of the community he continued to study rhetoric and philosophy, and to seek an outlet for his own free expression of the Christian faith.

In 371 he was consecrated by his brother Basil as Bishop of Nyssa, a small insignificant town in the region of Caesarea. This event was not entirely without political overtones and dubious motives. He later became Bishop of Sebaste, a much more influential and attractive city, but he eventually returned to Nyssa. The Arian conflict, and the vacillating allegiances of the rulers of the Empire, meant that Gregory spent the period from 376 to 378 in exile.

In 379 his brother Basil died and Gregory, released from his influence, wrote his most creative theological works. He critically engaged with his theological opponents while respecting both Scripture and tradition.

Gregory was a distinctive theologian. Orthodox in thought and theology, and passionate in his defence of Nicaea, he was not afraid to speculate and assimilate philosophy and learning from other sources into his theology, as long as it resulted in orthodox thought. No other Father of the fourth century made so extensive a use of philosophy as he did. Guided by excellent authors, making good use of his various sources, and required by controversies and theological debate to hone his doctrinal pronouncements to precision, Gregory made a significant contribution to the elaboration of church theology.

Gregory has been called the 'Father of Mysticism' and his mystic thought concentrates upon the unknowability of God. He stresses the constant journey and search of the soul towards God. The soul of the believer is aware of being the object of God's love, and the loving response of the soul is to desire more of God. For Gregory, love marks the soul, love draws the soul and love ignites the soul.

> The soul that looks upward towards God, and conceives that good desire for his eternal beauty, constantly experiences an ever new yearning for that which lies ahead.
>
> *Commentary on the Song of Songs*

Macrina

Macrina is one of the most significant Christian women of the Early Church. The first-born of a family of ten, she was the elder sister of both Basil of Caesarea (see 2 January) and Gregory of Nyssa. She was a woman of strong character, who was responsible for persuading Basil to become a priest instead of following the life of a professional rhetorician. Most of what is known about her life comes from the pen of Gregory of Nyssa. Gregory records that it was Macrina who was 'the religious conscience of the family' and the driving force behind the family's acceptance of asceticism.

From a highly influential Cappadocian family, Macrina took over the reins of the family when her father died, moving the whole household to their country estate at Annesi. Within her estate Macrina gathered around her both the like-minded and the needy, and with the addition of former domestic slaves and other new unrelated followers, an ascetic community was formed. Consequently Macrina is regarded as one of the founders of female monasticism.

Celibacy and virginity were a way of life for the community, and the decision to remain a virgin was marked by the wearing of a veil that covered both the head and the shoulders. Similarly personal poverty was a goal: Macrina is recorded as giving away her authority over her inheritance. Manual work was equated with the requirement for humility and obedience but was merely preparatory to spiritual work, and the community is recorded as practising unceasing prayer and hymnody, both day and night.

Gregory of Nyssa noted the likeness of the women of the community to angelic beings, in that

> they fell short of the angelic . . . only in so far as they appeared in bodily form, and were contained within a human frame, and were dependent upon the organs of sense. Perhaps some might even dare to say that the difference was not to their disadvantage. Since living in the body and yet after the likeness of the immaterial beings, they were not bowed down by the weight of the body, but their life was exalted to the skies and they walked on high in company with the powers of heaven.

20 July

Margaret of Antioch, Martyr, 4th century

In 303–4 the Emperor Diocletian began a persecution of Christians throughout the Roman Empire. The direct reason for the persecution is unknown, although there was an attempt to restore public morality and reinforce the imperial authority by ridding the Empire of a creed and organization which eroded its religious foundations. In the context of fourth-century Roman society, Christianity was seen as morally and socially disruptive.

In the Spring of 304 an edict was published which required pagan sacrifice to be offered on pain of death and confiscation of property. Margaret is reputed to have been martyred at Antioch in the Diocletian persecution. Nothing certain is known of her life or the manner of her death, although many legends have grown up surrounding her. She was honoured from a very early date in the Eastern Church, and then from the seventh century in the West.

Many of the legends which surround Margaret first appeared in the twelfth century. The most famous of these concerned her being swallowed by a dragon, and then bursting forth from its stomach. Somewhat perversely, she is the patron saint of childbirth. In the Late Middle Ages a cult surrounding her legend was popular, although it was suppressed by papal decree at a later date.

Although much of her life is clouded in mystery, and many of the legends beyond belief, Margaret is a reminder of the sacrifice that Christians made in the Early Church, and of the countless other unknown martyrs who have stood firm for Christ in the face of persecution and death.

Bartolomé de las Casas, Apostle to the Indies, 1566

Las Casas was born at Seville to a French family in 1474. He trained as a lawyer at Salamanca and in 1502 went out to the West Indies to assist the Spanish governor. Since Columbus' landing ten years earlier the Spaniards had been busy exploiting the wealth of Central and South America. But the *Conquistadores* were ruthless and had no regard for the indigenous peoples who were treated cruelly, often used as slaves and died in large numbers, having contracted European diseases against which they had no natural immunity.

Las Casas was ordained priest in 1510 and his new status released him from obligation to the colonial governor, giving him much greater freedom which he used to help the Indians, whose fate he viewed with horror. He did all he could to aid their cause and to draw their plight to public attention. When he returned home in 1515 he received much support from the Church and also from the Spanish government in publicizing the condition of the Indians who were being exploited in the name of Spain. Not surprisingly, he antagonized, and came to be hated by, the Spaniards in America who saw him as interfering in their business and resented what they regarded as his intolerant attitude to them. He returned to America with royal authority to protect the Indians and began a project to educate them separately from Europeans. But an Indian revolt in 1521, together with the implacable opposition of most Europeans there, resulted in the failure of his schemes.

He has been criticized on two main counts. First, for a tendency to exaggerate the plight of the Indians. Both orally and in his writings Las Casas acted as a propagandist rather than an accurate recorder of fact and in his desire to alleviate the sufferings of the indigenous population he was prepared to stretch the truth, sometimes to breaking point. Second, there was a curious lack of consistency in his sympathies for suffering races. It was ironic that in his desire to aid the Indians he supported the introduction of African slaves into Spanish territory in order to save the Indians from slavery. Though historical hindsight of the Atlantic slave trade induces revulsion in the modern reader, it should be noted that in the sixteenth century slavery was not considered to be unchristian.

In 1543 Las Casas became Bishop of Chiapas, in Southern Mexico, and in 1551 he retired to Valladolid in Spain where in due course he received a government pension. Though disappointed at the failure of his efforts on behalf of the Indians, he never stopped pleading their cause and addressed King Philip II on the subject shortly before his death, at the age of 92, in Madrid in 1566.

23 July

Bridget of Sweden, Abbess of Vadstena, 1373

Born in about 1303, Bridget was the daughter of a governor in Sweden and married Ulf Gudmarrson in her early teens. Initially living on his estates in Uppland, Bridget then became principal lady-in-waiting to Queen Blanche of Namur. Around this time Bridget began to receive visions and revelations, particularly of Christ on the cross. These visions, and her response to them, led to her being ridiculed by the other members of the royal court.

Together with her husband, Bridget made pilgrimages to holy sites in Norway and Spain, and after the death of Ulf in 1343 she lived the life of a penitent for three years. During this time she received visions and detailed instructions on the formation of a new religious order.

In 1346 Bridget founded a monastery at Vadstena, for 60 nuns and 25 monks. The rule of life that they accepted was harsh in terms of luxuries but generous in terms of education. All excess income was given away but the monks and nuns could have as many books as they needed. Her houses became popular throughout Europe, at one time numbering 70.

In 1349 Bridget sought papal approval for her order, known as the Bridgettine order, and travelled to Rome. She never returned to Sweden, spending the rest of her life either on pilgrimages or ministering to the sick and needy wherever she found them.

Bridget also attempted, as did many others, to mediate between the split papal courts of Rome and Avignon, although her recorded comments on the issue often contain the threat of divine punishment if the factions did not make peace. She was a continual challenge to the Church, pointing out and highlighting areas of spiritual decay, and campaigning for reform.

Although her visions continued throughout this time, the language that she used to deliver the messages of the visions was often condemnatory and harsh, and gradually the effect of her pronouncements on the royal and papal courts decreased. In reality she was remembered more for her acts of kindness and healing than for her visions and her writings are excellent examples of medieval spirituality.

> Blessed may you be, my Lord, my God, and my love most beloved of my soul. O you who are one God in three persons. Glory and praise to you, my Lord Jesus Christ. You were sent by the Father into the body of a virgin; and yet you ever remain with the Father in heaven, while the Father, in his divinity, inseparably remained with you in your human nature in this world.
>
> *Second Prayer of Bridget of Sweden*

26 July

Anne and Joachim, Parents of the Blessed Virgin Mary

There is no historical detail known of the life of Anne, nor of Joachim. Tradition ascribes to them the roles of parents of the Blessed Virgin Mary. The first mention found of them is in the apocryphal Gospel of James (second century) which has no historical validity. James says that after years of childlessness, an angel appeared to tell Anne and Joachim that they would have a child. For Joachim being without child was a source of shame and according to James, it was whilst he was praying in the desert that Anne received a visitation by an angel announcing that she would conceive. Anne promised to dedicate the child to God (in much the same way that Samuel was dedicated by Hannah).

Anne, as mother of Mary, has been honoured from as early as the sixth century, when a church was erected in her honour in Constantinople. Other relics and pictures of her found at Rome are from the eighth century. Her feast (The Conception of St Anne) has been kept from the tenth century. Anne was especially popular in the Middle Ages, particularly among miners and metalworkers and, conversely, the subject of much scorn and attack by the Reformers. There is a certain irony that the future Reformer, Martin Luther (see 31 October), himself a miner's son, was said to have prayed to St Anne for protection during a violent thunderstorm and if spared promised to enter the monastic life.

Similarly Joachim has been honoured since the sixth century, especially in Venice, but with less zeal elsewhere. He only came to be widely commemorated in the Late Middle Ages. Both Anne and Joachim are frequently represented in the art of this period which draws from the apocryphal Gospel of James for inspiration.

27 July

Brooke Foss Westcott, Bishop of Durham, Teacher of the Faith, 1901

Born in 1825, and educated at King Edward VI School, Birmingham and Trinity College, Cambridge, Westcott was elected a Fellow of the college in 1849. Ordained in 1851, he initially became a classics master at Harrow School. A devoted family man, he lived frugally with his wife and ten children, and the family were often to be seen on their bicycles in the lanes around Harrow.

While at Harrow he made his reputation with a series of scholarly works on the Bible, and began his renowned collaboration with F. J. A. Hort on a revision of the Greek text of the New Testament. This was eventually published in 1881 and formed the basis for many modern translations of the New Testament. In 1869 he became a canon at Peterborough and then in 1883 at Westminster, which posts he held alongside the Regius Chair of Divinity at Cambridge from 1870. In the 1880s he published three magisterial commentaries on John's Gospel, the Johannine Epistles and Hebrews. Along with Hort and J. B. Lightfoot, Westcott appeared to be leading a renaissance in biblical studies and theology in Britain. In demand for spiritual and vocational advice, he also founded and led Sunday afternoon religious discussions at King's College where he held a fellowship. He was much involved in the work of the newly-built Divinity School and was also involved in the foundation of the Clergy Training School at Cambridge, later re-named 'Westcott House' in his memory.

In 1890, Westcott was consecrated as Bishop of Durham. Durham had a tradition of scholar-bishops, but the industrial revolution had transformed the nature of the diocese and brought with it many social problems. Westcott had always maintained a deep interest in matters of social justice (he remembered the Chartist demonstrations in Birmingham in his youth) and in 1889 he became president of the newly-founded Christian Social Union. Though he never fitted the 'turbulent priest' stereotype, Westcott could be outspoken when he felt it necessary and constantly wrestled with the application of the gospel to social issues.

As Bishop of Durham this aspect of his ministry came to the fore and in 1892 he personally arbitrated in a bitter dispute between the miners and the colliery owners over proposed wage cuts. Nevertheless Westcott was able to maintain popularity with rich and poor alike. The Prime Minister Lord Salisbury, however, accused him of 'socialist tendencies' and declined to endorse Queen Victoria's suggestion that Westcott should be made Archbishop of York in 1890. He died in 1901, having preached at the annual miners' service in Durham Cathedral only the week before.

William Wilberforce, Social Reformer, 1833

Born in Hull in 1759, Wilberforce was educated at St John's College, Cambridge. In 1780 he was elected to Parliament, first for Hull, later for Yorkshire. He was converted to a living faith in his mid twenties, largely through reading William Law's *Serious Call* (see 10 April) and Philip Doddridge's *Rise and Progress of Religion in the Soul.* Initially he considered taking Holy Orders, but was persuaded by John Newton that he could do more good for the Christian cause in Parliament than in the pulpit.

In 1787 a *Society for the Abolition of the Slave Trade* was founded by Granville Sharp, Thomas Clarkson and a group of Quakers. Needing a Parliamentary spokesman, they approached Wilberforce who immediately saw this as an appropriate sphere of Christian service, commenting that 'God Almighty has set before me two great objects – the abolition of the slave trade and the reformation of manners.' In 1791 he moved the first of a long series of annual abolition resolutions in the House of Commons. Not until 1806 did the Commons vote for the abolition of the slave trade.

Wilberforce and his influential evangelical friends (known as the 'Saints' or the 'Clapham Sect' from their place of residence) were involved in promoting a wide variety of causes including the abolition of the state lottery and the opening up of India to Christian missionaries. Wilberforce supported Catholic emancipation and was involved in the foundation of many societies both to aid the spread of the gospel (Church Missionary Society, Religious Tract Society, British and Foreign Bible Society) and also the 'reformation of manners' – attempts to improve the moral tone of English society. These have come under criticism for attacking and abolishing many of the pleasures of the poor yet leaving the rich and influential free to amuse themselves as they pleased.

Though slave trade abolition had come into force in 1807, slavery remained legal in the British Empire and Wilberforce continued to campaign for an end to it, even after ill health forced his retirement from Parliament in 1825. The bill for the abolition of all slavery in British territories passed its crucial vote only three days before his death in July 1833. A year later 800,000 slaves, chiefly in the West Indies, were set free, initially being required to work as 'apprentices' for four years for their former masters until they received total freedom in 1838.

Ignatius of Loyola, Founder of the Society of Jesus, 1556

The youngest son of a Basque nobleman, Ignatius was born at his family's ancestral castle at Loyola in north-east Spain. He served as a page at the court of King Ferdinand V of Castile, and later entered military service, being seriously wounded at the French siege of Pamplona in 1521. During his lengthy convalescence (his leg never properly healed and he was left with a permanent limp) he read the life of Christ and biographies of various saints. The result was that he resolved to devote himself to the spiritual life. He went on pilgrimage to Montserrat (near Barcelona), where he hung up his sword over the altar and exchanged clothes with a beggar. He then spent about a year at nearby Manresa, first working in a hospital there, then living as a hermit in a cave. He studied Thomas à Kempis' *The Imitation of Christ* and it was probably during this year that he wrote the *Spiritual Exercises*, a manual of Christian prayer and meditation which has subsequently been used and valued by Christians of many denominations and traditions.

After a pilgrimage to Rome and Jerusalem, he returned to Spain in 1524 and studied at the universities of Barcelona, Alcalá and Salamanca (where he fell foul of the Inquisition because of his unauthorized preaching). He went on to Paris to continue his studies and it was there in 1534 that Ignatius and a group of six students (including Francis Xavier, see 3 December) vowed to go as missionaries to Islamic Palestine. In 1537 the group, now ten in number, finding that war prevented them travelling beyond Venice, offered their services to the Pope. By 1540 they had been ordained and with papal approval formed the Society of Jesus, with a vow of personal obedience to the Pope in addition to the traditional three monastic vows. Ignatius was elected the first general of the order and in the remaining 15 years of his life saw the order grow a hundred-fold and to be in the vanguard of both the Counter Reformation and the missionary work of the Roman Catholic Church.

He died on 31 July 1556. His prayer has become treasured by Christians of all traditions:

> Teach us, good Lord, to serve you as you deserve;
> to give and not to count the cost;
> to fight and not to heed the wounds;
> to toil and not to seek for rest;
> to labour and not to ask for any reward,
> save that of knowing that we do your will;
> through Jesus Christ our Lord.

4 August

Jean-Baptiste Vianney, Curé d'Ars, Spiritual Guide, 1859

Jean-Baptiste Vianney was born at Dardilly near Lyons in 1786, the son of a peasant farmer. With little education as a child, he worked as a shepherd before training for the priesthood. His training lasted nine years due, it is said, to his inability to learn Latin and because he spent over a year in hiding in order to avoid being conscripted into Napoleon's army. He was eventually ordained in 1815, the Bishop of Grenoble having decided that Vianney's zeal and devotion compensated for his lack of academic qualifications. After a curacy at Écully he was sent in 1818 as curé (parish priest) to the small village of Ars-en-Dombes near Lyons, where he remained for 40 years, becoming known simply as the 'Curé d'Ars'.

Vianney soon proved that the best parish priests are not always those who are the best academic theologians. He came to be regarded as both an excellent preacher and an outstanding confessor and counsellor. Indeed spiritual direction was his particular gift to the extent that at one stage of his ministry he was spending up to 16 hours a day hearing confessions. Whether he displayed charismatic gifts or just psychological insights, he nevertheless had the ability to discern the real issues that were on people's minds and the real causes of their problems. Consequently his fame spread and thousands (20,000 in 1855) beat a path to Ars-en-Dombes, some travelling hundreds of miles. Both the rich and the poor, the famous and the unknown came to hear him preach and to receive his spiritual direction and ministry of healing. Vianney's daily routine was to preach at 11.00 am and then spend the remainder of the day hearing confessions, sometimes from up to three hundred people a day.

Such a schedule could not be other than exhausting. Three times he attempted to resign and retire to a monastery, but each time he felt bound to return to deal with the needs of his people. He died, still at work in his parish, on 4 August 1859 at the age of 73. Famous far beyond his parish, Vianney was also respected by those who did not share his Roman Catholicism. The story is told that, when in vigorous debate with a Protestant peasant woman in his village, he asked her, 'Where was your Church before the Reformation?' She promptly replied, 'In the hearts of people like you.'

Oswald, King of Northumbria, Martyr, 642

Oswald was King of Northumbria from 634 to 642 and was one of the first Christian kings in England.

The son of King Ethelfrith of Northumbria, Oswald was forced to flee to Scotland when the rival king, Edwin, seized the Northumbrian Kingdom following the death of Ethelfrith in 616. Whilst living in exile in Scotland, Oswald was converted to Christianity through the monks of St Columba. He spent some time at the monastery of Iona which had been established by Columba (see 9 June) about 563, and returned to Northumbria to claim his crown when Edwin died in 633.

To establish his kingdom Oswald was forced to fight the Welsh king, Cadwallon. Before entering battle Oswald erected a wooden cross on the battlefield and ordered his soldiers to pray. He was successful in the fight and the field was named Heavensfield.

After securing his kingdom Oswald sought to establish Christianity in Northumbria. He sent to Iona for missionaries. The initial response of the community at Iona was to send a bishop who by reputation was severe in character and who met with little success. When he returned, discouraged, the community sent a monk called Aidan (see 31 August), who was known as a gentle character, to work in the region.

Oswald gave Aidan great support. In his first journey through the region Oswald acted as interpreter. The presence of the king can only have aided the work of Aidan in spreading the Christian message as, together with a small group of colleagues, Aidan began establishing churches. Eventually Oswald gave Aidan and his colleagues the island of Lindisfarne as a monastic base.

After eight years as King of Northumbria, Oswald was killed in battle by Penda of Mercia, who followed the ways of paganism, and who sacrificially mutilated Oswald's body, dispatching it to different parts of his kingdom.

Oswald was 38 when he died. He had united Northumbria, both politically and in terms of faith, and is recognized as one of England's foremost Anglo-Saxon Christian kings.

Bede records that

> As soon as he became King, Oswald greatly wished that all the people whom he ruled should be imbued with the grace of the Christian faith, of which he had received such signal proof in his victory over the heathen.
>
> *Bede: Ecclesiastical History, III.3*

John Mason Neale, Priest, Hymn Writer, 1866

To many modern Anglicans the name of J. M. Neale will be familiar from the small print in the hymn book, for Neale was the author of a number of hymns: *All glory laud and honour*; *Jerusalem the golden*; *O happy band of pilgrims*; *the Day of Resurrection*; *O come, O come Emmanuel*; and *Christ is made the sure foundation* being among the best known. Indeed he was prolific writer – more than one tenth of the hymns in the *English Hymnal* are his. But further examination of the hymn book's small print reveals that many were ancient hymns translated into English by Neale. And there lies the clue to Neale's real interest – the worship and liturgical practice of the Early Church.

John Mason Neale was born in London in 1818, educated at Sherborne and Trinity College, Cambridge, and was ordained in 1841. He suffered from chronic ill health throughout his life, and a breakdown in health occurring in the short time between presentation and institution to the parish of Crawley resulted in three years' recuperation in Madeira. Physically unable to cope with the rigours of parish ministry, he became instead the warden of an almshouse, Sackville College at East Grinstead, in 1846, a position he held for the rest of his life.

As well as writing hymns Neale was a founder member, with Benjamin Webb, of the Cambridge Camden Society and was much involved in its work of promoting what were perceived to be the 'correct' forms of church architecture and furnishings. His studies of the practices of the Early Church gave him a particular interest in the Eastern Orthodox tradition in which many ancient practices had been preserved. Neale began the study of Eastern Orthodoxy which had previously been ignored by Anglicans. At a time when the study and imitation of continental Catholicism was fashionable among Anglo-Catholics, Neale provided an important balance by pointing towards the Church's largely forgotten Eastern heritage. To Neale belongs the credit for reminding Anglicans that the Church's catholicity has an Eastern as well as a Roman dimension.

In 1854 Neale founded the Society of St Margaret, an order of women dedicated to the education of girls and nursing the sick, which eventually grew into one of the largest Anglican religious communities for women. An oratory was created in a former carriage house and Neale acted as the community's chaplain and led worship in an innovative Ritualist style centring on a daily Eucharist and the permanent reservation of the sacrament. Neale's translation of the Latin office Compline for the sisters' use was its first use in the Church of England. He died in 1866 at the age of 48.

8 August

Dominic, Priest, Founder of the Order of Preachers, 1221

Dominic was born in Spain, in Caleruega, Old Castile. He studied Arts and Theology and joined the order of Canons at Osma Cathedral. A philanthropist, he sold his books to feed the poor during a famine.

In 1201 Dominic accompanied Diego, the Bishop of Osma, to Northern Europe, where he became interested in missionary work. On his way home Dominic travelled through France and was shocked at the wide spread of heresy that he found. In particular he reacted against the Albigensians (a dualistic sect). After sitting up all night talking to an Albigensian innkeeper, and eventually seeing the innkeeper become an orthodox Christian, Dominic saw that the only effective way to rid the Church of heresy was good teaching. Much of the Albigensian doctrine was formed through a purely allegorical interpretation of the New Testament, and to counter this Dominic planned a monastic order devoted to teaching and preaching. He intended that the members of his order would be trained properly, and live a life of austerity. The order had its own schools and new members often went to universities.

The first house he founded was at Prouille (1206). Dominic taught that his preachers should live a life of poverty far greater than the teachers of false doctrine. He also taught that they should teach the true doctrine of the Church by persuasion, power and learning. Both of these ideals were a divergence from normal church practice at the time. Since there were many 'new' orders in the thirteenth century, Dominic was dissuaded from writing a new 'Rule' and adopted the Rule of St Augustine for his order. The Order of Preachers was given authority by Pope Honorius III in 1216.

In 1217 Dominic began to send his friars to other parts of the world, where they frequently attached themselves to universities. In 1220 an official gathering of the order established a constitution, and laid the foundation for an order of Dominican nuns.

Dominic had zeal for teaching and for combating heresy. He refused the position of bishop three times so that he could concentrate upon his mission. He flew in the face of accepted church action and rejected finery and position, preferring the way of humility and prayer. He took the gospel into hitherto unreached or ignored areas – the cities and the universities – and engaged those he met with persuasive teaching, grounded in an experience of God.

The 'Life of Dominic' attests to these attributes of humility and example:

> A general debate with the heretics being agreed upon, the bishop of the place wanted to attend in state with a pompous retinue, but Dominic addressing him, said: 'It is not in this fashion that we ought to meet them, but we should rather strive to win them over by our humility and virtuous example, than by mere show and display or by contentious words: and since the present meeting is not without its fears, let us arm ourselves with humility and go barefoot.'
>
> *The Life of Dominic, Ch. 2, c.1255*

9 August

Mary Sumner, Founder of the Mothers' Union, 1921

Mary Heywood was born in 1828 at Swinton near Manchester. The family moved to Hope End in Herefordshire and Mary was educated at home by her parents. In 1848, she married a young curate, George Sumner, son of the Bishop of Winchester.

In 1851 George became Rector of Old Alresford in Hampshire. For many years busy bringing up her three children, Mary became more and more concerned about family life and the fact that mothers received no particular support from the Church. In 1876 she began holding 'Mothers' Union' meetings in the parish, aiming to unite mothers of all social classes in bringing up their children in the Christian faith. Baptism and parental example were its two basic principles. At first a purely parochial organization, it eventually grew into an international concern, encouraging the ideal of a Christian home. This process began in 1885 when Mary made a speech at a conference in Portsmouth which gave rise to the Mothers' Union as a national organization. It enjoyed remarkable and rapid growth and in time grew from an organization in one parish to a world-wide society, today with over one million members, committed to supporting the family and based on five objects:

- To uphold Christ's teaching on the nature of marriage and to promote its wider understanding;
- To encourage parents to bring up their children in the faith and life of the Church;
- To maintain a world-wide fellowship of Christians united in prayer, worship and service;
- To promote conditions in society favourable to stable family life and the protection of children;
- To help those whose family life has met with adversity.

Mary Sumner died in Winchester in 1921.

Mary Sumner's Prayer:

> O Lord, fill us with thy Holy Spirit, that we may firmly believe in Jesus Christ, and love him with all our hearts. Wash our souls in his precious blood. Make us to hate sin and to be holy in thought, word and deed. Help us to be faithful wives and loving mothers. Bless us and all who belong to the Mothers' Union; unite us in love and prayer and teach us to train our children for heaven. Pour out thy Holy Spirit on our husbands and children. Make our homes, homes of peace and love and, may we so live on earth, that we may live with thee for ever in heaven; for Jesus Christ's sake. Amen.

10 August

Laurence, Deacon at Rome, Martyr, 258

Laurence was martyred at Rome under the persecution of the Emperor Valerian in one of the earliest and most brutal persecutions of the Church.

One of seven deacons at Rome when Sixtus was bishop (257–8), Laurence was responsible for the distribution of charity to the poor and needy. The most reliable account of his death tells of him being beheaded four days after the death of the bishop. The most 'romantic' account of his death tells how he was ordered to be roasted over a fire for his response to Emperor Valerian's demand to be given the treasure of the Church. According to this account, for three days Laurence gathered up all the poor of the city, amongst whom he had previously distributed alms, and declared to those who had come to claim the Church's money, 'Here is the treasure of the Church'. This act resulted in his slow death over a fire, a death which according to legend was borne cheerfully, without pain, and resulted in the conversion to Christ of many onlookers.

Whatever form of the legend is true, Laurence was honoured from a very early stage, and quickly became one of the foremost saints of the Roman Church. A chapel was built over his tomb by Constantine and he is regarded as the patron saint of deacons. The more legendary 'acts' of his life and death have popularized his memory, and in death he has risen to the position of archdeacon. His legend spread quickly, and he is often depicted in deacon's apparel bearing silver and gold to distribute to the poor.

Clare of Assisi, Founder of the Minoresses (Poor Clares), 1253

In 1212 the 18-year-old Clare heard the preaching of Francis of Assisi (see 4 October). She was so moved by his life and teaching that she gave up her possessions and lifestyle and joined him at the Portiuncula, a small chapel on the plain below Assisi, where she made her vows of commitment to God.

Initially Francis arranged for Clare to live in a Benedictine house, but eventually she moved to San Damiano, just outside the town of Assisi when Francis and his followers had restored a house for her. As her reputation for poverty and holiness spread, other women who wished to live the life as taught by Francis came to join her, including her mother and sisters. Clare was made abbess of this small community in 1215. The rule under which they lived was very austere, and included complete poverty. As with Francis, her followers soon began to found similar houses throughout Europe, with 47 being founded in Spain alone.

Clare remained in Assisi for the rest of her life. A remarkable contemplative, Clare cared deeply for the nuns in her charge. Her commitment to absolute poverty became an annoyance to the papal authorities, who tried to ensure that the community received a living allowance. It was a battle that Clare fought all her life. As most of the order's houses gradually relaxed the rule on complete poverty, Clare's community at San Damiano in Assisi remained one of the very few which held on to absolute poverty as a cornerstone of the community's ideals.

Stories soon grew up surrounding her, including the tale that twice she saved the city of Assisi from attack by her visible prayers in front of the attacking army. She would also undertake penance for the town in times of crisis.

Clare's personal practice of contemplation included a daily meditation on the Passion of Christ. Here is an example:

> Place your mind before the mirror of eternity
> Place your soul in the brilliance of glory
> Place your heart in the figure of the divine substance
> And transform your whole being into the image of the Godhead itself through contemplation
> So that you too may feel what His friends feel
> as they taste the hidden sweetness
> which God has reserved from the beginning
> for those who love Him.

> Since you have cast aside all things which, in this deceitful and turbulent world, ensnare their blind lovers, love Him totally who gave Himself totally for your love. His beauty the sun and moon.

John Henry Newman, Priest, Tractarian, 1890

Born in London in 1801 the son of a banker, Newman experienced an evangelical conversion at the age of 15. He went up to Trinity College, Oxford in 1817, but after graduation his association was with Oriel, first as Fellow then as tutor. Under the influence of Richard Whately and Edward Hawkins in the Oriel common room Newman's spiritual quest began to move away from evangelical Anglicanism to a more High Church understanding of the Christian faith. Ordained in 1826, two years later he became Vicar of St Mary's, Oxford.

His friendship with Hurrell Froude and the fallout from John Keble's 1833 Assize sermon, together with Newman's own studies in the Fathers, led him towards an explicitly Catholic understanding of Anglicanism as the *via media* between Rome and Protestantism. As the Oxford Movement took off it was Newman's incisive mind and pen that provided much of the momentum. It was he who pioneered the *Tracts for the Times*, personally writing three of the first four. Exalting the Fathers to a level with Scripture, Newman weighed the Church of England in the balance of antiquity and found it wanting.

Having come from an evangelical background, Newman came to reject its emphases, regarding its understanding of the Church as inadequate and insistence on the sole authority of Scripture as excessive. He sought to redress the balance:

> Surely the sacred volume was never intended and is not adapted to teach us our creed; however certain it is that we can prove our creed from it . . . From the very first the rule has been . . . for the Church to teach the truth and then appeal to Scripture in vindication of its own teaching.

Whereas Keble (see 14 July) and Pusey (see 16 September) never lost faith with the Anglican Church and strove throughout their lives to help it live up to its catholic and apostolic heritage, Newman was more easily discouraged by the controversies that assailed the Tractarians in the late 1830s. For him the crunch perhaps came with the furore following publication of *Tract Ninety* in 1841, in which he argued that the Thirty-Nine Articles could be interpreted in a 'catholic' sense since they were aimed primarily at the abuses and not the doctrines of Roman Catholicism. For most contemporary Anglicans Newman's agile mind was perceived to be performing mental gymnastics and no further tracts were written.

In 1842 Newman retired from Oxford to the nearby village of Littlemore. He resigned as Vicar of St Mary's in 1843, and in 1845 was received into the Roman Catholic Church. One of the most brilliant theological minds of the nineteenth century was lost to the Church of England. A year later he went to Rome, where he was ordained priest and entered the Congregation of the Oratory. Newman spent most of the remainder of his life in the house of the Oratory that he established near Birmingham. But though the Roman Catholic Church was his chosen spiritual home, he experienced suspicion from those, such as Cardinal Manning, who resented his greater ability and it was not until 1877 that Pope Leo XIII made Newman a cardinal. He died on 11 August 1890.

Jeremy Taylor, Bishop of Down and Connor, Teacher of the Faith, 1667

Jeremy Taylor was born in Cambridge in 1613 and remained there to study at Gonville and Caius College. In 1633 he was ordained and elected as a Fellow of the college. He came to the attention of Archbishop Laud, who nominated him for a fellowship of All Souls and appointed him chaplain to King Charles I in 1635.

While serving as royal chaplain, Taylor was suspected of Romanist tendencies because of his friendship with Christopher Davenport, a Franciscan chaplain to Queen Henrietta Maria. To defend himself he was obliged to preach a sermon asserting his opposition to Roman Catholicism. He joined the Royalist army as chaplain when civil war broke out in 1642, and after its defeat he was briefly imprisoned. In 1645 he retired to Wales as private chaplain to Lord Carbery. There Taylor had the leisure to study and write and produced a number of books. The most well known of these are the devotional treatises *The Rule and Exercises of Holy Living* (1650) and *The Rule and Exercises of Holy Dying* (1651), which have become regarded as spiritual classics.

In 1658 Taylor went to Ireland as a lecturer. At the Restoration in 1660 he was appointed Bishop of Down and Connor (to which was added the diocese of Dromore the following year) and Vice-Chancellor of Trinity College, Dublin. In the same year he published *Ductor Dubitantium, or the Rule of Conscience*, a comprehensive manual of moral theology. His episcopate was a troubled one and, facing strong opposition from both Presbyterians and Roman Catholics, Taylor was far from eirenic in his relations with non-Anglicans. He died in Lisburn on 13 August 1667.

A prayer of Jeremy Taylor:

> O God, whose days are without end, and whose mercies cannot be numbered; Make us, we beseech thee, deeply sensible of the shortness and uncertainty of human life; and let thy Holy Spirit lead us in holiness and righteousness all our days: that, when we shall have served thee in our generation, we may be gathered unto our fathers, having the testimony of a good conscience; in the communion of the Catholic Church; in the confidence of a certain faith; in the comfort of an assured hope; in favour with thee our God, and in perfect charity with all men. Grant this, we beseech thee through Jesus Christ our Lord.

13 August

Florence Nightingale, Nurse, Social Reformer, 1910

Born at Florence while her parents were travelling in Italy in 1820, Florence Nightingale was named after the city of her birth. She was raised mostly at Lea Hurst in Derbyshire. Brought up in the Unitarian Church, she later joined the Church of England but her personal beliefs were far from orthodox and prone to change. Nevertheless she experienced God's personal presence and sought to follow his promptings. Feeling called by God to some form of service at the age of 16, she decided that she must remain single and soon afterwards rejected a proposal of marriage.

In 1844, she came to believe that her calling was to nurse the sick and in 1849 she went to study hospitals in Europe. On 12 May 1850 she recorded in her diary, 'Today I am thirty – the age Christ began his mission. Now no more childish things. No more love. No more marriage. Now Lord let me think only of Thy Will, what Thou willest me to do.' Later that year she began nursing training at Alexandria in Egypt and subsequently studied at the Lutheran Deaconess Institute at Kaiserswerth in Germany. In1853 she became superintendent of the Hospital for Invalid Gentlewomen in London.

After the outbreak of the Crimean War in 1854, Florence used personal contacts in high places to allow her to take 38 nurses to serve at the military hospital at Scutari (Üsküdar) in Turkey and later at Balaklava in the Crimea. Through her tireless efforts to improve both nursing care and simple sanitation, the mortality rate among the sick and wounded was greatly reduced. At night, she would often patrol the wards, carrying a dim lamp, to check that all was well. The legend of 'the Lady with the Lamp' was born.

After the war she began the first professional nursing training in England at St Thomas's Hospital in London. Through her efforts the stature of nursing was raised to that of a medical profession with high standards of education and important responsibilities. But under the strain of ceaseless overwork, her own health broke, and she was an invalid for the last part of her life. She received many honours and in 1907 she became the first woman to receive the Order of Merit. She died in London on 13 August 1910, aged 90, and was buried at St Margaret's, East Wellow in Hampshire. Her tombstone bears the simple inscription, 'F. N. 1820–1910'.

Octavia Hill, Social Reformer, 1912

Octavia Hill was born in Wisbech, Cambridgeshire in 1838, the daughter of a corn-merchant and banker. She was influenced from an early age in social issues by her father's interest in prison reform and by her grandfather Thomas Southwood Smith, a national authority on sanitation and housing. Educated at home, she went to London in 1852 to work at the Ladies' Guild, a Christian Socialist co-operative managed by her mother, where she met John Ruskin and F. D. Maurice. She was soon put in charge of a branch engaged in teaching poor children to make toys, and so gained her first experience of the lives of the very poor.

In 1856 Octavia became secretary to the classes for women at the Working Men's College in Great Ormond Street, and a few years later she and her sisters started a school in Nottingham Place. It was while living there and visiting her poorer neighbours that she came to understand the urgency of addressing the housing problem in Victorian London. In 1864 she succeeded in interesting John Ruskin in her schemes for improving the dwellings of the poor and he advised her to put the work on a business footing. This proved to be sound advice, and her successful management led to a steadily increasing number of houses being placed under her charge. Perhaps the most important addition to her responsibilities was her appointment in 1884 by the Ecclesiastical Commissioners to manage a great part of their property first in Southwark and later elsewhere. Octavia Hill's help and advice were often sought in connection with the promotion of social reform by legislation. But her faith lay much more in the value of voluntary work, and it was with reluctance that she took part in political measures.

Though Octavia was involved in a number of voluntary organizations, she is particularly remembered for her joint initiative with Canon H. D. Rawnsley and Sir Robert Hunter in founding the National Trust in 1895 which has become Britain's leading charitable organization for preserving historical buildings and places of natural beauty. Always preferring voluntary to statutory schemes she was nevertheless persuaded to serve on the Poor Law Commission from 1905 to 1908. Her books include *Homes of the London Poor* and *Our Common Land*. Strongly motivated by her Christian faith, Octavia viewed human beings more as citizens of this world than as potential citizens of the next. Consequently she sought to make life on earth as positive an experience as possible, particularly for the poor and the disadvantaged.

Octavia never allowed her increasing fame to undermine her personal humility and lived quietly with her sisters in Marylebone Road, where she died on 13 August 1912.

Maximilian Kolbe, Friar, Martyr, 1941

Maximilian was born Raymond Kolbe to a pious Catholic family near Lodz in Poland in 1894. In 1906 he experienced a vision of the Virgin Mary, which he described in his own words:

> I asked the Mother of God what was to become of me. Then she came to me holding two crowns, one white, the other red. She asked if I was willing to accept either of these crowns. The white one meant that I should persevere in purity, a nd the red that I should become a martyr. I said that I would accept them both.

In 1910 he entered the seminary of the Conventual Franciscan Order at Lwow and in due course was sent to study in Rome where he was ordained priest in 1918. In 1917 he and six other young men had founded the 'Militia of the Immaculata' – a movement to encourage Marian devotion. When he returned to Poland in 1918 to teach in the Cracow seminary, he continued to develop this enterprise. In 1927, despite his indifferent health, he established a community near Warsaw called *Niepokalanow*, the 'City of the Immaculata'. By 1939 it had expanded from 18 friars to 650, making it the largest Catholic religious house in the world at that time.

But though in one sense a very conservative organization, in confronting the many changes in modern society, especially its secularization, the friars utilized the most modern technology including printing. This enabled them to publish countless catechetical and devotional tracts, a daily newspaper with a circulation of 230,000 and a monthly magazine with a circulation of over one million. Maximilian started a short-wave radio station and even planned a film studio. In 1930 he and four companions went to Japan where, despite daunting linguistic and financial difficulties, they established a magazine and a friary at Nagasaki. He envisioned further expansion overseas but by 1936 his health had so deteriorated that his superiors ordered him back to Poland.

Following the German invasion of September 1939 the friars were initially imprisoned but were then unexpectedly released and so were able to work among refugees and casualties of war. But as a Polish patriot who never feared to be outspoken in his contempt for the Nazis, Maximilian was not remain free for long. He was arrested and with countless others made the fateful journey by cattle truck to the death camp at Auschwitz. There he continued to minister to inmates awaiting death. Death came for him when he volunteered to take the place of another prisoner who had been condemned to die a slow death in a starvation bunker. Maximilian took his place, but eventually his Nazi captors ended his life with a fatal injection on 14 August 1941 – the eve of the Feast of the Assumption.

20 August

Bernard, Abbot of Clairvaux, Teacher of the Faith, 1153

Bernard was, by all accounts, a shy man, prone to illness, who would have much preferred a life of quiet contemplation to a life lived in the spotlight of the wider Church.

Born to a noble family at Fontaines, near Dijon in 1090, Bernard entered the monastic life at the age of 22 at the monastery of Cîtaux. After his three years of probation he was asked to establish a new Cistercian house at a place of his own choosing. He chose Clairvaux, which, under his leadership, gradually became established as a model monastic house. Initially Bernard was severe in his expectations of his monks, but responded to complaints and changed his methods. This soon became a central base for the Cistercian order (an order which emphasized personal mystical experience). Bernard was effectively the leader of the Cistercians for 30 years and renowned as a preacher. He founded new houses, frequently debated with and challenged the Benedictine order over purity, defending Cistercian spirituality. He was also a critic of contemporary society, and his refusal to accept high office gave him an authority and credibility within the world which he so distained. Although shy, Bernard was a 'prophetic' figure, a man who would speak out against injustice, corruption and heresy. Bernard was involved in the Second Crusade, persuading many to undertake the journey. The Crusade ended in failure, and Bernard returned to Clairvaux.

In 1130 Bernard entered papal politics, siding with Pop Innocent II when his election was challenged. He also campaigned against the growing secular business of the papal court. When Bernard died in 1153 he was known throughout Christendom, and the Cistercian order was experiencing rapid growth.

His writings were numerous. He yearned for mystical prayer amongst his followers and he stressed the human response to the suffering of Christ.

> You want me to tell you why God is to be loved and how much.
> I answer; the reason for loving God is God Himself;
> and the measure of love due to Him is immeasurable love.
>
> *On Loving God, Ch. 1*

> Why should not the creature love the Creator, who gave the power to love?
> Why should he not love Him with all his being, since it is by His gift alone that he can do anything that is good?
> It was God's creative grace that out of nothingness raised us to the dignity of humanity; and from this appears our duty to love Him, and the justice of His claim to that love.
>
> *On Loving God, Ch. 5*

William and Catherine Booth, Founders of the Salvation Army, 1912 and 1890

Born in Nottingham in 1829 and educated privately, William Booth was an apprentice pawnbroker when he experienced a religious conversion at the age of 15. He moved to London and in 1851 joined the Wesleyan Reform Union. Three years later he transferred to the more radical Methodist New Connexion, which accepted him as a ministerial candidate and an itinerant evangelist and preacher.

In 1855 Booth married Catherine Mumford, born at Ashbourne in Derbyshire, also in 1829, the daughter of a Wesleyan lay preacher. She had been expelled from the Brixton Wesleyan Church for 'excessive zeal'! Despite being in constant pain Catherine bore four children and later started and ran the women's work of the Salvation Army. She ensured that from the first women had a place in the Army's leadership. A gifted teacher in her own right, she became affectionately known as the 'Mother of the Salvation Army' until her death from cancer in 1890.

After separating from the Methodist New Connexion in 1861, William Booth continued his ministry independently. In 1865 the Booths founded the Christian Mission at Whitechapel in East London to propagate the Christian faith and to furnish spiritual and material aid to those in need. Much later, in 1878, at the height of 'jingoism' when Britain nearly went to war with Russia over Constantinople, the mission, which for some time had informally been using military ranks and terminology, officially changed its name to the 'Salvation Army'.

Members of the Army, equipped with uniforms and flags, drums and cornets, were often greeted with riotous demonstrations when they first appeared on the streets. Some suffered assault and some were arrested for breach of the peace.

Having famously asked his son the question, 'Why should the devil have all the best tunes?', William encouraged Salvationists to set their hymns and songs to the 'pop' tunes of the day:

> The Army is coming – amen, amen!
> To conquer this city for Jesus – amen!
> We'll shout 'Hallelujah' and praise his dear name,
> Who redeemed us to God through the blood of the Lamb.
> The sound of its footsteps is rolling along;
> The kingdom of Satan triumphant so long,
> Is shaking and tott'ring, and downward shall fall
> For Jesus the Saviour shall reign over all.

The Army's work of evangelism and social action rapidly progressed, and branches were established in all parts of the world. William Booth wrote several books, the best known of which was *In Darkest England and the Way Out* (1890). In 1912 he was 'promoted to glory' and his son, William Bramwell Booth, succeeded him as general.

27 August

Monica, Mother of Augustine of Hippo, 387

Monica was a citizen of Thagaste, North Africa, and a Christian from childhood. She was married to a wayward husband, Patricus, who after years of licentiousness and abuse was finally converted to Christianity at the age of 40. Her mother-in-law also lived with the family at Thagaste, and contributed to the difficulties Monica encountered there.

A devout and strong-willed woman, Monica prayed continually for the conversion of her three children, whom she brought up as devout Christians. However, her eldest son caused her most grief, rejecting the faith at the age of 17. Grieved by his behaviour and company she would ban him from the house. However, after a conversation with a priest, Monica ceased hounding her son to become a Christian and instead prayed continually for his conversion. When the son left Thagaste for Italy (in the middle of the night so as to avoid his mother), she followed him, travelling through Carthage and Rome, eventually catching up with him in Milan, all the time praying for his conversion. There she came under the influence of Bishop Ambrose (see 7 December), and joined his court.

Her wayward son was Augustine (see 28 August), who would become one of the most influential and significant Christian theologians in the history of the Church. It was through the teaching of Ambrose, and the prayers of his mother that Augustine recommitted his life to Christ.

Monica arranged for her son to marry, but Augustine refused, deciding to remain celibate. On the return journey to Africa, after Augustine's baptism, Monica died. She was 55.

> Then we went in to my mother, and told her what happened, to her great joy. We explained to her how it had occurred and she leaped for joy; and she blessed You, who are 'able to do exceedingly abundantly above all that we ask or think'. For she saw that You had granted her far more than she had ever asked for in all her pitiful and doleful lamentations. For You did so convert me that I sought neither a wife nor any other of this world's hopes, but set my feet on that rule of faith which so many years before You had showed her in her dream about me. And so You turned her grief into gladness more plentiful than she had ventured to desire, and dearer and purer than the desire she used to cherish of having grandchildren of my flesh.
>
> *Augustine, immediately after his conversion*
> *Confessions, 8.xii*

28 August

Augustine, Bishop of Hippo, Teacher of the Faith, 430

Born in Thagaste, North Africa, of a pagan father and a Christian mother, Augustine was raised as a Christian, but not baptized. He initially studied rhetoric at Carthage, North Africa before moving to Rome to study philosophy. His study of philosophy and especially of Manicheaism led him to renounce his Christian faith.

Non-exclusive cohabitation (concubinage) was an accepted way of life and for 15 years Augustine lived with a woman (whose name has not been recorded) and together they had a child, a son called Adeodatus who later died aged 15.

Augustine taught rhetoric and grammar at Carthage before concentrating on philosophy. He was always seeking to break free from his mother's zealous practice of the Christian faith, and in 383, in the middle of the night so to avoid her, Augustine left Carthage for Rome. Undeterred, his mother followed him, eventually catching up with him in Milan, where he had been appointed Professor of Rhetoric.

Augustine's long journey back to Christianity is recorded in his *Confessions*, and reached a crux at Milan, where he heard the preaching of Ambrose. Augustine records how he reflected on the necessity of faith to achieve wisdom, and he tells of how he concluded that the authority on which faith rested was the Scriptures.

Less than ten years after his conversion, Augustine was a bishop. He spent the intervening time preparing for baptism, living a monastic life, researching and writing. In 388 Augustine returned to North Africa, and in 391 he travelled to Hippo intending to found a monastery. However, at Hippo he surprised himself by undergoing ordination. He was consecrated coadjutor (assistant) bishop in 395/6, taking control of the diocese in 397.

Augustine's time as a bishop not only saw the production of many books but it was also a time of intense pastoral leadership. He worked unceasingly for the African Church, preaching daily, overseeing care for the poor, giving judgements in cases of dispute and giving much time to the formation and care of the clergy. He was also to be found at the church councils in Africa and beyond, and he was extremely active in the explanation and defence of the faith to those opposed to it.

Augustine was a complex character: a philosopher, theologian, mystic and poet, as well as a highly gifted pastor and preacher. Although often thought of as academic and condemnatory, Augustine came to believe that the Church was a place where outside influences and human weaknesses could be accommodated, and that the unity of the Church was more important than its purity.

In a time of uncertainty for the Empire, and consequently impoverishment for the poor, Augustine showed a deep care and practical concern for others. He used his own finances to feed the poor and is recorded as melting down church treasures to pay ransom for captives.

Augustine's theology has been highly influential, although some parts bear the unmistakable stamp of fifth-century assumptions about society. The problems that he sought to explain and the way of thinking that he instigated affected both Christian and secular thought for centuries. He is the prime example of the African contribution to the spread of Christianity and doctrine throughout the history of the Church. Augustine's desire for God is evident throughout his work:

> The life of a Christian is an experience of an ever-deepening desire for God. What you desire you cannot, as yet, see; but the desire gives you the capacity, so that when you eventually see you are satisfied . . . Let us desire, my brothers and sisters, for we are to be filled.
>
> *Commentary on First Epistle of John, IV, 6*

> You stir mankind to take pleasure in praising you, because you have made us for yourself, and our hearts are restless until they rest in you.
>
> *Confessions, I.i*

30 August

John Bunyan, Spiritual Writer, 1688

John Bunyan was born in 1628 at Elstow, near Bedford, the son of a brazier or tinker. He served an apprenticeship at his father's trade, and during the Civil War served for a time in the Parliamentary army. In about 1648 he married Margaret Bentley, and as a result of her Christian witness he attempted to reform his life. After several years of striving to reform and despairing of his efforts he came to both a living faith and an assurance of salvation. He joined the Independent congregation in Bedford and later began a preaching ministry there. After his wife's death, Bunyan remarried and became a popular preacher, speaking to larger audiences and at the same time coming into conflict with the local clergy who resented uneducated and unordained preachers.

After the Restoration of Charles II in 1660, the Church of England reasserted its authority and action was taken against unlicensed preachers. Bunyan, who refused to stop his preaching ministry, spent most of the next twelve years in Bedford jail (although during a part of this time he was allowed a degree of freedom and was able to support his family by making shoelaces). With little to read other than the Bible and John Foxe's *Book of Martyrs*, Bunyan began to write religious tracts and pamphlets and, most importantly, his spiritual autobiography, *Grace Abounding to the Chief of Sinners* (1666).

Bunyan was released in 1672, but by 1675 he was back in prison serving a six-month sentence for unlicensed preaching. It was during this time that time he probably wrote a large part of his major work, *The Pilgrim's Progress*, a prose allegory of the pilgrimage of a soul in search of salvation, which was published in 1678. The main character, Christian, with his companions, first Faithful then Hopeful, journeys from the City of Destruction to the Heavenly City, encountering *en route* such hazards as the Slough of Despond, the Hill Difficulty, Doubting Castle, By-Path Meadow and Vanity Fair.

The instant popularity of *Pilgrim's Progress* can be deduced from the fact that ten editions were printed during the remaining ten years of Bunyan's life. It eventually became the most widely read book in the English language after the Bible and it greatly influenced later English writers. Noted for its simple, biblical style, *The Pilgrim's Progress* is now generally considered one of the finest allegories in all of English literature – not just among spiritual writings – and has been translated into many languages.

Aidan, Bishop of Lindisfarne, Missionary, 651

Aidan was a monk of Irish origin and Celtic faith. He lived at the monastery in Iona, and was sent to Northumbria in answer to a request from the King of Northumbria, Oswald (see 5 August), for missionaries. Iona was the powerhouse of Celtic Christianity and the principal monastery of the Irish and Picts. Aidan was chosen to lead the second group of missionaries to Northumbria. The first mission was under the leadership of a severe bishop who returned home complaining of the uncouthness of the people.

Aidan was given the island of Lindisfarne by King Oswald, and was consecrated bishop in 635. He travelled widely on the mainland, often in the company of Oswald, who initially acted as his interpreter. He is recorded as being a man of charity, miracles and kindness.

We learn much of Aidan's life from Bede, who writes of him with praise and affection and states simply that Aidan was held in high regard because he lived as he taught. He introduced monastic values of penance and prayer to his converts, celebrated Easter according to the ancient Celtic date and tradition, and established monasteries as centres of faith and education. As such, Aidan is the supreme example of the passion and power of Celtic Christianity.

After the death of Oswald at the hands of Penda, the pagan ruler of Mercia, Aidan continued to evangelize the region, aided by more monks from the monastery at Iona. He supported King Oswin of Deira, and continued to enjoy freedom to preach and travel. During his time Christianity was firmly rooted in Northumbria, and Lindisfarne established as a leading monastic base. A representative of the Celtic tradition, Irish by birth, Scottish by education and monastic by formation, Aidan Christianized Northern England, and established Celtic Christianity as a credible force, which Bede (see 25 May) acknowledges

> [Aidan] loved to give away to the poor who chanced to meet him whatever he received from kings or wealthy folk. Whether in town or country, he always travelled on foot unless compelled by necessity to ride; and whatever people he met on his walks, whether high or low, he stopped and spoke to them. If they were heathen, he urged them to be baptized; and if they were Christians, he strengthened their faith, and inspired them by word and deed to live a good life and to be generous to others.
>
> *Bede: Ecclesiastical History, III.5*

1 September

Giles of Provence, Hermit, c.710

According to tenth-century tradition, Giles was an eighth-century hermit who lived in a forest near the mouth of the River Rhône in Provence and who built a monastery in the region.

To these few facts legend has been added liberally. Apparently Giles lived in solitude, eating only herbs and the milk of deer. One day Flavius Wamba, King of the Visigoths, was out hunting in the forest. A hind that he was chasing sought refuge in Giles' presence. Wamba who was undeterred in his pursuit of his prey, shot an arrow at the hind, hitting Giles instead. Wamba was so impressed by Giles' calm reaction and his life of holiness and asceticism that he donated land to him for the creation of a monastery. The area surrounding the monastery became known as Saint-Gilles. As interesting as this legend is, it is also attached to other hermit saints and its true provenance is unknown.

Further legendary acts of Giles include his visit to Rome to receive official recognition for his monastic community from the Pope. On this occasion the Pope is supposed to have given to Giles two ornate wooden doors for his community. On receiving the doors Giles promptly threw them in the River Tiber, and upon his return to Gaul, found the doors waiting for him, washed up on a nearby beach.

The memory of Saint Giles became very popular in the Middle Ages, due to the belief of the power of his name, and of the story of the protection of the hind. Further legendary tales were added to his story, including miraculous works in Greece as a child, and accounts of his challenging rulers and kings over unconfessed sins. Crusaders were responsible for carrying the cult of St Giles further afield, but the monastery itself fell into poverty by the Late Middle Ages after relying too much on the gifts of pilgrims.

Giles is the patron saint of cripples, beggars and blacksmiths.

2 September

The Martyrs of Papua New Guinea, 1901 and 1942

Papua New Guinea's inhabitants already had a bad reputation – cannibalism and head-hunting being among their customs – when the interdenominational London Missionary Society first viewed Papua as a mission field in the late 1860s. For this reason European missionaries did not initially reside on the mainland. Instead they landed Polynesian teachers there and kept them supplied by ship from Darnley Island in the Cook Strait. The first resident missionary – W. G. Lawes – settled at Port Moresby in 1874. Three years later he was joined by James Chalmers, who transferred to Papua after ten years on the Pacific island of Rarotonga.

Chalmers' task was to superintend the extension of the mission in the south east of the island and to penetrate the interior. Chalmers was a born pioneer, an affable, warm-hearted Scot, who later achieved unsought fame when his exploits were published in Britain. A colleague described him as 'the Livingstone of New Guinea'. Chalmers spent the remainder of his long missionary career in Papua, outliving two wives in the process. As the mission grew in size, largely thanks to Chalmers' pioneering work of exploration and opening up new mission areas, the Society sent out more personnel from Britain. One of these was Oliver Tomkins from Great Yarmouth, who arrived in Papua in 1900. He joined Chalmers in his pioneering work and the two were murdered at Dopima on Goaribari Island in the Gulf of Papua on 8 April 1901.

Chalmers and Tomkins were the first European martyrs on Papua New Guinea, but Chalmers himself recognized the debt owed to the Polynesian teachers and the disproportionate risks they faced, with many largely unrecorded martyrdoms: 'They have to bear the brunt of the fight, and we, the white missionaries, follow in and get the bulk of the credit'.

Neither were Chalmers and Tomkins to be Papua's last European martyrs. Further missions were attracted to this huge island – Methodist, Roman Catholic and Anglican. The Anglican presence was largely on the north coast and this took the full force of the Japanese invasion in 1942. Bishop Philip Strong urged his clergy to remain in the war zone and he himself set the example. But this selflessness was not without its cost: there were arrests by the Japanese and a number of the mission personnel were executed, 2 September 1942 being the day of greatest carnage. There was no distinction in death between ordained and lay, women and men, old and young Europeans, Australians and native Papuans – members of all these groups were killed indiscriminately. Vivian Redlich, John Barge, Bernard Moore, Leslie Gariadi, Lucian Tapiedi, Mavis Parkinson, May Hayman, Lilla Lashmar, Margery Brenchley and Henry Holland were among those who paid the ultimate price for their faith. Altogether 333 Christians lost their lives at the hands of the Japanese invaders of Papua. Perhaps most crucially for the future of the Christian faith in Papua was that the Church in Papua now had its own indigenous martyrs.

3 September

Gregory the Great, Bishop of Rome, Teacher of the Faith, 604

Known as the Father of the medieval papacy, Gregory's list of achievements is lengthy. As well as being an accomplished law student, Gregory founded monasteries, contributed finance to many works, reformed the church leadership in Rome, set out liturgical reform and organized missionaries to the Anglo-Saxons.

Gregory was born in 540 to an aristocratic family of piety and scholarship that had already produced two popes. Brought up in the climate of cultural renewal, Gregory studied grammar, dialectic and rhetoric. He was made Prefect of Rome in 572 where he honed the administrative and political skills which would equip him for his later roles. He entered the monastic life in 574, establishing and endowing six monasteries on his family land, and one in Rome itself. In 579 he was sent to Constantinople where he stayed until 586. It was during this period that he wrote his best theological commentaries.

On his return to Rome, Gregory acted as adviser and secretary to Pelagius II, whom he succeeded as Pope in 590. Gregory discovered Rome in a miserable state devoid of real leadership, not only in the Church, but also in the wider city. In 592–3 the Italian peninsula was under threat from the Lombards, and rather than allow the invaders to deal with an inadequate state leadership Gregory took over the responsibility from state control, organizing bread supplies and providing for the city's defence. Such was his administrative ability and leadership that by the end of the sixth century, and with the Lombards repelled, the whole peninsula came under papal rule.

One of Gregory's projects was the sending of missionaries to the Anglo-Saxons and he commissioned both Augustine (see 26 May) and Mellitus (see 24 April). The enormous numbers of letters that he wrote to these two missionaries meant that his influence was felt even after his death.

Gregory's period as Pope marks the transition from the ancient world of imperial Rome to a medieval Christendom united by the Roman Catholic Church. The reach and extent of papal authority increased dramatically. As Europe entered the Middle Ages it was as a Christian civilization, not only united by the Catholic Church, but to a great extent led by its supreme ruler – the Pope in Rome.

Despite the great changes that occurred during his life, Gregory is recorded as a man of humility and peace and his preferred title as Pope was the 'servant of the servants of God'. He was unafraid to stand for Christian truth in a changing and challenging world and challenged those in his charge to do so also.

> If a preacher does not denounce the wicked, he himself will be reckoned guilty. For only one who is not afraid to say what they rightly feel and does not blush to do so ought to be a defender of the truth. The preacher is . . . a physician, who does not blush to prescribe the medicines.
>
> *Gregory the Great, Ezekiel I.xi.22; I.x.17*

4 September

Birinus, Bishop of Dorchester (Oxon), Apostle of Wessex, 650

Birinus was consecrated a missionary bishop by Asterius, Archbishop of Milan, at Genoa. Probably of Germanic stock, he was sent by Pope Honorius I to evangelize the remote and unreached areas of England. Birinus landed in Wessex in 634 and on his journey north he encountered the West Saxons. Birinus found them so pagan that he decided not to continue his journey northwards, but to stay and evangelize them instead.

Birinus was greatly aided in his evangelism by the approach of King Cynegils of the West Saxons, who asked him to teach him the ways of Christianity. Birinus eventually baptized Cynegils and two of his children.

Cynegils' daughter married the Christian King Oswald of Northumbria (see 5 August), and the two kings jointly gave Birinus the town of Dorchester (in what is today Oxfordshire) as his episcopal seat. Birinus duly settled at Dorchester, which was heavily influenced by a Roman population and style, and made his headquarters there, engaging in mission to the surrounding areas. He eventually built the first church at Winchester, and when the diocese of Dorchester was divided Winchester became the centre of a new diocese.

Birinus was a missionary bishop initially under the jurisdiction of the Bishop of Genoa, and consequently he paid little attention to the Archbishop of Canterbury or to the central ecclesiastical structures of the country he came to evangelize.

Bede described Birinus as 'a good and just man, who in carrying out his duties was guided rather by an inborn love of virtue than by what he had read in books'.

Allen Gardiner, Missionary, Founder of the South American Missionary Society, 1851

Born at Basildon near Wallingford in Berkshire in 1794, Allen Gardiner entered the Royal Naval College in Portsmouth in 1808 and went to sea two years later. He served in many parts of the world and saw action most notably in 1813 when he earned distinction for his part in the capture of an American frigate off the coast of Chile. A successful naval officer, he had reached the rank of commander when he resigned from the service in 1826.

Brought up in a Christian family, Gardiner's faith had been 'on hold' until the death of his mother while he was away at sea when he began a process of his rediscovery of the truth of Christianity. A visit to South America on HMS *Dauntless* in 1821 first aroused an interest and concern for the indigenous peoples of that continent, for so long abused and exploited by Europeans. He made the decision to devote his life to mission work and, following the death of his first wife Julia in 1834, he set out to work among the Zulus of South Africa. But attacks on Zulu territory by the Boers made effective mission work impossible and with his second wife Elizabeth he sought new spheres for missionary service.

He and his family went first to South America, crossing the continent overland by pack mule from Buenos Aires to Santiago distributing Scripture. But he made little headway with the suspicious Indians who regarded English missionaries with the same hostility as their Spanish conquerors. Gardiner's next project was in Papua New Guinea, but the hostility of its Dutch rulers frustrated this plan.

But Gardiner's vision for South America remained and to further it he founded the Patagonian Missionary Society in 1844. A Bible-distributing mission to the Gran Chaco in 1845 aroused the hostility of the local Roman Catholics so he turned to the far south. A preliminary expedition in 1847 convinced him that it was right to target Tierra del Fuego, where he returned with companions in 1850. But native hostility and the lack of food in this remote area doomed the expedition to starvation. Gardiner died on Picton Island probably on 6 September 1851, four months before the arrival of HMS *Dido*, which buried Gardiner and retrieved his journal, which was still in his hands and in which he had written the words, 'Let not this mission fail'. An answer to this prayer became apparent as the Patagonian Missionary Society was revitalized by news of Gardiner's tragic death. In 1864 it was renamed the South American Missionary Society and became the Church of England's principal channel of mission to that continent.

Charles Fuge Lowder, Priest, 1880

Born at Bath in 1820, the son of a banker, and educated at Exeter College, Oxford where he was influenced by the Tractarians, Charles Lowder became one of the best-known 'slum priests' in Victorian London.

Ordained in 1843, he worked initially in the West Country before moving to London to join the staff of St Barnabas, Pimlico at a time of riot and legal prosecution because of the parish's advanced ceremonial practices. While in Pimlico he was involved in the foundation of the Society of the Holy Cross 'to defend and strengthen the spiritual life of the clergy, to defend the faith of the Church, and to carry on and aid Mission work both at home and abroad'. At a time of hostility and persecution the society brought together Ritualist clergy for mutual support, prayer and encouragement.

Inspired to engage in urban mission by reading a life of St Vincent de Paul (see 27 September), Lowder moved across London in 1856 to become curate of St George's in the East, another parish that was to suffer from the mid-Victorian phenomenon of anti-Ritualist rioting because of its style of worship. Lowder's task was to run the St George's Mission in Wapping, one of the worst slum areas of the East End. To him, mission was not a short-lived campaign but a permanent Christian presence in an area where the Church had no foothold and where it would have to earn the respect and confidence of the local people. The mission started with a single room as a base, and progressed in due course to a borrowed iron church. Lowder's residence in their midst greatly endeared him to the local people, to whom he was affectionately known as 'Father Lowder', especially after his efforts on their behalf in the East End cholera outbreak. Eventually the iron church was superseded by a purpose-built brick church for the new parish of St Peter's, London Docks that was carved out of St George's parish, with Lowder as its first vicar in 1866.

Exhausted by his long years of work, Lowder resigned the living of St Peter's in 1880 and retired to Chislehurst. He died soon afterwards and, amidst scenes of obvious grief, large crowds of East Enders attended his funeral to mourn the priest who had served them so selflessly and for so long.

John Chrysostom, Bishop of Constantinople, Teacher of the Faith, 407

The literal translation of 'Chrysostom' is 'Golden-Mouth'. Such was the power, eloquence and skill in John's preaching that during his time as priest in Antioch people began to call him by this nickname which was both descriptive and well deserved. His sermons were full of biblical exposition and practical application. He combined this with a flair for words and a fierce commitment to practical Christianity. His lifestyle matched his words. John's early ascetic life meant that he was as spiritually sensitive as he was linguistically eloquent.

Born in Syria in the middle of the fourth century, John started to live the ascetic life after his baptism. His desire for authentic Christianity led him into the desert, where he placed himself under the authority of an old Syrian monk for four years, before moving on to live in isolation in a cave for a further two. Ill health finally forced him back into the city, and he was ordained priest in 386. During the twelve years he spent at Antioch he made great use of the skills of public speaking that he had learnt as a youth, and was given special responsibility for preaching. His sermons were directed towards the instruction and moral reformation of a nominally Christian society. He was appointed a special assistant to the bishop, with responsibility for the poor of the city.

In 398 John was chosen to be the Bishop of Constantinople. There is no reason to suppose that he did not welcome the move to a city which was the seat of power of the Eastern Emperor and which surpassed Rome in terms of authority and prestige. John was quietly whisked away from Antioch without his or his people being told of his election as Bishop of Constantinople to avoid popular demonstrations.

In Constantinople Chrysostom inherited an undisciplined clergy living in luxury. The disparity between the huge fortunes of the ruling class and the needs of the poor was often emphasized in his preaching. He instigated many practical works to redress the balance, which meant that in turn he was both loved and hated by the citizens of the city. The Emperor's wife Eudoxia took a particular dislike to his highlighting of the moral and practical aspects of Christianity.

The Empress, incensed at John's preaching, erected a statue of herself outside the Church of Hagia Sophia to provoke Chrysostom. Charges were brought against him, alleging that he had called the Empress a 'Jezebel'. Other charges were concocted and brought against him but John refused to defend himself or tone down his preaching. The Empress had him exiled, only to recall him a short time later when the city was hit by a earthquake. John never moderated his position, preaching against excess and continuing to rein in the worst excesses of the Church. He was exiled in 404, again at Eudoxia's instigation, and this time sent to Pontus. He was made to walk the journey, and given no rest, and he died *en route*.

Chrysostom's flair for words is evident in his writing on prayer:

> By prayer, I understand not that which is found only in the mouth, but that which springs up from the bottom of the heart. Indeed, just as trees with the deepest roots are not broken or uprooted by a violent storm... so too, prayers that come from the depths of the heart, rooted there, ascend to heaven with confidence. They are not turned aside under attack from any distracting thought at all.
>
> *On the Incomprehensibility of God, Fifth Discourse*

15 September

Cyprian, Bishop of Carthage, Martyr, 258

Cyprian was an Orator, teacher of rhetoric and advocate before becoming a Christian in 245. After his conversion he concentrated upon Christian studies. He was a student of Tertullian, the great African Christian scholar, whom he regarded as his master. Cyprian renounced his inheritance as a landowner, giving the money to the Church, and was ordained priest. This fast progress continued when he was consecrated Bishop of Carthage in 248, only three years after his conversion. Cyprian was constant in his care for the poor, and was praised for his teaching, his character, his thought, and his time as a bishop. His reign however, was not without controversy.

As Bishop of Carthage during the persecution of the Church by Emperor Decius in 250, Cyprian fled to the countryside, saying that it was better that he guide his Church by letter than give his life and leave them leaderless. He returned to the city in 251.

During the persecution some Christians offered the required sacrifice to the pagan idols, or bought certificates stating that they had done so. Cyprian was faced with the question of how to readmit these believers to the Church. The decision was a difficult one, and he disagreed with his priest Novatius, who admitted them back into the Church without any requirement being placed upon them. Cyprian was also involved in heated controversy with Bishop Stephen of Rome over the validity of baptism administered by schismatics and heretics. Cyprian rejected its validity, demanding rebaptism, Stephen accepted it. These two disagreements colour the whole of Cyprian's period as bishop. His desire for the unity of the Church was equalled by a desire to preserve its purity.

Cyprian united the Church in Carthage behind him. By the time of Valerian's persecution in 257, the African Church was a powerful force, not only standing against the Church in Rome in theological matters, but also standing with the regional government which was beginning to seek freedom from the overbearing influence of the Emperor.

Cyprian's martyrdom occurred in the persecution of 257, which targeted the Church leadership. Cyprian refused an imperial order that stated that all bishops had to participate in pagan ceremonies. He was exiled for a year, and on his return was rearrested and subsequently beheaded. The African Church, not prepared to dilute her belief in the purity of the faith in theological debate, was unwavering in her faith in the face of persecution.

> When we pray it is not for one person, but for the entire people; because, we the whole people, are one. God, who is the Teacher of prayer and peace, taught us peace. He wished each one to pray for all, just as he, himself, has borne all together in one.
>
> *Commentary on the Lord's Prayer, Ch. 8*

16 September

Ninian, Bishop of Galloway, Apostle of the Picts, c.432

Although a Briton by birth, Ninian had received his education in Rome, before returning to the Isles, and settling in Galloway. Ninian evangelized the district beyond Hadrian's wall reaching up into the region of the Picts (Forfar, Perth and Sterling). He also built the first known stone church in Britain in 397 in Galloway and established a monastery in the area of Whithorn.

Ninian was influential in the establishment and success of Whithorn as a base for study and spirituality for Irish and Welsh monks. As such he played a great part in the gradual move north of the Christian faith in the fifth century.

Bede records Ninian as being the Apostle to the Picts: 'The southern Picts . . . accepted the true faith through the preaching of Bishop Ninian, a most revered and holy man of British race'. While there is speculation as to how much influence Ninian had in the far north of this region, there is a consensus that he was involved in a mission to the Picts in some way. More credibility is placed upon his work in the Galloway region. There is a recognition that much of the success of Columba in establishing Christianity in the northern regions of Britain was down to the earlier work of Ninian.

He was buried in Whithorn, and his resting place quickly became a place of pilgrimage.

16 September

Edward Bouverie Pusey, Priest, Tractarian, 1882

Edward Pusey was born near Oxford in 1800, and educated at Eton and Christ Church. In 1828 he was ordained and appointed Regius Professor of Hebrew and Canon of Christ Church Cathedral. Previously, in 1823, he had been elected a Fellow of Oriel College and it was in the senior common room at Oriel where he became acquainted with John Keble (see 14 July), John Henry Newman (see 11 August) and others who were to take the lead in the Oxford Movement, which developed rapidly after Keble's Assize sermon in 1833. This group wished to rediscover and to emphasize the spiritual rather than the national side of the Church of England by stressing the Church's Catholic and apostolic origins. Their means of disseminating their ideas was the publication of a series of *Tracts for the Times*, to which Pusey contributed tracts on fasting and baptism. When Newman left the Church of England in 1841, Pusey found himself somewhat unwillingly assuming the leadership of a group who were popularly known to their supporters as 'Tractarians' and to their detractors as 'Puseyites'. But as the Ritualist phase of the movement began to build up steam in the late 1850s he became increasingly detached from the direction it was taking.

The death of his wife in 1839 greatly affected Pusey, deepening his feeling of great personal unworthiness. From 1846, he adopted a strict ascetic lifestyle which, paradoxically, made him an inspiring figure in the eyes of many. In 1843 his sermon, *The Holy Eucharist, a Comfort to the Penitent*, was condemned by the university authorities and he was suspended from preaching in the university pulpit for two years. He was actively involved in the foundation of Anglican religious communities for women. He promoted auricular confession and the doctrine of the Real Presence and took sides in a number of learned theological disputes. In many ways he was a reluctant controversialist, but was always prepared to defend newly re-discovered Catholic doctrines and practices against their opponents.

Despite his great erudition, his preaching was both pastoral and practical. Bishop Gray of Cape Town noted in 1867 that Pusey's language 'was full of love and tenderness, and savouring more of Low Churchmanship than of High'. In the great cholera epidemic of 1866, Pusey did outstanding work in caring for the sick. He died at Ascot Priory in 1882 and was buried at Christ Church Cathedral. After his death his library was made the centrepiece of Pusey House – a permanent memorial to him at Oxford.

17 September

Hildegard, Abbess of Bingen, Visionary, 1179

Hildegard was the tenth child to be born to a noble family in the Nahe valley, in the Rhineland. From early childhood Hildegard was the recipient of supernatural visions and experiences. At the age of eight she was put by her parents into the care of Jutta, a female recluse who lived close to a Benedictine Monastery at Diessenberg. Seven years after, at the age of 15, Hildegard took vows and became a nun in the monastic community that had gathered around Jutta. On Jutta's death in 1136, Hildegard herself became the abbess.

As well as a visionary and mystic, Hildegard was a remarkable woman who excelled in many areas. She was not a nun removed from the world and enveloped by mystery. She was versatile and energetic, producing varied works and affecting others wherever she went. Hildegard corresponded with many people, including royalty. She saw herself as standing in the prophetic tradition and was not afraid to castigate or reprimand. She wrote musical compositions including hymns, chants and songs. Her theological works include commentaries on creeds and Gospels, and on the Rule of St Benedict. Hildegard's medical handbooks and books about nature are remarkable for their content and conclusions. She also wrote a play.

Between 1141 and 1151 Hildegard began to receive visions and, with the approval of the Archbishop of Mainz, recorded some them. The collection of her visions is called her *Scivias* and contained 26 visions. Hildegard writes on the nature of man, and the Last Judgement. *Scivias* includes a collection of dramatic songs.

The community grew too large for their premises and moved to Rupertsberg, near Bingen. From this base Hildegard travelled throughout Rhineland and founded a daughter house at Eibingen.

Hildegard was concerned that the writings about her visions be approved. Pope Eugenius gave her the necessary permission and, as her writings spread, so did her fame. The mystical quality of her writings, and the nature of her music have led to Hildegard being appropriated by many people, not all of whom recognize the theological and spiritual base to her life. Hildegard was, above all else, a woman devoted to God, whose visions and writings sprang out of a desire for him.

> O how precious is the maidenhood of this virgin, she of the shut door whose womb the holy Godhead filled with His fire so that a flower bloomed in her and the son of God from that secret place went forth like the dawn.
>
> Thus the sweet seed, who was that Son, through the shut door of her womb unlocked paradise.
>
> And the Son of God from that secret place went forth like the dawn.
>
> *Responsory 63*

Theodore of Tarsus, Archbishop of Canterbury, 690

Theodore was Archbishop of Canterbury at a time of crisis for the Roman Church in England. In 664 Archbishop Deusdedit died and, as a severe plague had greatly reduced the number of bishops and high-ranking clergy in Britain, finding a successor proved to be a hard task. Three years after the death of Deusdedit, Wighard was chosen to be archbishop, but he too died of the plague on the journey to Rome for his consecration. By this time the Pope was concerned about the delay and chose Hadrian, an African monk, as the next Archbishop of Canterbury. Hadrian refused the position, feeling that he was not worthy of the task, and recommended Theodore, a Greek monk living in a Roman monastery. Although Theodore was not ordained the people reluctantly agreed. Theodore was immediately ordained deacon, and when he had grown his hair long enough (four months later) was ordained priest and consecrated bishop.

Both Theodore and Hadrian travelled to Britain in the company of Benedict Biscop (see 12 January). It was a long and arduous journey during which Theodore learnt the English tongue. They arrived in Britain in May 669. On arrival they found a Church lacking in leadership, although relatively healthy at root level. Theodore appointed three bishops immediately, and set off on a tour of the Church. He called a synod at Hertford in 672, and issued canons designed to establish principles of administration and order. The date of the celebration of Easter was affirmed, and bishops were required to confine their activities to their own dioceses. This measure was aimed at limiting the activities of the Celtic Bishops, who were able to wander wherever they willed, having a more pliable jurisdiction. Theodore established a yearly meeting of the whole Church, and moved to increase the number of bishoprics throughout the land. He sought to bring unity to a fragmented Church.

A major area of contention for Theodore came in the Northumbrian region, the area most loyal to the Celtic traditions, and the areas least open to the decisions made at the Synod of Whitby (664). Theodore had several disagreements with Wilfrid (see 12 October), Bishop of Ripon (a vast area), which included Wilfrid's expulsion (677) and reinstatement at a lower level of authority and influence. Theodore introduced into Northumbria the Roman diocesan system of church government whilst allowing the Northumbrian Church freedom to blend both Celtic and Roman principles. In doing so he confirmed the decisions taken at Whitby whilst retaining the characteristics of both Roman and Celtic traditions within the same united body. Theodore's actions shaped the Church for ages to come, and began to sow the seeds of a common identity of the Church in Britain.

Although remembered as the principal force behind the common Church in Britain, Theodore was also known as a gifted teacher and theologian. He taught science, astronomy and law as well as Latin and Greek at the school he founded in Canterbury. An astute politician and a visionary leader, Theodore oversaw one of the most fruitful periods of the Church in Britain.

The process of integration of the various elements of the Church was completed after Theodore's death. The monastic community on Iona conformed in 716. Wales was the last bastion of Celtic independence, finally submitting to the authority of Rome in 768.

20 September

John Coleridge Patteson, First Bishop of Melanesia, and his Companions, Martyrs, 1871

Born in 1827 and brought up in a highly privileged environment, John Coleridge Patteson was ordained in 1853. The following year he was recruited by Bishop George Selwyn of New Zealand (see 11 April), to oversee the Church's work in the Melanesian part (today's Vanuatu and Solomon Islands) of that vast diocese, leaving Selwyn free to concentrate on New Zealand itself. An exceptional linguist, he learned Maori on the outward voyage so as to be able to use it on arrival in New Zealand. In due course he was to master 24 of the 96 languages of Melanesia. In 1861 the diocese of New Zealand was split and he was consecrated missionary Bishop of Melanesia. The long distances he was required to travel in order to minister to the people of his widespread diocese and the isolation and loneliness that he experienced gradually took their toll. His health declined and those who met him were shocked at how quickly he had aged. Yet his warm personality and a distinct lack of episcopal pomp endeared Patteson to all those with whom he came into contact. The Presbyterian missionary John Geddie, for example, described the bishop as 'a man of the most lovely Christian character and singular devotedness'.

An innovator in missionary work, Patteson began to query the traditional Victorian connection between Christianity and literacy, questioning its relevance for adults in a non-literate society. He also affirmed the value of indigenous cultures, so often routinely condemned by European missionaries:

> I have for years thought that we seek in our missions a great deal too much to make English Christians of our converts. We consciously and unanimously assume English Christianity to be necessary. One mistake of this kind was to suppose clothing essential.

He aimed to disturb as little as possible the manners and customs of the people among whom he worked and lived.

Patteson was clubbed to death on Nukapu Island in the Santa Cruz group on 20 September 1871. Joseph Atkin and Stephen Taroaniara, his companions, were hit by a hail of arrows, and subsequently died of tetanus. This was almost certainly a revenge killing after local men and boys had been kidnapped to work on the Queensland cotton plantations. When Patteson's body was later recovered from a boat floating in the island's lagoon, it was found to bear five wounds clearly caused after death, and in his hands was a palm branch with five knots. Historians have suggested that these symbolized revenge for five men who had been kidnapped from the islands, but to the Melanesian faithful a comparison with the *stigmata* of Christ was irresistible.

Lancelot Andrewes, Bishop of Winchester, Spiritual Writer, 1626

Lancelot Andrewes was born near to the Tower of London in 1555 and educated at Merchant Taylors' School and Pembroke Hall, Cambridge, where he was elected Fellow in 1575. He was ordained in 1580. In 1589 he became Vicar of St Giles, Cripplegate, where he soon developed a reputation as a preacher, before returning to Cambridge as Master of Pembroke Hall. In 1601 he became Dean of Westminster and four years later was consecrated Bishop of Chichester.

One of the most learned men of his time, he was present at the 1604 Hampton Court conference out of which emerged the new translation of the Bible which became known as the Authorized (or King James) Version. Andrewes himself worked on the first part of the Old Testament. In an age of Calvinist theology and largely Low Church ceremonial, Andrews was an articulate exponent of a more sacramental pre-Tractarian form of High Church Anglicanism, giving respectability and academic underpinning to a movement that was later to be associated with Archbishop Laud (see 10 January).

But, unlike Laud, Andrewes was not himself a controversial or combative figure. He was essentially a scholar and it was upon sound learning and a desire that Anglican worship should be based on ordered ceremonial that he adopted and developed practices in worship to complement his belief in the Real Presence and to honour the incarnate Christ. His ceremonial practices were largely a personal matter in his private chapel and where others adopted them it was by Andrewes' example not by his persuasion. He was an outstanding theologian of the High Church movement in the Church of England, writing from a uniquely Anglican point of view about the Church, the sacraments and episcopacy. He counted Richard Hooker (see 3 November) and George Herbert (see 27 February) among his friends.

But in his own day he was best known as a preacher. He preached regularly at the court of James I and many of his sermons were published. Over three hundred years later T.S. Eliot took some words from Andrewes' 1622 Christmas sermon ('A cold coming they had of it . . .') for the opening five lines of his poem *The Journey of the Magi.*

Andrewes was translated from Chichester to Ely in 1609 and in the same year he was appointed a privy councillor. He was further translated to Winchester in 1619. He died at Winchester Palace in 1626 and is buried in Southwark Cathedral.

A morning prayer of Lancelot Andrewes:

> O Thou who sendest forth the light, createst the morning, and makest the sun to rise on the good and the evil: Enlighten the blindess of our minds with the knowledge of thy truth; lift up the light of thy countenance upon us, that in thy light we may see light, and, at the last, in the light of grace the light of glory; through Jesus Christ our Lord.

Sergei of Radonezh, Russian Monastic Reformer, Teacher of the Faith, 1392

Sergei (or Sergius), Abbot of Radonezh, in Russia, was one of the most influential and humble men in Russian history. He is remembered as one who changed the course of a nation thorough humility and holiness.

Born in 1314 in Rostov and baptized with the name Bartholomew, Sergei and his family were driven from their home by civil war and after a period farming at Radonezh near Moscow he started to live the life of a hermit when he was 20 years old, living in the forest at the edge of his village. From there he entered the monastic life, and his reputation as a man of wisdom, humility and deep spirituality grew. Eventually Sergei became the abbot of a monastic community, and in 1378 he refused the offer of being appointed Bishop of Moscow. So high was his reputation as a man of God that Grand Prince Dimitri frequently turned to him as peacemaker and mediator in political matters.

In 1380 Russia had been under the control of the neighbouring Tartars for a hundred years. An army of 400,000 was gathering to attack Moscow. Prince Dimitri was faced with the decision of whether to defend or surrender. In this most critical time in Russian history, Dimitri chose to consult Sergei. The normally quiet, reticent Sergei, who shied away from giving explicit commands, on this occasion was firm: 'Go forward, and fear not. God will help you.' And later, Sergei had a further word of encouragement for the prince: 'Be in no doubt, my Lord; go forward with faith and confront the enemy's ferocity; and fear not, for God will be on your side.'

Prince Dmitri was persuaded not to surrender, but to fight for freedom. After a fierce battle the Russian forces were victorious, the Tartars were defeated, Russia liberated and the Christian tradition preserved.

During his life Sergei was said to have founded 40 monasteries and was constantly sought after for spiritual advice. The most loved of all Russian saints, Sergei remained close to his peasant roots in touch with the ordinary people. He held up the service of others as an important part of the monastic vocation and emphasized personal and communal poverty.

In his lifetime Sergei was widely respected and honoured as one upon whom God's spirit was seen to rest and he was said to have undergone on occasions physical transfigurations by light. Today he is Russia's patron saint and each year many pilgrims visit his shrine at Zagorsk's Trinity monastery.

Wilson Carlile, Founder of the Church Army, 1942

Wilson Carlile was born in Brixton, London in 1847 and had a patchy education owing to the chronic back trouble from which he suffered all his life. But he excelled at languages and music. He was highly successful in business until recession and serious illness combined to end his career at the age of 31. A breakdown followed which was in turn followed by his conversion. He later commented:

> I have seen the crucified and risen Lord as truly as if He had made Himself visible to my bodily sight. That is for me the conclusive evidence of His existence. He touched my heart, and old desires and hopes left it. In their place came the new thought that I might serve Him and His poor and suffering brethren.

Initially he offered his services to the Americans Moody and Sankey, at that time holding a mission in London. He accompanied Sankey on the harmonium, learned a great deal about methods of evangelism and was inspired to become an evangelist himself. Consequently he was confirmed into the Church of England and then entered the London College of Divinity to train for his ordination in 1880. He served his curacy at St Mary Abbots in Kensington but the lack of contact between the Church and the working classes was a cause of real concern to him and he began outdoor preaching in order to reach those who would not come to church.

Carlile left Kensington in order to work in a slum mission, and from 1882 began the process of uniting local Anglican parish missions into a national organization, which in keeping with the popular use of military terminology in church life at that time took the title 'Church Army'. A training college for men was founded in 1884 followed by one for women three years later. After some initial hesitancy the Church of England incorporated the Church Army into its structures and in due course the office of Evangelist was founded for Church Army officers and sisters. The Church Army's work included evangelism and social and moral welfare work and this was supplemented by work among the troops during the First World War. Carlile was careful to ensure that the Church Army always worked within official church structures. He remained honorary chief secretary until his retirement in 1926, having been made a prebendary of St Paul's Cathedral in 1906. He died in 1942.

Vincent de Paul, Founder of the Congregation of the Mission (Lazarists), 1660

Born the son of peasant farmer at Pouy in the Landes, south-west France around 1580, Vincent was educated by the Franciscans and at the universities of Dax and Toulouse. While travelling by sea from Marseille to Narbonne in 1606 he was captured by pirates and sold into slavery in Tunisia, but escaped after a few months and returned to France.

Ordained in 1600, he spent ten years in uneventful parish ministry but eventually he underwent a marked change of attitude to the poor and the suffering. In Paris, Vincent visited prisoners condemned to be galley slaves and, appointed by Louis XIII as royal almoner of the galleys (in effect, chaplain to the galley slaves), he continued this ministry, both pastoral and evangelistic, at Marseille and Bordeaux.

In 1617 he founded the first Confraternity of Charity, made up of wealthy women working among the sick and poor near Lyons. For a number of years he was the personal chaplain to the wealthy Gondi family who encouraged and supported Vincent in his charitable and mission work. With their support he founded the Congregation of the Mission – an institute of priests initially organized for rural mission.

A community of the Congregation was formally established at the Collège des Bons-Enfants in Paris in 1626, where Vincent served as Principal. The alternative name 'Lazarist Fathers' was given to the group when it established headquarters at the former priory of St Lazare, in 1632. Vincent not only headed the order but also founded with others several charitable organizations, notably the Daughters of Charity, in 1633. This was notable in being the first non-enclosed community of women which was devoted to caring for the sick and the poor. From 1628 the Congregation of the Mission organized several seminaries for the training of priests as a result of work done by Vincent with young men about to be ordained. He was also concerned with relief work during the religious wars in France. His implacable opposition to the Jansenists (a group considered heretical within the Roman Catholic Church) was believed to have been responsible for its suppression, yet paradoxically in an age of religious conflict he was unusually courteous towards Protestants, insisting that they be treated as brothers, with respect and love.

Vincent died in Paris on 27 September 1660. It was said that 'the poor of Paris lost their best friend and humanity a benefactor unsurpassed in modern times'.

30 September

Jerome, Translator of the Scriptures, Teacher of the Faith, 420

Jerome (also known as Eusebius Hieronymus) was born around the year 342 at the edge of the Latin-speaking world in the city of Strido in Dalmatia (modern Croatia). He was highly influential in the history of Christian thought and his translations were crucial to the spread of Christianity and Christian study. However, he was an extremely temperamental individual, sarcastic, impervious to gossip (many of his close friendships were with women), and had a habit of making enemies wherever he went. He could, by all accounts, be equally gregarious and an enthusiastic friend when his confrontational side was not to the fore.

The man who became known as the 'prince of translators' began by studying grammar and rhetoric at Rome. During his time in the city he was baptized, and then left for Trier in Gaul where, with a group of friends, he was persuaded to enter the monastic life.

After an argument, the group split, and Jerome left the community. With some of the group, Jerome journeyed to Antioch, and by the time he had reached the city in 374 two of his travelling companions had died, and Jerome himself was seriously ill. It was during this period that he is believed to have had a dream in which God condemned him for living more like a person from classical literature (a Ciceronian) than as a Christian. On his recovery he started to live as a hermit in Syria, and during this time learnt Hebrew – a language he found difficult and coarse, and from which he frequently retreated.

He was ordained priest in Antioch, before studying in Constantinople under Gregory of Nazianzus. Jerome's ordination to the priesthood was strange. He never served as a priest in any capacity, and there is no evidence of his ever celebrating the Eucharist. He seems to have been ordained simply to fulfil the desires of others, and saw himself as having primarily a monastic vocation.

It was in Constantinople that his reputation as a translator began to emerge, and he was much in demand as an interpreter but once again he found relationships difficult and his work took him back to Rome. In Rome he began a work on a Latin text of the Bible, which eventually became known as the Vulgate. Jerome's translation was to become the standard version of the Bible in the Western Church for over a thousand years. He was supported in his work by a group of Christian women, which resulted in some scandalous gossip. As ever with Jerome this relationship did not last long. He eventually settled in Bethlehem in 386, founding a monastery where spent the last 35 years of his life as a monk and a scholar.

During this period of his life Jerome wrote many books, some vehement in their response to what he considered false teaching. His single-mindedness in pursuit of his own point of view led to the loss of his great friendship with Rufinus, and he also locked horns with Augustine.

Jerome was an intensely knowledgeable man, gifted in translation, and devout in his personal life. His difficult personality and frequent quarrels have led many to speculate at his designation as a saint. However, Jerome's immense literary output, his translation of texts from the original Hebrew into Latin, his Bible translation, his adaptation, revision and continuation of Eusebius' Church History, and his biblical commentaries, mark him out as one of the most gifted and erudite Fathers of the Church. His correspondence is refined and detailed, drawing from the best of Eastern and Western theology.

> It shall come, it shall come, that day when this corruptible shall put on incorruption, and this mortal shall put on immortality
>
> *Letter 14*

1 October

Remigius, Bishop of Rheims, Apostle of the Franks, 533

Remigius is one of the most famous bishops of Rheims, and according to Gregory of Tours was bishop for 70 years, having been ordained at the age of 22. Born in Gaul, he became known as the 'Apostle to the Franks' for his role in the conversion of Clovis I, the Frankish ruler, and the subsequent baptism of 3,000 of his subjects.

Clovis I became King of the Salian Franks in 481, and expanded his kingdom rapidly, spreading into Roman Gaul and other territories. He converted to Christianity after marrying Clotilde, a Burgundian Princess, who was a devout Christian. Alongside her influence was the healing of a sick child that Clovis interpreted as divine intervention. Similarly Clovis won a significant battle victory, which he saw as a sign from God. When the battle was going away from him, Clovis called out to 'Clotilde's God' and promised that he would be baptized if the battle was won.

Clovis was then trained in the Christian faith and baptized by Remigius some time between 496 and 506. There was close co-operation between Clovis and Remigius, and consequently between the Church and the State. Whatever the cause of Clovis' conversion, be it the healing of a child, or a battle victory, there is no doubt as to the effect of the baptism of the king upon the country, and subsequently upon Western Christendom. Once Remigius enjoyed the protection of the king he was free to preach the gospel all through the Frankish lands where he founded many churches and bishoprics.

1 October

Anthony Ashley Cooper, Earl of Shaftesbury, Social Reformer, 1885

Born in London in 1801, and educated at Harrow and Christ Church, Oxford, Anthony Ashley Cooper had an intensely unhappy childhood. Abandoned by his parents to the care of servants, he was fortunate that his childhood nurse Maria Millis taught and nurtured him in the Christian faith. His childhood experiences gave him a deep sympathy with the sufferings of poor and unwanted children, and his evangelical faith gave him the sense of duty to seek the path of serving suffering humanity rather than pursuing personal pleasure, as was the norm in the aristocracy at that time. He had entered Parliament in 1826 as Conservative member first for Woodstock and from 1831 for Dorset, and on his father's death in 1851 he entered the House of Lords as the seventh Earl of Shaftesbury.

Shaftesbury was far from pietistic in his clear evangelical faith, believing that 'Christianity is not a state of opinion and speculation. Christianity is essentially practical.' In Parliament he was an important force in early British reform legislation being responsible for numerous social reforms aiding factory workers, women and children in coal mines, the insane, chimney sweeps and poor children. He took the trouble to find out for himself about the conditions of the poor, visiting slums and factories, going down mines and visiting asylums and schools. Outside of Parliament he was indefatigable in his support of Christian causes, being involved in the Ragged School Union, the British and Foreign Bible Society, the NSPCC, the London City Mission, and the Church Pastoral-Aid Society to name but a few. All this activity underpinned what he described as the 'single object' of his life – 'the advancement of God's ever blessed name, and the Temporal and eternal welfare of all mankind'.

Shaftesbury was related through marriage to Lord Palmerston, Prime Minster for all but fourteen months of the years from 1855 to 1865. Knowing little about the Church, Palmerston consulted Shaftesbury in all his ecclesiastical appointments in order to find suitable candidates for senior posts in the Church of England. Hostile to Tractarianism within the Church of England (though he and Pusey – see 16 September – were cousins), but not to Roman Catholicism, Shaftesbury struck up a friendship with Cardinal Manning, the leader of the Roman Catholic Church in England. After Shaftesbury's death Manning, on reading his biography, commented, 'what a retrospect of work done. It makes me feel that my life has been wasted.'

Lord Shaftesbury died in 1885. Refusing to allow a statue of himself, he is commemorated by the statue of Eros in Piccadilly Circus, appropriately situated at the end of Shaftesbury Avenue.

Francis of Assisi, Friar, Deacon, Founder of the Friars Minor, 1226

The son of Pietro Bernardone, a wealthy cloth merchant, Francis worked with his father until he was 20. He was well known in Assisi for his love of parties and celebrations. In 1202, as a result of a border dispute between Assisi and Perugia, Francis was taken prisoner and held for a year. On his release he returned to Assisi and continued his energetic way of life. However, after a long period of illness and a further taste of army life, Francis began to grow weary of his lifestyle. He made a pilgrimage to Rome, and was greatly affected by the beggars that he met in the city.

When he returned to Assisi Francis resigned from his father's business and left his old friends behind. He stole a bag of cloth from his father and sold it, using the proceeds to repair church buildings. He was never reconciled with his father. While he was working on the Church of Saint Damiano one morning he heard a reading from Matthew chapter 10, in which Jesus asks his disciples to leave all behind them. Francis understood these words to be directly spoken to him.

People soon began to join the man who by now had a reputation for simple living and charity rather than for extreme behaviour and partying. He formed a group of followers, who called themselves the 'Friars Minor' and they quickly developed into a religious order.

The order spread, and Francis travelled. He attempted to reach Africa, but illness forced him back to Italy. He journeyed with the Crusaders, but preached a spiritual crusade rather than a physical war. He returned to Italy, and divided his rapidly growing order into manageable districts. He appointed other people to be in charge and wrote a 'Rule of Life'. Francis resisted seeking full approval for his order from the Papacy until 1223. By the time of his death there was a men's order, a women's order (instituted by Clare – see 11 August) and a lay order. He received the gift of *stigmata* in 1224, and died in 1226.

Francis is known as a gentle and generous man who radically altered his life in response to God. Fully devoted to God, and fully prepared to give everything for others, his life of humility and action have led to him to be remembered as one of the most influential men of medieval times.

Most High, Glorious God,
enlighten the darkness of our minds.
Give us a right faith,
a firm hope
and a perfect charity,
so that we may always
and in all things
act according to Your Holy Will.

Francis of Assisi: Vocation Prayer

6 October

William Tyndale, Translator of the Scriptures, Reformation Martyr, 1536

William Tyndale was born in Gloucestershire in the early 1490s and studied at Magdalen Hall, Oxford. He moved to Cambridge to further his studies and it was possibly there, where the influence of the Continental Reformation had taken the greatest hold in England, that he conceived the project of translating the Bible into English direct from the original languages. Ordained in 1515, he served for a time as tutor at Little Sodbury Manor near Bristol where he fell foul of the local clergy when he attempted to preach on College Green in the city centre. A brilliant linguist, his intention was to make the truths of the Scriptures available to ordinary people in their own language and to produce plentiful copies at the lowest possible price. It is said that, in the course of a dispute with a prominent clergyman who disparaged this proposal, Tyndale said, 'If God spare my life, ere many years I will cause a boy that driveth the plough to know more of the Scriptures than thou dost.'

He offered to work in the household of Bishop Tunstall of London, but the bishop refused to support him and a London merchant Humphrey Monmouth became his patron. But with an increasing clampdown on 'heretics' by both government and the church authorities, Tyndale crossed the Channel where he could work in greater safety. Initially based in Hamburg, he travelled to Wittenberg in 1524 and met Martin Luther (see 31 October). But even in Europe he had to keep on the move. Narrowly escaping arrest at Cologne, he was able to publish his New Testament at Worms in 1525. Eighteen thousand copies came off the press and were smuggled into England in bales of cloth from Antwerp. The growth of English Protestantism was clearly aided by the easy availability of the New Testament.

Tyndale continued to work on his translations. He made inroads on the Old Testament (though he only published the Pentateuch and Jonah) and in 1534 he produced a revised version of the New Testament. But he was betrayed and arrested at Vilvorde near Brussels where, after 16 months of imprisonment, he was strangled and burned at the stake on 6 October 1536. But official attitudes were changing in England. Miles Coverdale continued Tyndale's work and in 1537, the *Matthew Bible* (i.e. Tyndale plus Coverdale) was published with the Royal Permission. Ninety per cent of the 1611 Authorized Version was based on Tyndale's work. He was thus a formative influence, not just on Christianity in the English-speaking world, but on the English language itself.

9 October

Denys, Bishop of Paris and his Companions, Martyrs, c.250

Denys, an Italian by birth, was one of a group of seven Christians who were sent to Gaul by the Church early in the third century as missionary bishops. Denys was made Bishop of Paris after establishing a Christian base on what was then an island in the Seine, from which he taught and preached successfully.

The year 250 saw the Valerian persecution sweep the Roman Empire, and Denys was subject of much opposition. He was arrested and martyred along with his companions, Rusticus, a priest, and Eleutherius, a deacon. Legend says that they were beheaded at the top of a hill in Paris, now known as Montmartre, the 'Hill of the Martyrs'. Their bodies were thrown into the Seine but were recovered and their final resting place eventually became the Abbey of Saint Denys.

In the ninth century Denys' legend became confused with that of Denys the Areopagite and then that of Pseudo-Dionysius, leading to widespread commemorations. This confusion was apparently intentional, at the behest of Hilduin, an abbot of Saint-Denis, and as a result the cult of St Denys gained in prominence and importance until the fabrication was uncovered.

Today Denys is a reminder of the price paid by early Christians as they spread the gospel throughout the Roman Empire. Denys is the patron saint of France.

9 October

Robert Grosseteste, Bishop of Lincoln, Philosopher, Scientist, 1253

Robert Grosseteste was born in Stowe (Suffolk), and educated at a cathedral school (possibly Hereford). He joined the household of the Bishop of Hereford in 1192. He was noted for his studies in liberal arts, canon law and medicine.

The Bishop of Hereford died in 1192, and Grosseteste's life becomes difficult to trace with any certainty from that point on until 1225, when he was given a parish in the diocese of Lincoln. In 1229 he was made Archdeacon of Leicester, became a canon in Lincoln Cathedral, and taught theology in Oxford. Grosseteste became seriously ill in 1232, and took this to be a sign of divine displeasure at his holding more than one office at the same time. He resigned all his positions, except that of canon at the cathedral.

When Hugh of Lincoln (not to be confused with his predecessor commemorated on 17 November) died in 1235, the cathedral chapter elected Grosseteste as his replacement. He remained bishop of the largest diocese in England for the next 18 years. He wrote on many subjects including liberal arts, astronomy and cosmology and played a pivotal role in the introduction of Aristotle to scholastic thought, writing commentaries and translations of his works. His theological works include a tract on the theology of penance and confession. Grosseteste aimed to produce theology that was not only useful to the ordinary parish priest but that also met the intellectual standards of academia.

As the diocese of Lincoln at the time contained Oxford, Grosseteste had responsibility for the oversight of theology teaching within the university. Through this link he was able to influence many students, particularly by his translations of Scripture and his emphasis on the necessity of understanding the Greek text.

Grosseteste was known as a brilliant but demanding church leader. His high standards for Christian practice and ministry landed him in a number of disputes with various parts of his diocese and his own cathedral chapter. When the chapter refused to allow an inspection of the cathedral in 1239 the only way Grosseteste could achieve his aim was via a lengthy court case. In the course of this court case he wrote a comprehensive manual of church leadership with particular emphasis upon the authority and role of leadership within the Church. Grosseteste clashed with the Archbishop of Canterbury on more than one occasion and was happy to lecture the Pope over the complacency and lethargy of the papal office when he appeared before the papal court in 1250. Grossteteste saw the Archbishop of Canterbury as the principal cause of the then unhealthy state of the Church in England.

Robert Grosseteste was an intellectual visionary, unafraid to confront others when he saw the need, who was a figure of immense importance to the thirteenth-century Church.

Paulinus, Bishop of York, Missionary, 644

Paulinus was a monk sent to Kent by Gregory the Great (see 3 September) in 601 to support the mission of Augustine to the Anglo-Saxons.

After working in Kent, he was ordained Bishop of York in 625 when Edwin, King of Northumbria asked to marry Ethelburga, the sister of the King of Kent. Ethelburga was a Christian, whilst Edwin was not. This initially caused consternation to the King of Kent, and he only agreed to the marriage of his sister when Edwin declared that he would allow her complete freedom in her faith, and was, in fact, considering the claims of Christianity for himself. Paulinus was consecrated bishop and sent to Northumbria with Ethelburga, partly as support for her, and partly in an attempt to convert the king.

The king was as good as his word in allowing Ethelburga freedom of faith, but less so when it came to his own conversion. Not only did Paulinus have to use every means of persuasion at his disposal, but he also resorted to bribery, with letters and gifts being received from the Pope as a means of persuading Edwin of the claims of the gospel. Eventually, as a result of the preaching of Paulinus, the lifestyle of Ethelburga, and a favourable political climate, Edwin accepted Christianity in 627. Paulinus baptized the king, his court, and numerous nobles throughout Northumbria. These baptisms would take place in rivers throughout the north of the country, and records show services occurring at the River Swale, the River Trent, and in particularly at Yeavering in Glendale, near to the Scottish border.

Paulinus began to build a cathedral at York, but his work in the north was cut short in 633 when Edwin was defeated and killed in battle by the pagan warrior Penda of Mercia and his Welsh Christian ally Cadwallon. Now a widow, and without a court, Ethelburga returned to Kent, in the company of Paulinus, who considered the continuing work of preaching the gospel in Northumbria too dangerous without the protection of the king. This action has been questioned by some, but was in line with the prevailing Roman attitude of serving under, and with the blessing of, an established authority. On his return south, Paulinus was made Bishop of Rochester, serving in the region until his death in 644. The Church in the north suffered under the hands of a pagan ruler, although Bede mentions that Aidan's missions to the region approximately five years later (see 31 August) found Christians still keeping the faith.

Thomas Traherne, Poet, Spiritual Writer, 1674

The son of a shoemaker, Thomas Traherne was born in Hereford in 1637. A relative with the financial means provided for his education at Brasenose College, Oxford. Ordained in 1660, he held the living of Credenhill in Herefordshire until his death. But he was largely an absentee, spending most of his time at Oxford, where he took a BD degree, with only occasional visits to his parish. In 1667 he moved to London as chaplain to Sir Orlando Bridgeman, the Lord Keeper of the Seals to Charles II. When Bridgeman retired, Traherne remained his personal chaplain and lived with him at Teddington until his own death in 1674.

Traherne's only published work during his lifetime was *Roman Forgeries* (1673), a polemical work which claimed that significant Roman Catholic documents were forged, and the year after his death *Christian Ethicks* was published.

Traherne was largely forgotten until the late 1890s, when two handwritten volumes of poetry and prose were discovered, quite by chance, at a London bookstall. Thought at first to be by the metaphysical poet Henry Vaughan, they were eventually identified as works of the long-forgotten Traherne. Edited for publication, they appeared as *Poems* in 1903 and *Centuries of Meditation* in 1908. Another manuscript volume, containing a considerable number of unpublished poems, was discovered in the British Museum and published as *Poems of Felicity* in 1910

Traherne's poetic style is marked by a distinctive musical quality and strikingly original imagery. There is a sense of rejoicing and the celebration of innocent wonder, and a delight in the presence of God in his creation. Two stanzas of the poem *Wonder* give some flavour of Traherne's style and subject matter:

> The skies in their magnificence,
> The lively, lovely air;
> Oh how divine, how soft, how sweet, how fair!
> The stars did entertain my sense,
> And all the works of God, so bright and pure,
> So rich and great did seem,
> As if they ever must endure
> In my esteem.
>
> A native health and innocence
> Within my bones did grow,
> And while my God did all his glories show,
> I felt a vigour in my sense
> That was all spirit. I within did flow
> With seas of life, like wine;
> I nothing in the world did know
> But 'twas divine.

Ethelburga, Abbess of Barking, 675

Ethelburga was from a wealthy family with royal connections and was the sister of Erconwald, the Bishop of London. She was abbess of the double monastery (a religious house for both men and women, with a common superior) at Barking, and quite possibly the owner of the property also. The double monastery allowed the sharing of resources for worship and protection from external forces, but also maintained the strict segregation of the sexes throughout the rest of the life of the community.

Ethelburga had joined the monastery at an early age, and was taught in the ways of monasticism by Hildelith, a French nun, who had the unenviable task of teaching a wealthy, well-connected and influential young lady the ways of monastic life. In the time of Ethelburga's stay at the monastery, Barking became celebrated for the fervour of the nuns in both faith and study.

Bede, writing 70 years after her death, waxes lyrical about Ethelburga, telling not only of her holiness, but also of the miracles that surrounded her life. These included the miraculous light that revealed the site for the community cemetery, and the visions in the community that preceded her death. A plague was afflicting the monasteries and death for many of the community seemed certain. The sisters were unsure whether to site the community cemetery inside or outside their walls and, as Bede tells it, a great light came from heaven not only covering the nuns but also indicating the location of the cemetery.

> As they were singing their customary praises to our Lord, a light from heaven like a great sheet suddenly appeared and shone all over them all, so alarming them that they even broke off their singing in consternation.
>
> *Bede: Ecclesiastical History, IV.7*

Ethelburga was honoured for her holy lifestyle as well as for the miracles that surrounded her life. Bede noted that 'none who knew her holy life can doubt that when she departed this life the gates of her heavenly home opened at her coming'.

James the Deacon, companion of Paulinus, 7th century

In 633 Edwin, King of Northumbria, a recent Christian convert, died in battle. When he received this news Paulinus, the Bishop of York (see 10 October), who was instrumental in Edwin's conversion and influential in the spread of Roman Christianity throughout Northumbria, abandoned his Northumbrian base and retreated to Kent as part of the court of Edwin's widow and son. This action was in line with the prevailing Roman attitude of serving under, and with the blessing of, an established authority. Paulinus left a solitary deacon as the only representative of the Roman Church's mission to Northumbria. The deacon's name was James.

James remained in Northumbria, living mainly at a village near Catterick (now in North Yorkshire), and took an active part in the preaching of the gospel throughout the region. James represented Christianity in the face of hostility from Penda of Mercia ensuring the survival of Roman Christianity in the region. Preaching the gospel under a pagan ruler was a risky occupation, and James was often in danger of his own life. It is largely due to the efforts of James and his associates that when the Northumbrian mission arrived in the area approximately five to ten years later there was still evidence of active Christianity to be found.

In more peaceful times, after the death of Penda and the re-establishment of Christian rule, James taught music, especially Gregorian Chant to the emergent churches of the region, and is praised by Bede as being a man of honour and integrity. He was present at the Synod of Whitby in 664, which met to discuss the differences between the Celtic Northumbrian Church of the north and the Roman Church of the south. James stood for Roman Christianity in an area which was far more sympathetic to the Celtic form of the Faith. His life was commemorated by the ordinary Christians, both Celtic and Roman, that he had served in the days after the flight of Paulinus.

12 October

Wilfrid of Ripon, Bishop, Missionary, 709

Wilfrid was a Northumbrian nobleman, and an early disciple of the Celtic Church. Though a man of intense spiritual energy and commitment, he never relinquished his immense wealth nor the position in society given to him by birth.

Wilfrid's adolescent years were spent at Lindisfarne, most probably for educational reasons, and in 653 he joined Benedict Biscop (see 12 January) on one of his frequent journeys to Rome. There he was greatly influenced by Gallic Christianity which was similar to the Celtic tradition, and he eventually sought to instil some of these principles into the Northumbrian Church.

On his return from Rome, Wilfrid was somewhat dubiously ordained by Agilbert, a dispossessed bishop of the West-Saxons. He was a spokesman for the Roman Church at the Synod of Whitby in 664, and soon after that he was appointed as Bishop of Northumbria. Although the Church after Whitby was held to be united, Wilfrid considered ordinations performed by bishops from Scotland to be uncanonical, and so he journeyed to Gaul to be installed. He stayed there for two years, far longer than was necessary, and on his return found that Oswy, King of Northumbria, had grown tired of waiting, and had installed Chad (see 2 March) in his place. Wilfrid finally took up the position of Bishop of Northumbria when Archbishop Theodore (see 19 September) insisted on it, three years later.

Wilfrid's career was then the subject of much turbulence and disagreement. In total he was deprived of his see three times, twice appealing to Rome for reinstatement. He disagreed with the Northumbrian kings, and fell foul of Theodore, the Archbishop of Canterbury who was modernizing the government of the Church. When he died his once vast diocese had been reduced by the archbishop to that of his monastery at Hexham.

Wilfrid was a man of many colours and allegiances. Greatly influenced by the idea of papal support, he had an intense and colourful image as a bishop, more regal than ecclesiastical. He laid claim to having introduced the Rule of St Benedict to Northumbria, and had a papal charter giving his monasteries independence from outside interference. He encouraged female participation in the Church, protected the Northumbrian Queen Etheldreda (see 23 June) in her dispute with her husband over her virginity – at one point helping her to escape. His travels to Rome included missionary preaching (in Frisia in 679) and he greatly influenced the kingdom of Sussex for the gospel. His final reinstatement to the position of Bishop of Ripon and Hexham was followed by three days of feasting.

Wilfrid was a nobleman who retained his wealth, leaving much to his family at his death, and bequeathing two shares to the abbots of Ripon and Hexham that they might be able to 'purchase the friendship of kings and bishops'. His colourful character allowed Wilfrid to gain a foothold for the gospel in areas that were otherwise inaccessible, and his spiritual energy should not be underestimated.

Elizabeth Fry, Prison Reformer, 1845

Elizabeth Gurney was born in Norwich in 1780, the daughter of John Gurney, a member of the prominent Quaker banking family. In 1800 she married Joseph Fry, a London merchant and also a Quaker. Elizabeth's Christian beliefs were accompanied by a large measure of social concern and in 1808 she founded a school for girls at Plashet in East London.

As far back as 1798 she had felt called to ministry after a word directed to her at a Quaker meeting:

> Deborah Darby then spoke . . . she addressed part of it to me; I only fear she says too much of what I am to be. A light to the blind; speech to the dumb; and feet to the lame; can it be? She seems as if she thought I was to be a minister of Christ. Can I ever be one? If am obedient I believe I shall.

Thirteen years later, in 1811, she was recognized by the Society of Friends as a preacher and minister.

After a visit to Newgate prison in 1813 she became aware of the plight of women and children imprisoned in inhuman conditions and felt that her Christian responsibility was to attempt to relieve their plight. Initially she began daily visits to the women prisoners at Newgate, where she read the Bible to them and taught them to sew. In 1817 she began a campaign to secure certain basic rights for female prisoners: classification of criminals, segregation of the sexes, female supervision of women, and provision for education. In 1818 she gave evidence to a Parliamentary Select Committee who were examining prisons and later saw many of her proposed reforms carried out.

Elizabeth's efforts on behalf of the less fortunate were prodigious, though the bankruptcy of her husband in 1828 did curtail some of her work. In 1820, having observed the problems of homelessness and begging in the capital she established a 'Nightly Shelter for the Homeless in London', the first of many in later years. Recognizing the problems encountered by those who had served their sentences, she founded a society for the care and rehabilitation of released prisoners. It was said that for 20 years she personally inspected every ship containing female convicts before it sailed from Britain. She made frequent visits to the Continent and did much to foster prison reform there: between 1838 and 1842 she visited all the prisons in France, reporting to the Interior Minister, and travelled through Belgium, Holland, Switzerland, Germany and Denmark on similar missions.

Elizabeth inspected prisons and mental hospitals in Scotland and Ireland; instituted a nursing order; provided libraries for coastguard stations; and struggled for housing and employment for the poor. Ill-health prevented further travels, but everywhere she had been the authorities put her suggestions to practical effect. The book she produced in 1831, *Texts for Every Day of the Year*, remained in print for many years and was widely read. She died at Ramsgate in Kent, on 12 October 1845.

Edith Cavell, Nurse, 1915

Edith Cavell was born at Swardeston in Norfolk in 1865, where her father was the vicar. Initially she worked as a governess before training as a nurse at the London Hospital. Subsequently, he worked in a number of locations including Maidstone, St Pancras, Shoreditch and Manchester.

In 1907 Edith was invited become matron of a large training centre for nurses in Brussels. She worked there for seven years until the First World War broke out and Belgian neutrality was violated by the German armies seeking a direct route to Paris and the Channel ports. Belgium found itself a war zone and the Brussels nursing school became a Red Cross hospital. Edith refused the opportunity of returning home to England and was much involved in tending wounded soldiers from both German and Allied armies. This even-handed approach to the wounded became more difficult after the German occupation of Brussels in 1915, as did Edith's clandestine work of assisting in the process of smuggling British soldiers across the border from Belgium into the Netherlands. Some two hundred were enabled to escape by this means.

In August 1915 Edith was arrested and kept in solitary confinement for a number of weeks before being tricked into making a confession to a charge which carried the death penalty. But she showed neither regret for what she had done, complaint of her sentence nor bitterness to her captors. On the night before her execution she was visited by the Anglican Chaplain in Brussels, the Revd Stirling Gahan. Together, they said the words of *Abide with me* and Edith received Holy Communion. Gahan reported her words: 'I am thankful to have had these ten weeks of quiet to get ready. Now I have had them and have been kindly treated here. I expected my sentence and I believe it was just. Standing, as I do, in view of God and eternity, I realize that patriotism is not enough. I must have no hatred or bitterness to anyone.' Unsuccessful appeals for postponement of her execution were made by the American and Spanish ministers to Germany; she was shot by a firing squad on 12 October 1915.

After the war her body was exhumed and returned to England. Vast multitudes attended her memorial service at Westminster Abbey. She was buried at Norwich Cathedral and a commemorative statue was erected in St Martin's Lane, near to Trafalgar Square in London.

Edward the Confessor, King of England, 1066

Born at Islip some time in the period 1002–1004, the son of Ethelred II (the 'Unready'), Edward was sent to Normandy in 1013 to be educated at the court of Duke Richard of Normandy, his uncle. Three years later, in 1016, his father lost his throne to the Danes and fled to Normandy himself. The Danish kings Sweyn, Canute and Harthacanute showed every sign of establishing a dynasty in England and the rest of Edward's life could have been spent in the vain pursuit of noble pleasures. But the unexpected death of Harthacanute in 1042 found Edward acclaimed as king and he began his reign by marrying the daughter of the powerful Saxon Earl Godwin.

In many ways Edward's death in 1066 is both more interesting and certainly more well-known than his life. The fact that he had, at different times, promised the succession to the throne to two different people – Harold Godwinson and William of Normandy – set the stage for an epic confrontation, the most famous battle in English history, and a transformation of England's future.

Less than a century after Edward's death he was canonized by Pope Alexander III in 1161. What were the grounds for this? Edward had a general reputation for both religious devotion and for generosity to the poor and sick, but canonization required greater evidence of supposed saintliness. First was his supposed chastity. The fact that he and Queen Edith were childless led to the stories that the marriage was unconsummated and the growth of a legend that he had taken a vow of chastity. Second was the rather better attested fact that Edward was the first known king to touch for the healing of scrofula – the 'King's Evil' – a tradition continued by English monarchs until Queen Anne. Third, a vow Edward really did take was to make a pilgrimage to St Peter's tomb at Rome. But the political situation made this inexpedient and the Pope commuted the vow into the building of a monastery dedicated to St Peter. Thus began the building of Westminster Abbey, which has been a focus of national devotion ever since. In fact Edward was too sick to attend the Abbey's consecration, which took place the week before his death. A fourth factor in his canonization was the number of miracles he allegedly performed after his death. When Thomas Becket (see 29 December) translated Edward's body to the Abbey in 1163 it was claimed to have been undecayed.

15 October

Teresa of Avila, Teacher of the Faith, 1582

Born at Avila in 1515 to an old Spanish family of partly Jewish ancestry and educated in an Augustinian convent, Teresa entered the local Carmelite Convent of the Incarnation in 1535. There she fell seriously ill, was in a coma for a while, and partially paralysed for three years. The illness made her lax and lukewarm in her prayers and devotions. However, her prayer life eventually deepened and she began to have visions and a vivid sense of the presence of God. At times she felt sharp pains that she claimed were caused by the tip of an angel's lance piercing her heart. In 1555, after increasingly rigorous religious exercises, she underwent a profound spiritual awakening, experiencing visions of Christ and a state of spiritual ecstasy. She was thus converted to a life of extreme devotion. But her new seriousness about her faith did not fit with the relaxed attitude of the Carmelites, where the nuns retained their own property and freely accessed the world outside their convents.

So in 1560 Teresa took it upon herself to reform the Carmelite order which had, in her view, departed from the order's original intention and become far too lax. Her proposed reforms included strict enclosure of the nuns within the convent, where they would be required to engage in prayer and study, and required to go barefoot ('discalced') as a symbol of their poverty, humility and simplicity. Not unnaturally, her proposed reforms were not popular amongst most Carmelites and it took papal intervention on her behalf for her to establish, in 1562, the Convent of St Joseph at Avila, the first community of reformed, or Discalced, Carmelite nuns. In 1567 she was authorized to establish similar religious houses for men and in this she was aided by John of the Cross, the Spanish mystic (see 14 December). Though she was constantly harassed by those hostile to her intentions, Teresa helped to establish 16 foundations for women and 14 for men. Two years before her death the Discalced Carmelites received papal recognition as an independent order. Teresa died in Alba de Tormes in 1582.

As well as being a monastic reformer Teresa was also a unique spiritual writer, the first to describe states of prayer between meditation and ecstasy. In her life of Christian service Teresa gave the lie to the viewpoint that the contemplative life and practical action are incompatible, and urged her followers to 'accustom yourself continually to make many acts of love, for they enkindle and melt the soul'.

Nicholas Ridley, Bishop of London, and Hugh Latimer, Bishop of Worcester, Reformation Martyrs, 1555

Nicholas Ridley (c.1500–55)

Nicholas Ridley was born near Willimoteswyke in Northumberland about 1500, and educated at Pembroke Hall, Cambridge, and the universities of Paris and Louvain. He returned to Cambridge around 1530 where he became known to Thomas Cranmer (see 21 March). After Cranmer became Archbishop of Canterbury he appointed Ridley as his chaplain in 1537. He became chaplain to King Henry VIII in 1541. On Edward VI's accession in 1547 Ridley became Bishop of Rochester, being translated to the more important diocese of London in 1550.

Ridley helped Cranmer to compile the Prayer Book and Articles and was appointed to help establish Protestantism in the University of Cambridge. After the death of Edward and with the future of the Reformation in doubt Ridley, along with many other Reformers, resorted to desperate measures and gave his support to Lady Jane Grey as Edward's successor to the throne and publicly pronounced both of King Henry VIII's daughters, Mary and Elizabeth, illegitimate.

Ridley was in the vanguard of the English Reformation in two particular respects. He was the first of the English Reformers to accept and propagate the distinctive teaching on the Eucharist of the ninth-century Benedictine monk Ratramnus. Here the presence of Christ is affirmed but in a spiritual, not physical, form in the hearts of believers receiving the consecrated bread and wine, not in the elements themselves. At a time when Cranmer was still a believer in the (physical) Real Presence, 'Dr Ridley did confer with me, and . . . drew me quite from my opinion'. Ridley's influence on Cranmer was of the highest significance and the distinctive 'Cranmerian' flavour of the Prayer Book Communion service thus owes much to Ridley. Secondly, as Bishop of London from 1550 Ridley forced the pace of the English Reformation by requiring the removal of stone altars from churches in London diocese and their replacement with wooden communion tables. This was at a time when the political will to move in this direction nationally was lacking and Ridley's initiative broke the log jam and was widely followed, providing a reformed context for the Eucharist.

When Mary, a Roman Catholic, was proclaimed queen, Ridley was imprisoned in the Tower of London, where he wrote statements defending his religious opinions. In 1554, refusing to recant, he was declared a heretic and excommunicated, and in 1555 he was tried and condemned for heresy. Ridley was burned at the stake in Oxford along with Hugh Latimer on 16 October 1555.

Hugh Latimer (c.1485–1555)

Born the son of a yeoman farmer at Thurcaston in Leicestershire about 1485, Hugh Latimer was educated at Cambridge and elected Fellow of Clare Hall in 1510. After ordination he quickly gained a reputation as a highly able speaker and preacher and used these gifts to promote reform of the university and social justice on a wider scale.

Cambridge was a hotbed of Protestant opinions and in the early 1520s Latimer began to align himself with them. When required by the Bishop of Ely to preach a sermon against Martin Luther (see 31 October), he refused and was for a time suspended from preaching. He regained his licence to preach after a successful interview with Cardinal Wolsey.

Latimer's preaching style was direct, homely and witty, demonstrating a clear knowledge of both Scripture and human nature. He preached before Henry VIII in Lent 1530 and the king's favour was demonstrated by Latimer's presentation to the living of West Kington in Wiltshire. But as Latimer's preaching and doctrine became unmistakably Protestant he received a censure from Convocation in 1532. After the break with Rome, however, Latimer's advice was increasingly sought by the king and in 1535 he became Bishop of Worcester. He resigned the see four years later when the king turned against reform and the conservative Act of Six Articles was enacted. In great danger at this time, Latimer was imprisoned for some months then forbidden to preach and required to leave London. By the end of Henry VIII's reign he was imprisoned in the Tower, but was released on Edward VI's accession and once again became a popular and influential court preacher, still with an emphasis on justice as he denounced both social and ecclesiastical corruption and abuses.

On the accession of Queen Mary in 1553 he was again imprisoned. After refusing to recant his theological opinions he was condemned and burnt with Ridley at the same stake in Oxford on 16 October 1555. Whether he did indeed comfort the younger and more fearful Ridley with the words recorded by John Foxe is not known, but they have nevertheless entered into Anglican folklore: 'Be of good comfort Master Ridley, and play the man. We shall this day light such a candle by God's grace in England, as (I trust) shall never be put out.'

17 October

Ignatius, Bishop of Antioch, Martyr c.107

Ignatius, second Bishop of Antioch, was sentenced during the Roman Emperor Trajan's reign to be devoured by wild beasts. Trajan decided that Christians, although guilty of 'anti-state behaviour', were not to be sought out for arrest, but rather should be arrested and tried only if they were obvious in their faith and refused to reject Christ when asked.

Ignatius was arrested in Syria and transported to Rome for his punishment. On this long and arduous journey Ignatius travelled through Asia Minor, and stopped at Phrygia and Smyrna. As news spread of his arrest and journey he received visits by prominent Christians, including Polycarp (see 23 February). He wrote letters to the Churches of each area he passed through, and also wrote to the Christians in Rome informing them of his impending arrival. Ignatius was convinced of the need for unity in the Church, and he encouraged this whenever he could. He saw this unity as ideally illustrated in relationships between bishops of the Church. He emphasized the need for constant community worship and celebration of the Eucharist. His letters reveal him to be a man completely devoted to Christ and passionate for unity.

Ignatius was also keen to receive martyrdom, and in his letters he emphasized that on no account was anyone to attempt to prevent his death. For him, martyrdom was the ultimate imitation of Christ, and a gift from God. Although there is no account of his martyrdom it is widely assumed that he died upon the completion of his journey at Rome.

Ignatius called Christians 'fellow travellers' 'bearers of God' and 'Christ-bearers' and emphasizes whole-hearted devotion to Christ: 'Even the things you do in the flesh are spiritual, for you do all things in union with Jesus Christ.'

Henry Martyn, Translator of the Scriptures, Missionary in India and Persia, 1812

Born in Truro in 1781, Henry Martyn was educated at Truro Grammar School and St John's College, Cambridge, where he graduated as Senior Wrangler (highest marks in the mathematics examination). He had also undergone a conversion experience during his time in Cambridge under the influence of Charles Simeon (see 13 November), the Vicar of Holy Trinity. Consequently he abandoned his intended legal career and was ordained in 1803 to serve as curate (under Simeon) of the Cambridgeshire village of Lolworth, a post which he combined with a fellowship at St John's College.

In the early nineteenth century the East India Company (a private company which controlled all of British India) did not allow Christian missionaries to operate in their territory lest Hindu susceptibilities be offended. This policy was being challenged in England but in the meantime the Clapham evangelicals and Charles Simeon were using their contacts and influence to have evangelical clergy appointed as East India Company chaplains. Officially they ministered to the Company's employees and to the expatriate British community. Unofficially they also sought to begin mission work among indigenous Indians. It was to such a chaplaincy in India that Henry Martyn embarked in 1805 on a nine-month voyage to Calcutta. The last-minute rush when a passage to India became available meant that he had to leave his sweet-heart, Lydia Grenfell, without becoming engaged to her. They were never to meet again.

Martyn's main contribution to mission work was two-fold. First, what today would be called 'dialogue' – seeking to learn all he could about Indian religions by discussion with Hindus and Muslims. Second, his translation work. As well as his brilliance in mathematics he had a real ability in languages (he had spent his spare time at Lolworth learning oriental languages as a means of relaxation). In his six short years in India, he translated the New Testament into both Urdu and Persian, revised an Arabic translation of the New Testament, and translated the Psalter into Persian and the whole Book of Common Prayer into Urdu. But his health rapidly declined. He almost died of tuberculosis at Cawnpore in 1809, and he was given unlimited leave of absence. He left India in 1811, returning home via Persia, hoping to make further translations and to improve his existing ones. But he fell ill *en route* to Damascus and died on 16 October 1812 at Tokat, where he was given an honoured burial by the Armenian Church.

25 October

Crispin and Crispinian, Martyrs at Rome, c.287

According to eighth-century historical records, Crispin and Crispinian were brothers, initially from Gaul and shoemakers by trade, who fled Rome during the persecution of Diocletian in 303. They settled at Soissons (France), working as shoemakers by night and preaching by day. They accepted only the payments that were offered to them for their goods. They are recorded as being martyred in 287.

Unfortunately, as the date of their martyrdom (287) and the date of Diocletian's persecution (303) shows, accounts of their life are flawed. Crispin and Crispinian were probably from Rome, not Gaul, and their remains transferred to Gaul at a later date. Their memory was accepted in Roman Christianity in the Carolingian (eighth century) era. They are known as shoemakers only because of a play on words between Latin and Greek (*crepida* being shoemaker in Latin).

Shakespeare cites them in a speech made by Henry V on the eve of the battle of Agincourt which took place on 25 October 1415, in which he drew from English legends that suggested that the brothers settled in Kent rather than Soissons.

In the midst of the confusion concerning their memory few facts remain: Diocletian indeed perpetuated an intense persecution of the Early Church in the years 303–4, and Crispin and Crispinian suffered in some way for their faith. The resulting tradition of memory grew up surrounding their story and gained particular following in Soissons which developed a link to the brothers.

Alfred the Great, King of the West Saxons, Scholar, 899

Alfred was born in Wantage in 849, son of Ethelwulf, King of Wessex. Alfred became king at the age of 22 in 871, a most difficult and dangerous time for Wessex, engaged as it was in a struggle against the Danes who occupied most of north and east England. However he bought time and peace by paying 'Danegeld'. But from 875 the Danes went on the offensive again and much of Wessex was overrun. Alfred went into hiding at Athelney in the Somerset marshes, quietly gathered about him as many loyal Saxons as he could find in preparation for a counter-attack and, when he engaged the Danes at Edington in 878, won a famous victory. The Danes were obliged to withdraw to north and west England (the 'Danelaw') and their leaders were required to submit to baptism, probably in order to lessen the possibility of persecution of Christian English by pagan Danes in the Danelaw. In the south and west, Wessex, under Alfred, was now supreme since the successive Danish invasions had crushed out of existence most of the individual Anglo-Saxon kingdoms. Alfred made Wessex a rallying point for all the Saxons and by freeing the country from the invaders unwittingly unified England and prepared the way for the eventual supremacy of his successors. Although there were further invasions, incursions and battles, Alfred was able to maintain his supremacy in the south and west and the Danes gradually settled down to peaceful occupations in the north and east.

Historically, great wartime leaders have not always proved so successful at peacetime government. Alfred, however, proved an able and farsighted ruler, though he suffered from an unknown chronic illness, possibly psychosomatic. A priority was defence: Alfred created the first English navy, improved the efficiency of military call-up and created a system of fortified boroughs for defence in time of war. Religious, educational and legal matters were also important to him. Though brought up illiterate he learned to read and write in his late thirties and did much to encourage Anglo-Saxon scholarship, especially the translations of key religious texts into the vernacular. It was a source of some regret to Alfred that, having acquired a thirst for knowledge comparatively late in life, Wessex lacked scholars to teach him as much as he desired.

The only English monarch ever to be called 'the great', Alfred died on 26 October 899, and was buried in the Old Minster at Winchester. He was a man of rigorous and sincere personal spirituality unusual for a lay person in Anglo-Saxon England. He compiled a personal prayer book of psalms, readings and the daily office, much of which he learned by heart, and always carried it with him. Alfred also endowed a number of monasteries as key spiritual educational and social centres and he codified the English legal system, giving it a clear Christian basis.

26 October

Cedd, Abbot of Lastingham, Bishop of the East Saxons, 664

Cedd was a pupil of Aidan (see 31 August), who had established Christianity within Northumbria during the reign of King Oswald. Cedd spent some time at the monastery of Lindisfarne, where along with his brother Chad (see 2 March), he was taught by Aidan. There were four brothers in all: Chad, Cynebill, Caelin and Cedd. All four became priests and two became bishops.

Cedd was from the region of East Anglia, but practised Celtic Christianity rather than the Roman Christianity associated with the south of England. He is known as of the Lindisfarne monks who travelled great distances to preach the gospel.

In 653 Cedd and his brothers were sent by King Oswy of Northumbria to evangelize the Middle Angles in Mercia. He was also sent to Essex on a similar mission sometime later. Such was the success of his missions that he was consecrated Bishop of the East Saxons in 654 by Finan of Lindisfarne. While in this post he established monasteries at West Tilbury and Ythancester (Bradwell-on-Sea).

Cedd was present at the Synod of Whitby (664), which was called to establish uniformity over the celebration of Easter between the Churches of the Celtic and Roman traditions, and to clarify other ecclesiastical customs. Able to speak both Gaelic and Anglo-Saxon, Cedd acted as interpreter at the gathering. The council was called by King Oswy, a Celtic Christian who had married Eanfleda, a Roman Christian. The differences in Easter practices in the royal household were becoming contentious. Although eventually influential for the history of Christianity in Britain, the Synod of Whitby was only attended by a few representative bishops. It was many years before uniformity became apparent within the Church, and practices merged. The process of convergence between Celtic and Roman traditions was long and gradual. Bede, an English Roman Christian writing 70 years after the Synod, made this council the crux of his account of church history, and subsequent medieval histories distorted the facts for political motives.

In a journey back to Northumbria in 658 Cedd established the monastery at Lastingham, after being given land by Ethelwald, Oswy's son. He died of the plague whilst living at Lastingham in 664.

James Hannington, Bishop of Eastern Equatorial Africa, Martyr in Uganda, 1885

James Hannington was born at Hurstpierpoint in Sussex in 1847. After leaving school in Brighton he worked in business, then in the army. In 1868 he entered St Mary Hall at Oxford to train for the Anglican ministry. Ordained in 1874, he served curacies at Martinhoe in Devon (where he had a conversion experience) and at Darley Abbey near Derby. In 1875 he returned to Hurstpierpoint as minister of St George's Chapel.

In 1882, influenced by the news of the deaths of missionaries in Buganda (part of modern-day Uganda), Hannington offered to serve with the Church Missionary Society. Though the Kabaka (king), Mutesa, welcomed Christian missions, Buganda was land-locked and a long trek from the coast was required in order to get there. This was to be Hannington's undoing on two occasions. On his first tour of duty in East Africa in 1882–3 he was overcome by fever and dysentery on the trek westwards and had to be carried back to the coast, twice being given up for dead. On his return the CMS Medical Board ruled that he should never return to the region.

Yet in 1884 when a separate diocese was created for Eastern Equatorial Africa, this ruling was reversed and Hannington, fully recovered in health, was consecrated bishop by Archbishop Benson at Lambeth. He arrived in Africa early the following year and began visiting his clergy in the coastal settlements. One commented, 'he was beloved by every missionary. There never was a bishop who could be so firm, and, at the same time, so kind and considerate.'

Yet the time came in July 1885 when Hannington prepared to visit his flock inland in Buganda. The old Kabaka, Mutesa, had died the previous October. His son Mwanga was no friend of European missionaries and Hannington had already received word of the suffering of both missionaries and converts at Mwanga's court. So, wishing to be with them as soon as possible the courageous and impetuous Hannington ignored advice from all quarters and travelled the quickest route, which unfortunately was the invasion route traditionally taken by Buganda's enemies. German imperialists had been unsettling the Bugandans, who seemed unable to distinguish between different nationalities of white men. On entering the border region, the bishop's party was detained by the local chief who asked Mwanga for instructions as to the fate of his prisoner. When the order came, Hannington and his party were speared to death on 29 October 1885.

Though by no means the first Christian martyr in Uganda (George Shergold Smith and Thomas O'Neill of the original CMS Nyanza mission party were martyred in 1877) nor, sadly, the last (see 3 June), Hannington was Uganda's most high-profile martyr until Archbishop Janani Luwum in 1977 (see 17 February).

Martin Luther, Reformer, 1546

Martin Luther was born at Eisleben in Saxony in 1483, the son of a copper miner. After Erfurt University, fearful of death and judgement, he entered the Augustinian monastery in Erfurt but did not find the peace with God he anticipated. Taking his vows as a monk in 1506, he was ordained priest in 1507. He turned to the study of theology at which he excelled and by 1512 he had received both his doctorate and the chair of theology at Wittenberg University.

At some point between 1512 and 1515 Luther had his so-called 'Tower experience' which marked a fundamental shift in his theology and faith. Through studying the Scriptures – notably Romans 1.17, 'the righteous shall live by faith' – he came to believe that Christians are saved not through their own efforts but by the gift of God's grace, which they accept by faith. Once he had grasped this truth he was transformed from someone fearful of God's wrath into a fearless critic of a Church that was failing to teach this fundamental truth.

Luther's increasing disillusion with the Catholic Church was brought to a head by the indulgence controversy which resulted in his Ninety-Five Theses, published on 31 October 1517. What was intended to initiate an academic debate quickly got out of hand and Luther was excommunicated in 1521. But his views struck a chord with others, and a bloc of anti-Catholic states began to emerge in Germany. By 1529 the word 'Protestant' had been coined to describe their beliefs.

Though reform not schism was his aim, Luther stuck to his beliefs when Rome declined to reform itself, even along the conservative lines favoured by Luther. In addition to the doctrine of justification by faith he asserted the priesthood of all believers, the concept of national Churches, vernacular Scripture and liturgy, the use of hymns in worship and the freedom for clergy to marry.

Luther was successful in challenging the might of the Catholic Church partly because the intellectual changes of the Renaissance made such challenges acceptable, partly because the political situation in Germany was favourable to a new religious dimension, and partly because the technology to disseminate his ideas (the printing press) had recently been invented. But, most importantly, it was his personal courage and willingness to risk his life for the truth that allowed the Reformation to be born and to develop. He died at Eisleben in1546.

A very human being who spoke from the heart – often in violent and earthy imagery – Luther saw life as a constant spiritual struggle in which he was only able be victorious through Christ's grace freely bestowed on him. His hymns often reflected this sense of battle, as in these translated verses of a hymn in German from 1529:

With our own might we nothing can,
Soon are we lost and fallen;
But for us fights the righteous man,
Whom God himself hath callen.
Ask ye, Who is this?
Jesus Christ it is,
Our sole King and Lord,
As God of Hosts adored;
He holds the field forever.

Though earth all full of devils were,
Wide roaring to devour us;
Yet fear we no such grievous fear,
They shall not overpower us.
This world's prince may still
Scowl fierce as he will,
He can harm us none,
He's judged; the deed is done;
One little word can fell him.

3 November

Richard Hooker, Priest, Anglican Apologist, Teacher of the Faith, 1600

Richard Hooker was born at Heavitree near Exeter around 1554, and educated at Corpus Christi College, Oxford. He became a Fellow of the college in 1577 and deputy professor of Hebrew in 1579. He was ordained in 1581 and, being required to vacate his fellowship upon his marriage to Joan Churchman in 1584, was appointed Rector of Drayton Beauchamp.

From 1585 to 1591 he was Master of the Temple Church in London. Towards the end of his life he returned to rural ministry, first at Boscombe in Wiltshire from 1591 to 1595, then at Bishopsbourne in Kent where he remained until his death in 1600.

When Hooker arrived at the Temple Church in 1585 he found the Puritan Walter Travers already installed as afternoon lecturer. Possibly Travers was resentful that he had been passed over for the mastership, certainly Hooker would have objected to Travers' Puritan preaching. Whatever the cause, a dispute flared until Archbishop Whitgift took Hooker's side and Travers was removed.

But perhaps the Travers incident was significant in that it indicated Hooker's implacable opposition to the growth of Puritanism within the Church of England, which was the inspiration of his major work, the treatise *On the Laws of Ecclesiastical Polity*, published in eight volumes from 1594 (only the first five during his lifetime). In this work Hooker sought to respond to the attacks on the 1559 Elizabethan Settlement of the Church of England from the growing Puritan party in the Church.

As Queen Elizabeth's reign progressed, it become increasingly clear to all concerned that, as far as the queen was concerned, the 1559 Settlement was not the first step on the road to reform but the last. While for many Anglicans this presented no problem, for the Puritans, looking wistfully over their shoulders at Geneva, it was time to agitate. The 1580s and 1590s saw increasingly acrimonious disputes. This was the backcloth against which Hooker was writing. He sought to demonstrate the advantages of episcopacy in the Church of England against the presbyterian system proposed by many Puritans. Yet he was not dogmatic, regarding episcopacy as the best but not the only legitimate form of church government. Anglicanism was rooted in both Scripture and tradition as befitted a Church both Catholic and Reformed. And as the Church was a dynamic, living institution, human reason – a gift of God – was a vital element in interpreting both Scripture and tradition.

Richard Hooker was the first real apologist for the seemingly untidy compromise that came to be known as Anglicanism. So crucial has Hooker been to Anglican thought over the centuries that evangelicals, Anglo-Catholics and central churchmen have all attempted to claim him as one of their own.

Martin of Porres, Friar, 1639

Martin of Porres was born in Lima, Peru in 1579, the child of a Spanish officer and an Indian woman from Panama. He grew up in the chaos and brutality of the aftermath of the Spanish conquest of Peru and the heavy-handed process of attempting to impose European order and religion on a society that was previously part of the ancient Inca civilization. He became an apprentice to a barber-surgeon so that he would have a trade. At 15, he was accepted as a lay brother in the Dominican friary in Lima, where he was to spend the rest of his life. He worked at various times as barber, farm labourer, almoner and infirmarian.

The painful experiences of his childhood never left him, but he was able to use them as a positive force, giving him understanding of the problems experienced by others and spurring him on to show compassion and generosity to those in need. Martin provided medical care for the sick of Lima. Though surgery was primitive, he had a vast knowledge of herbal medicines and with them he treated illnesses ranging from infections and fevers to intestinal ailments and sprains. In addition to his medical work, he distributed food and clothing to the poor each week – all of which he had first begged from the wealthy families in the city. He founded an orphanage for abandoned children and staffed it with the best nurses and teachers he could find to provide love, care and security for the children. On the hills near Lima, he planted fruit orchards for the poor. He is also remembered for his love of animals, including even vermin.

It is said that Martin wore the oldest, most patched garments he could find, and spent long hours in prayer. It was perhaps inevitable that he was credited with supernatural powers – levitation whilst praying, for example, along with more conventional spiritual gifts such as prophecy. And there were those in distant parts of the world – Africa, Japan, the Philippines – who claimed to have seen Martin despite the fact that he never left Lima. He died of fever at the age of 60, and was mourned by all sections of Lima society, who recognized his obvious holiness. His beloved poor never allowed his memory to fade, and today he is one of the most popular saints in the Americas – the patron saint of social justice and interracial harmony.

Leonard, Hermit, 6th century

Leonard is one of those people whom the Church of England commemorate, whose existence can neither be affirmed nor denied. Although given a sixth-century date, Leonard is in all probability a creation of an eleventh-century mind. *The Life of Leonard* first appeared in 1030, only two years after the first mention of Leonard within the documents of the Church. *The Life* tells how Leonard was of noble birth and held position in the court of Clovis, King of the Franks. He was said to have received the help of God in repelling an army enabling Clovis to win a battle. (Clovis, whose historicity is not in doubt, was converted to Christianity by Remigius –see 1 October – around the year 500).

The Life tells how Leonard refused to become a bishop, and led his life as a hermit in the forest. His seclusion was broken when, one day, he encountered Clovis and his pregnant wife in the forest, and ensured the safe delivery of their child. For this he was granted as much land as he could ride around in one day and upon which he founded a monastery in Noblac.

Leonard is popularly remembered as a result of thanksgiving being offered at his shrine in the eleventh century by crusaders journeying home after their release from prison camps. He became one of the most popular saints of the Middle Ages, honoured especially as someone who cared for prisoners. He is also the patron of peasants and of the sick.

William Temple, Archbishop of Canterbury, Teacher of the Faith, 1944

William Temple was born in 1881, son of the Bishop of Exeter. After education at Rugby and Balliol College, Oxford, a vocation to ordained ministry was nearly still-born, when Temple's personal integrity meant that he openly expressed his difficulties with some aspects of the doctrines of the virgin birth and the bodily resurrection of Christ as they were then understood. This openness and honesty resulted in a delay of two years in his ordination since Bishop Paget of Oxford refused to ordain him. Temple was subsequently ordained by Archbishop Randall Davidson of Canterbury.

After a spell as headmaster of Repton School and then as Rector of St James, Piccadilly, Temple resigned the living in order to lead 'Life & Liberty', a movement pressing for more accountable structures within, and greater autonomy for, the Church of England. A member of the Labour party (until becoming bishop) he was a convinced supporter of social and economic reform and served as the first president of the Workers' Educational Association. Born to privilege himself, he sought to extend basic privileges to all, believing that 'human status ought not to depend on the changing demands of the economic process', and that 'it is a mistake to suppose that God is only, or even chiefly, concerned with religion'.

He rose rapidly in the hierarchy of the Church of England, from Bishop of Manchester (1921–9) to Archbishop of York (1929–42) and then, for the last two years of his life, of Canterbury. He was also active in promoting the ecumenical movement. A gifted communicator with a razor-sharp mind, he was never fussy or pompous and possessed the common touch – as much at home on a beach mission at Blackpool as addressing the House of Lords.

Like St Paul, Temple had a 'thorn in the flesh', throughout his life suffering from gout, which constantly caused him debilitating pain. His early death at the age of 63, only eight months before the end of the Second World War, was a cruel blow, depriving both Church and nation of a wise and visionary leader at a time of national reconstruction and leaving a void that proved impossible to fill.

Temple left one of the classic definitions of Christian worship:

> Worship is the submission of all our nature to God. It is the quickening of conscience by his holiness; the nourishment of mind with his truth; the purifying of imagination by his beauty; the opening of the heart to his love; the surrender of the will to his purpose – and all this gathered up in adoration, the most selfless emotion of which our nature is capable.

Willibrord of York, Bishop, Apostle of Frisia, 739

Willibrord was born in 658 in Yorkshire, the son of Wiligis, who retired to live as a hermit near the Humber Estuary when Willibrord was aged six. Willibrord is known as the Apostle of Frisia (today the German/Dutch borderlands), for his campaign to establish Christianity in that land.

Willibrord was a disciple of Wilfrid (see 12 October) at Ripon where he received his education. Wilfrid was an enthusiastic, if controversial, bishop who was exiled to Ireland in 678. He was an unswerving servant of Roman Christianity, who clashed with the Archbishop of Canterbury on many occasions, and who was at times more regal than episcopal.

Willibrord travelled with him and spent twelve years in Ireland, some of which was as a member of the monastic community at 'Rath Melsigi', where he was ordained priest. In 690 he returned to England, and encouraged by King Egbert he set out to evangelize Friesland (Holland), taking with him eleven companions. In 692 on a visit to Rome he received full missionary status from Pope Sergius I who further ordained him Archbishop of the Frisians in 695.

Willibrord's campaign was relatively successful, although patchy, and he established his cathedral at Utrecht. In 698 he journeyed to Echternach (in Luxembourg), where he began a Benedictine monastic community.

Opposition from Radbod, King of the Frisians, led to difficulties for the Church, and the eventual exile of Willibrord. Undeterred, Willibrord continued his mission into Denmark, Heligoland and Thuringia (Germany). It was not until after Radbod's death in 719 that Christianity finally achieved acceptance in the land. Willibrord was greatly assisted in the last stage of this campaign by Boniface (see 5 June), missionary Bishop of Frisia from 722, who continued to work with the Church in the area after Willibrord's death.

Willibrord was a gracious man, who worked to normalize relationships between established Churches and missionary converts. Legend tells how in his missionary activities he once destroyed a pagan idol and suffered no harm. Similarly the killing of sacred cows for food brought no response.

Margery Kempe, Mystic, c.1440

Margery lived from 1373 to c.1440. She was the daughter of a prosperous businessman in Kings Lynn, and was married to John Kempe. They had 14 children.

Margery lacked a formal education. She never learnt to write, and all her books were dictated to others. She was not a recluse, neither was she a submissive wife. She was highly emotional, could be incredibly rude (especially to senior male clerics), and would emotionally engage with the liturgy, all of which led to a distrust of her actions from established clergy, and a search for any heretical element in her sayings.

Margery experienced depression, possibly connected with the birth of her first child, and it was this depression that initiated a life of spiritual experience. Locked away in a room, forcibly restrained on the orders of her spiritual director, and suffering from depression, Margery saw a vision of Jesus, who said to her, 'Daughter, why have you forsaken me, and I never forsook you?'

This convinced her that both her guilt and fear were misplaced, and brought her into a personal and intimate relationship with Christ.

In 1436 Margery wrote *The Book of Margery Kempe*. It is essentially a spiritual autobiography. It is honest, but with a dubious historical chronology. It is not a diary. The book was written down by someone else, and edited, after much persuasion by a priest. Extracts of it were published in the sixteenth century, in a carefully edited edition. The discovery of the complete manuscript in 1934 led to a re-evaluation of the book and of Margery herself.

Margery is honest. She reveals her love of clothes, her envy of other people, her lack of scruples and her fantasies. Yet she is also honest in her dealings with her relationship with Christ. She finds in Christ a fulfilment she could find nowhere else, and this fulfilment leads her on a journey of gradual transformation.

Remembered initially as a mystic, Margery is now known to be a more complex and challenging character. Her achievements, despite all her failings, have often been met with puzzlement, or even hostility. At times overcome by joy, at others too honest for comfort, Margery is the embodiment of an honest soul on a quest for God.

> Then said the Archbishop to her, 'You shall swear that you shall neither teach nor challenge the people in my diocese.'
>
> 'No sir I shall not swear' she said, 'for I shall speak of God and reprove those who swear great oaths wheresoever I go . . . for God almighty forbids not, sir, that we should speak of him . . . and therefore sir, I think that the gospel gives me leave to speak of God.'
>
> 'Ah, sir', said the clerks, 'here we know well that she has a devil within her, for she speaks of the gospel.'
>
> *The Book of Margery Kempe, Ch. 52*

10 November

Leo the Great, Bishop of Rome, Teacher of the Faith, 461

All that is known of Leo's early life is that he was born in Rome, and that he held significant positions within the Church before his election as Bishop of Rome. In 440 he was living in Gaul, acting as a peacemaker between two warring generals when news reached him of his appointment as bishop.

Leo is remembered as the 'Father of the Papacy' – the bishop who formed the papacy into a political force and built on the pre-eminent position of Rome within Christianity. His influence was felt in doctrinal, political and organizational affairs throughout his reign. He was a prolific writer, author of many doctrinal works as well as a whole host of sermons and letters.

Leo was first and foremost a cleric, and throughout his reign was active in theological controversies with Manichaeism, Pelagianism and Nestorianism. Although Leo did not attend the Council of Chalcedon in 451 personally, his representatives took a leading role in the proceedings, and here they emphasized and cemented the pre-eminence of the Roman Bishop's position in the Church. Leo saw his authority as Bishop of Rome as being grounded in the Apostle Peter.

Leo was Bishop of Rome at one of the most crucial moments of history, when the western part of the Roman Empire was dissolving and fracturing under attacks from the Barbarians. Surrounded by hostile forces and disintegration, representing a Church in a city with a weak and incapable government, Leo took over the task of negotiating with the invading parties, when others proved inadequate.

Leo oversaw the rebuilding and administration of the city of Rome as the Empire crumbled all around, not only protecting the city, but enabling its survival. His political activities, conducted against a backdrop of weak regional government, forged a link between the secular and the sacred which was to become a powerful union for the growth of the Church and the position of the papacy in years to come.

> We should not be afraid that our wordly resources will decrease while we practise mercy. For Christian poverty is always rich because what it has is more valuable than what it doesn't have ... For the value of our charity is determined by the sincerity of our feelings.
>
> *Leo the Great, Sermon 42*

> Christians remember your dignity! As you become a partner in God's nature, refuse to return to the old, wicked behaviour. Remember the Head and the body which you are members of. Remember that you were rescued from the powers of darkness and brought out into God's light and kingdom
>
> *Leo the Great, Sermon 21*

Martin, Bishop of Tours, c.397

Martin was born at Sabara (now in Hungary), and by family tradition was forced to follow his father into the army. He served as a cavalry officer under the Emperors Constantius and Julian. A man of charity, he was noted for his good works while still in the army. He was said to have seen a vision of Christ in a naked beggar to whom he gave half his cloak. According to Sulpicius Severus, his biographer, Martin was so moved by this vision that he sought baptism. Martin struggled to reconcile his faith with his military position, and eventually became convinced that his faith prevented him continuing his role as a soldier. 'I am Christ's soldier; I am not allowed to fight.' This refusal to fight, on grounds of conscience, led to his imprisonment for the remainder of his term of service. He left the army in 356, at the age of 20.

Martin spent time as a hermit on the island of Gallinara, and also travelled, until in 360 he entered the monastery in Poitiers. Under the care of Hilary, Bishop of Poitiers (see 13 January), Martin led a community of ascetics, and became Bishop of Tours in 371, a position that he did not seek. Martin was not an intellectual but a visionary, a rough character and a man of action. The role of bishop gave him opportunities to preach the gospel and to confront injustice. Martin worked where he was able, and brought Christianity to regions of Gaul where the gospel had not previously been preached. He was prepared to travel by whatever means necessary to reach the outlying areas of his region. This led to his being held in great affection by those he went to meet. For 25 years Martin worked in the Loire region of Gaul. He was known as a missionary, founding many churches and monasteries and removing pagan shrines, sometimes forcibly, in both rural and urban areas. His reputation as a wonder-worker spread as he healed the sick and fought for the poor and oppressed. Martin was not averse to prophetic action, using symbolic acts to counter injustice and to proclaim the gospel.

He was widely acclaimed in life and death as the story of his life, written before his death, spread his reputation far and wide. He was one of the first non-martyrs to be venerated as a saint.

> [The devil said to him]
>
> 'Wherever you go, or whatever you attempt, the devil will resist you.'
>
> Then Martin, replying to him said 'The Lord is my helper; I will not fear what man can do unto me.'
>
> Upon this his enemy immediately vanished out of his sight.
>
> *Sulpicius Severus: Life of St Martin, Ch. 5*

Charles Simeon, Priest, Evangelical Divine, 1836

Born in Reading in 1759, Charles Simeon was educated at Eton and King's College, Cambridge. Here, a requirement to attend Holy Communion in the college chapel caused him weeks of mental agony and resulted in his conversion in 1779. In 1782 he became a Fellow of King's and was ordained. After a curacy at St Edward's, Cambridge, Simeon became Vicar of Holy Trinity in 1783. He remained at this parish in the centre of Cambridge for 53 years. Initially his parishioners did not welcome his evangelical style of ministry but his assiduous pastoral care eventually won them over.

He set up a regular weekly prayer and Bible class, out of which developed a system of group meetings, which gave him the opportunity to aid individuals' spiritual growth. He also began a specifically student-orientated ministry, later to be followed in many churches in university towns, with his famous Friday evening 'conversation parties'. By this means he was able to influence the future ministry of the Church of England by encouraging vocations in able students. He also encouraged some of them (most notably Henry Martyn – see 19 October) to become East India Company chaplains. In 1799 he was involved in establishing a more systematic form of missionary enterprise by the foundation of the Church Missionary Society.

But Simeon's legacy to Anglican ministry was not yet complete. He was particularly concerned with the quality of preaching from Church of England pulpits. By his example and by his books on the art of preaching he perhaps did more than anyone else to draw English preaching away from the long moral lectures fashionable in the eighteenth century to systematic biblical exposition. Yet he was clear that quantity did not equal quality: 'Never weary your hearers by long preaching,' he told his students and 'leave off whilst your congregation are still hungry. That will bring them back for more.'

Simeon was also concerned that work such as his should not be undone after his death by the appointment of an anti-evangelical successor. He began the process of systematizing patronage by buying up advowsons (the right of presentation to a parish) and assigning them to trustees to administer. After his death they became the 'Simeon Trustees' and remain today one of the largest evangelical patronage societies. His ideas were later adopted by those of other traditions and, though sometimes criticized for polarizing parishes, have assisted in creating continuity of ministry over the long term.

In September 1836 Simeon travelled from Cambridge to Ely to see his new bishop. There he caught a cold, which developed into a fatal fever, and he died on 13 November.

14 November

Samuel Seabury, first Anglican Bishop in North America, 1796

Born at Groton, Connecticut in 1729, Samuel Seabury studied theology at Yale and then crossed that Atlantic to study medicine at Edinburgh. In 1753 he was ordained by the Bishop of Lincoln and returned to America as a missionary for the Society for the Propagation of the Gospel in New Brunswick. He later had charge of several parishes in New York.

But this was a period of great tension between the American colonists and the mother country as relations deteriorated and the slide into war gathered pace. Seabury took the minority view among the colonists, supporting the maintenance of the colonies' loyalty to the Crown. During the War of Independence he remained loyal to the Crown and after putting his views in debate suffered brief imprisonment in 1775 and opposed the Declaration of Independence in 1776.

But with the war over and American independence a fact in 1783 Seabury was elected Bishop of Connecticut and Rhode Island by the now independent Protestant Episcopal Church of America and given leave to go to England to seek consecration as a bishop. But America's recently won independence from Britain caused an insuperable barrier to this proposal since Seabury could not now take the Oath of Allegiance to the king and by law no English consecration could take place without it. So he was advised to go instead to Scotland where the Anglican Scottish Episcopal Church, disestablished after the Glorious Revolution of 1688, had no link with the State and its bishops were free agents.

Consequently in Aberdeen on 14 November 1784, Samuel Seabury was consecrated bishop by the Bishop of Aberdeen and two others. Two links were forged between the Scottish and American Episcopal Churches as a result. First, as a recognition of its episcopal origins the flag of the American Episcopal Church contains the Cross of St Andrew. Second, Samuel Seabury promised the three Scottish bishops that, in return for his consecration, he would do his best to persuade the American Church to use the longer Scottish prayer of consecration of 1637 rather than the much shorter 1662 prayer in use in England.

Seabury's was both the first and last such consecration. Recognizing that the problem was likely to recur, an Act of Parliament of 1786 empowered the two archbishops to consecrate bishops for territories outside British jurisdiction. Seabury's consecration at the hands of Scottish bishops was a potent reminder that the Anglican Church was already a wider communion than just the Church of England overseas and that pluralism and diversity as an Anglican hallmark now had an international dimension.

Margaret, Queen of Scotland, Philanthropist, Reformer of the Church, 1093

Margaret was born about 1045, probably in Hungary. A tradition has it that Margaret's father and uncle were sent to Hungary for safety during the reign of the Danish king Canute. She was the grand-daughter of the Saxon King Edmund Ironside (c.981–1016). She returned to England with her father in 1057. Ten years later Margaret and her family were again facing exile after the Norman invasion. Her ship landed on the coast of Fife in 1087 (whether intentionally sailing to Scotland or blown off course while trying to cross the North Sea to Europe is disputed). King Malcolm Canmore of Scotland (Malcolm, son of Duncan, in Shakespeare's *Macbeth*) took the refugee party under his protection. It is said that Margaret was contemplating entering a religious order, but Malcolm persuaded her to marry him instead in 1070.

Margaret now used her influence as queen in the cause of advancing and reforming the Christian faith in Scotland. Among the reforms for which Margaret was responsible were the regulating of the Lenten fast and Easter Communion and observing the prohibited degrees of marriage. In all matters she sought to bring the Scottish Church into line with the common usage of the Western Church. Her private life, it was said, was given up to prayer and practices of piety. There are popular accounts of her caring for the prisoners in the royal dungeons, washing the feet of beggars and tending to the sores of lepers. Orphans and the poor received her special interest and she encouraged the founding of schools, hospitals, and orphanages. Her attempts to prevent feuding among the Highland clans were less successful. Margaret and Malcolm had six sons and two daughters. One son became King David I of Scotland and continued to implement his mother's ideals. A daughter, Matilda, married King Henry I of England.

Margaret and Malcolm restored the ruined abbey on Iona and founded several churches, including Dunfermline Abbey in 1072, built as a setting for Margaret's greatest treasure, a relic of the true Cross. Her jewel-encrusted Gospel book (which according to legend was miraculously recovered from a river into which it had fallen) is now in the Bodleian Library at Oxford.

She died in 1093, four days after her husband's death, on a date she is said to have previously foretold, and was buried at Dunfermline Abbey.

Edmund Rich of Abingdon, Archbishop of Canterbury, 1240

The son of a businessman, Edmund was educated at Oxford and Paris. He taught in the Arts faculty in Oxford from 1195 to 1201, before moving to Paris to study theology. He then lived with the Austin Canons at Merton (Surrey) for a year, and took a further course in theology at Oxford, graduating in 1214.

In 1222 he became treasurer of Salisbury, lecturing in the cathedral school where he became known for utilizing the literal sense and historical context of the Bible, as well as the more allegorical or spiritual understanding of Scripture. In 1223 Edmund was appointed Archbishop of Canterbury by Pope Gregory IX after three earlier suggestions from Canterbury had been rejected. He was regarded as very much an outsider posting, and struggled to stamp his authority on the more corrupt or independent elements of the Church, although ultimately it was his defence of the national Church against the claims of Rome that led to his downfall.

Edmund became known as a reforming archbishop, mainly through his desire to end corrupt practices and mismanagement within the Church. He disliked the administrative responsibilities that went with his office, and he chose his advisers well, delegating much responsibility to them. He was determined to visit each diocese and monastic community, and was prepared to go through the courts if permission was not granted. The Benedictine monks especially were resentful of his visits, as was his own monastic community at Canterbury.

Edmund was also more than able to stand up to royal interference, and was able to unite the Church in England in political activity. Edmund campaigned against both royal mismanagement and papal interference. His protests were full and forthright but ultimately unsuccessful. His 'Constitutions' (a set of guidelines or rules) for the government of the Church were issued in 1236, but were largely ignored by corrupt churchmen, and seeking support from the Pope for his reforms he journeyed to Rome. Although Edmund had preached on the Pope's behalf in support of a Crusade, Gregory IX rejected Edmund's appeals, and, feeling betrayed and unsupported, Edmund retired to Pontigny where he died in 1240.

Edmund was a scholastic theologian whose writings include both works of theology and devotion. In particular the *Speculum Ecclesiae*, a restatement of early monastic teaching on contemplation, spiritual progress and the journey of the soul, proved popular beyond his time. He is remembered for his generous charitable giving and practical acts of care as well as his time as archbishop.

Hugh, Bishop of Lincoln, 1200

Hugh, born at Avalon, in Burgundy about 1140, was groomed by his father to become a member of an order of canons. However, he preferred the harsher religious life of the Carthusians, a contemplative monastic order, and he joined their community at Chartreuse when he was 25.

By way of penance for the murder of Thomas Becket (see 29 December) in 1170, King Henry II was in the process establishing the first Carthusian house in England. Having heard of Hugh's reputation, Henry attempted to persuade him to accept the position of prior of this new venture at Witham in Somerset. Hugh, however, was not abashed to negotiate with the king, making the rehousing and compensation of those villagers displaced by the new monastery a precondition of his acceptance. Around 1175–8 (the actual date is uncertain) Hugh crossed the Channel to take up his new post and under his leadership the community flourished.

In 1186 Henry appointed Hugh as Bishop of Lincoln. Once again Hugh showed his freedom of spirit by refusing to accept the position until he had been elected by a free vote of the cathedral chapter. Lincoln was then the largest diocese in England, and Hugh was particularly careful in the quality of the people to whom he delegated much of the work. Highly thought of by King Henry II and consequently frequently called upon for advice or counsel, Hugh was not afraid to demonstrate his independence from royal control. Like Thomas Becket before him he always championed the freedom of the Church from State intervention and had no hesitation in speaking his mind when the need arose.

Hugh also refused to raise money that was demanded by King Richard II to pay for his participation in the Crusades. This was the first time of note that a royal request for money had been refused by the Church. But Hugh's action only served to enhance his reputation. His relationship with King John was less successful, however, as Hugh constantly challenged the king over matters of faith and conduct to which the king refused to respond. In response to an Easter Sermon by Hugh, King John walked out halfway through, unable to stomach the demands upon kingly authority that Hugh was making.

Hugh was perhaps a typical representative of twelfth-century monasticism. Although a bishop, he would spend some time each year at the monastic community in Witham. His fairness as a judge gave him a substantial reputation, as did his heavy workload within the diocese and for the State. He had several disagreements with the Archbishop of Canterbury, Hubert Walter. When Hugh was dying, the Archbishop suggested that he should take the opportunity of repenting of his rudeness to him. Hugh refused, and replied that he wished he had been ruder still.

Hugh has been said to combine something of the power and attractiveness of Cuthbert (see 20 March) with the love and compassion of Francis of Assisi (see 4 October). His understanding of the suffering of Christ greatly affected his work and his relationship with others. His tomb at Lincoln became a place of popular pilgrimage, second only to that of Thomas Becket at Canterbury.

18 November

Elizabeth of Hungary, Princess of Thuringia, Philanthropist, 1231

Daughter of King Andrew II of Hungary, Elizabeth was sent to Thuringia (south central Germany) for an intended political marriage. At this time she was four years old. In 1221, at the age of ten, she married Ludwig IV of Thuringia. Her marriage was, by all accounts, a happy one. She gave birth to three children, and enjoyed life in the royal court. In the early years of her married life she was influenced by the Franciscans. She developed a reputation for charity, giving much money away, and caring for others. She founded hospitals, and provided for orphans. She took a spiritual director, Conrad of Marburg, in 1225, when she was 14.

In 1227 her husband died of the plague, contracted whilst on the Crusades. Elizabeth was then driven out of the court by Ludwig's brother Henry. He accused her of wasting too much state money on charity. This act led her to begin a life of poverty. Thus, at the age of 17 she renounced all her goods, and began to live at Marburg under the guidance of Conrad. She became a Franciscan Tertiary (a voluntary as opposed to a full member of the order).

Conrad, her spiritual director, had once been an inquisitor of heretics, and he ordered for her a life of great austerity, including physical suffering. Elizabeth refused to return to Hungary, preferring to remain with those she cared for, even though she herself suffered enormously under the direction of Conrad. She spent her days caring for the sick and the poor, and in visiting others. She died in 1231, aged 24.

One story concerning Elizabeth was from the years of her brief marriage: In disobedience to her husband's instructions Elizabeth was carrying food to the poor – bread concealed in her apron – when her husband intercepted her and demanded to know what her apron contained. She told him that it contained roses and when he demanded to see its contents the apron was indeed full of roses. Of course such a legend begs as many questions as it answers – particularly regarding obedience, truthfulness and miraculous deception! It nevertheless gives some indication of the commitment to the poor that Elizabeth was said to have exhibited.

Hilda, Abbess of Whitby, 680

Hilda was a princess within the Deiran (Northumbrian) dynasty, with connections to the East Anglia royal family. She was baptized by Paulinus, Bishop of York (see 10 October).

Hilda's sister became Queen of the East Angles. This region was greatly influenced by the Gallic Church, and this spurred Hilda to travel to Chelles, near Paris, with the aim of taking her monastic vows. However, before Hilda reached Gaul she was recalled by Aidan (Bishop of Lindisfarne – see 31 August) to Northumbria. After living a solitary life for a short period of time, she was made abbess of a religious house at Hartlepool in 649.

In 657 Hilda founded a religious community at Streasnaeshalch, later named Whitby by the Danes. Whitby came to have a significant role in the development of the faith in England. Whitby was a double monastery (a community of both men and women, but governed by a single head) and was a royal establishment. No fewer than five bishops were trained there, and the community became famous for its learning.

Whitby was the location for the celebrated Synod of 664, and Hilda was hostess for the gathering. The Synod was called in 664 to decide upon the date of Easter, which was a point of contention between the Celtic and Roman Churches in Britain. At this Synod, Hilda argued for the defence of Celtic church customs, and although the argument was eventually lost, she accepted the decisions of the Synod with grace, and worked to unite the Church throughout the land.

The existence of a written form of Hilda's life, and her position as abbess of a double community show the importance of women at this stage of English Christian history. She was a woman of note and influence, asked for counsel by rulers, kings and ordinary people. She is reputed to have encouraged Caedmon to write Christian poems – the first Christian poetry to be composed in English.

> Now we must laud the heaven-kingdom's keeper,
> the Ordainers might and his mind's intent,
> the work of the Father of Glory:
> in that he, the Lord everlasting,
> appointed of each wonderous thing the beginning;
> he holy Creator,
> at the first created heaven for a roof to the children of men;
> he, mankind's Keeper, Lord everlasting, almighty Ruler,
> afterwards fashioned for mortals the middle earth, the world.
>
> *Caedmon's Hymn, 7th century*

Mechthild, Béguine of Magdeburg, Mystic, 1280

Mechthild was born around 1207. Most of what is known about her is taken from her own writings.

She began to receive spiritual visions at the age of 12, and in 1230, when she was 23, she left her home to live in Magdeburg with a community of Béguines (the Béguines lived an ascetic life, but did not take formal monastic vows). She remained in the town and community for 40 years, eventually moving to Helfta, after a brief stay with her relatives.

Helfta was a well-known spiritual centre, controlled by Dominicans, under the rule of Gertrud von Hackeborn. It was famous for mysticism, poetry and learning, and was a centre of women's intellectual achievement. Mechthild died in Helfta in 1280.

Whilst Mechthild was at Magdeburg she was guided by Heinrich von Halle, a spiritual director. It was he who encouraged her to write down her mystical experiences and visions. Thus from 1250 onwards Mechthild recorded her visions. Her writings were simple, and straightforward. She wrote in both poetry and prose, and also composed hymns. She wrote six books while in Magdeburg, with a further book being written at Helfta. Her work combines liturgy and dance. She uses songs that were in vogue at the time, that speak of love and sorrow. She draws heavily on her past experiences in a household court: describing knighthood and court life in detail. Her themes all revolve around metaphors of love, an individual's relationship with God, the creation of souls, and an awareness of the Creator in creation.

Although encouraged by Heinrich, the writings are the work of Mechthild alone. The books, once translated and copied, soon gained popularity and were to be found throughout Europe. She is an outstanding example of ecstatic mysticism, and of the tradition of female religious writers throughout the medieval period.

> I cannot dance Lord, unless you lead me.
> If you want me to leap with abandon
> You must intone the song.
> Then shall I leap into love,
> From love into knowledge,
> From knowledge into enjoyment,
> And from enjoyment beyond all human sensations.
> There I want to remain, yet want also to circle higher still.
>
> *The Flowing Light of the Godhead, Book I*

It is my nature that makes me love you often
For I am love itself.
It is my longing that makes me love you intensely
For I yearn to be loved from the heart.
It is my eternity that makes me love you long,
For I have no end.

How God answers the Soul

20 November

Edmund, King of the East Angles, Martyr, 870

Information concerning Edmund is scanty and illustrates well the difficulty of disentangling history from legend. Edmund was born about 840, though differing accounts suggest for his birthplace locations as wide apart as East Anglia, Kent and Nuremburg. What is more certain is that at the age of 15 he became King of the East Angles.

No details of his reign are known for certain, but he would appear to have been a just and equitable ruler who ignored the flattery of his courtiers and there is a legend that he retired for twelve months to his royal tower at Hunstanton and there learned the whole Psalter by heart, in order that he might afterwards recite it regularly. This however probably owes more to the wishful thinking of a later monastic chronicler than to hard fact! Indeed, the information on Edmund's death came via St Dunstan (see 19 May) who, as a young man, had first heard it from an old man who claimed that in his youth he was Edmund's sword-bearer. Such are the tenuous sources of the only available evidence!

But Edmund was clearly a Christian: the pagan Anglo-Saxons who came to Britain in the years following the end of the Roman occupation had become settled communities of farmers who had been gradually Christianized by contact with both Celtic and Roman Christianity.

But by the late ninth century further pagan invasions were taking place, this time from Scandinavia. In 870 Edmund is said to have repulsed the two Danish chiefs Inguar and Hubba who had invaded East Anglia. They soon returned with overwhelming numbers and Edmund's army was defeated, possibly at Hoxne on the Norfolk/Suffolk border. Whatever terms were then forced upon him, he felt unable to accept because of his Christian faith. Consequently he was beaten and flogged and was said to have called upon the name of Jesus. He was then used for archery practice by the Danes and subsequently beheaded.

The cult of Edmund the martyr was not long in developing with many legends surrounding his memory. In the tenth century his bones were moved to Beodricsworth in Suffolk, which soon became known as Bury St Edmunds and the abbey built there became a place of popular pilgrimage. From 1914 it became the cathedral city of the newly created diocese of St Edmundsbury and Ipswich.

Priscilla Lydia Sellon, a Restorer of the Religious Life in the Church of England, 1876

Lydia Sellon was born, probably in 1821, the daughter of a naval commander. She never enjoyed good health and was about to go abroad for a warmer climate in 1848 when she changed her plans and responded to an appeal from Bishop Henry Phillpotts of Exeter for workers amongst the destitute in Plymouth, Devonport and Stonehouse. Her genius for organization was crucial to the success of this venture and the group of women she gathered around her adopted a conventual lifestyle and, with the advice and assistance of Dr Pusey (see 16 September), she founded the Devonport Sisters of Mercy. They immediately had their baptism of fire in the 1849 cholera outbreak and to strengthen them in their work requested a daily communion. The incumbent of St Peter's in Plymouth, George Rundle Prynne, responded positively with the first daily Eucharist in the Church of England since the Reformation.

Despite their selfless work the sisters experienced much local opposition in the prevailing atmosphere of religious intolerance in the early 1850s. In 1856 the Devonport sisters joined with the first community founded – the Society of the Holy Cross (also known as the Park Village Sisterhood) – to form the Society of the Most Holy Trinity. Lydia assumed the title of abbess of the combined sisterhood and led her community in starting schools and orphanages in addition to sisters nursing the sick in slum districts. Some went to the Crimea with Florence Nightingale (see 13 August) to nurse in the military hospitals, others to Hawaii at the request of Queen Emma, who had a great respect for the sisterhood, to establish a school. Mother Lydia travelled to Hawaii herself in 1867 where she established St Andrew's priory in the grounds of the future St Andrew's Cathedral in Honolulu.

It was not just service but worship that Mother Lydia saw as crucial to the revival of the religious life. The monastic offices had been used since the cholera outbreak and, after the amalgamation in 1856, the Rule laid down that the sisters were to offer 'day and night throughout the four and twenty hours . . . the voice of mourning for sin, of interceding for grace, of adoration of the majesty of the Divine Trinity and of the love of Jesus'.

In her last years, she was an invalid, dying in her mid-fifties on 20 November 1876. Dr Pusey described her as 'the restorer after three centuries of the Religious Life in the English Church'.

Cecilia, Martyr at Rome, c.230

The life of Cecilia is unknown. Believed to have been martyred at Rome in 230, she is the subject of a fifth-century legend. This legend tells of how Cecilia, a Christian woman of noble birth, was to be married to a pagan man called Valerian. Valerian, and his brother Tiburtius, became Christians and were martyred. Cecilia was arrested whilst burying the brothers and sentenced to death. She died after several unsuccessful attempts by incompetent Roman guards to kill her.

Although this legend has no historical reliability, Cecilia has been venerated from the fifth century, when stories about her spread. There is, however, some evidence of the martyrdom of Valerian and Tiburtius.

Yet a church in Rome was founded by a woman called Cecilia, and the two ancient stories have been combined, with the result that her story became more believable. Relics uncovered at the church in the sixteenth century were found in a well-preserved state, adding to the legend.

The fifth-century 'acts' which first told of her life recalls her singing to the Lord as she was married to her then pagan husband. For this reason she was chosen as patron saint of church music in the sixteenth century. This patronage has led to many poems and songs being written in her honour, including compositions by Purcell, Handel and Britten. Chaucer used her legend in his *Canterbury Tales* (The second Nun), and Cecilia is also depicted in many paintings and mosaics.

Clement, Bishop of Rome, Martyr, c.100

According to the oldest list of Roman bishops, Clement was the third Bishop of Rome. He is believed to have been bishop from AD 92 to100.

Legend records that the Apostle Peter himself consecrated Clement, and that Clement relinquished the position to Linus, only to take it up again after Linus' death. Early Church historians point out that Clement knew both Peter and Paul. There is little evidence to suggest that Clement was martyred, his 'life' being written in the fourth century and legendary in character.

The Letter of Clement to Corinth, composed just before the persecution of Domitian, was still read frequently in the city at the end of the second century. The letter shows the position of Rome as Church of honour and authority in relation to other, younger Churches. The Letter, which can be ascribed to Clement with certainty, shows him to be a man concerned with unity and peace, one who sought to restore order to the factious Corinthian Church, and who emphasized the emerging role of bishops and priests at the Eucharist. Clement emphasizes apostolic succession, the responsibility of all to preach the gospel, and stresses the duty of the Church to pray for those in power.

> Let him who has love in Christ keep the commandments of Christ. Who can describe the bond of the love of God? What man is able to tell the excellence of its beauty, as it ought to be told? The height to which love exalts is unspeakable.
>
> Love unites us to God. Love covers a multitude of sins. Love bears all things, is long-suffering in all things. There is nothing base, nothing arrogant in love.
>
> Love admits of no schisms: love gives rise to no subversion: love does all things in harmony. By love have all the elect of God been made perfect; without love nothing is well-pleasing to God.
>
> In love has the Lord taken us to Himself. On account of the Love he bore us,
> Jesus Christ our Lord gave His blood for us by the will of God;
> His flesh for our flesh, and His soul for our souls.
>
> *Clement: xlix*

Catherine of Alexandria, Martyr, 4th century

The Life of Catherine was written in the eighth century, and she owes her place in history to this legend.

According to tradition, Catherine was of a royal family and at the age of 18 she protested against the persecution of Christians by the Emperor Maxentius. Maxentius brought in 50 philosophers to convince her of the errors of Christianity. After prolonged debate some of these philosophers were converted to Christ, but all were killed because of their failure to silence Catherine.

Catherine is said to have refused a proposal of marriage from the Emperor himself and as a consequence was thrown into jail. She then converted all her fellow prisoners and jailers. Maxentius was furious, and ordered her to be tied to a spiked wheel (later called a Catherine Wheel). The wheel broke, and Catherine was subsequently beheaded.

Catherine's legend flourished throughout the Middle Ages, particularly through the period of the Crusades. She became the patron saint of young girls, students and nurses. Her legend spread partly through paintings and other artistic representations of her life.

Isaac Watts, Hymn Writer, 1748

Isaac Watts was born in Southampton in 1674 and educated at the grammar school there. Having considerable academic ability he came to the attention of a local benefactor who offered to send him to university. But rather than Anglican Oxford or Cambridge Watts chose the highly regarded Dissenting Academy at Stoke Newington in Middlesex. Leaving there in 1694 he worked first as a private tutor before entering the Independent ministry, first as assistant in 1699, then three years later as pastor of Mark Lane Chapel in London.

Because of deteriorating health he resigned his ministry at Mark Lane in 1712 and retired to Abney Park, Stoke Newington, where for the remaining 36 years of his life he lived under the patronage of the Abney family. Here his limited financial independence allowed him the freedom to write and yet he was said to have given away to the poor a third of his modest allowance. Watts has sometimes been accused of harbouring Unitarian sympathies but this was probably an inaccurate inference from his known opposition to a proposal in 1719 to require Nonconformist ministers to subscribe to the doctrine of the Trinity. It would appear to have been the proposed compulsion rather than the doctrine itself that he opposed.

Physically unprepossessing, it was his serene and spiritual manner and his unswerving faith that endeared him to others and is reflected in the words of many of his hymns. In fact he wrote over six hundred hymns though few of these are now in regular use. Among his hymns still sung are *Jesus shall reign where'er the sun*, *Joy to the world* and, one of the finest English hymns of any age, *When I survey the wondrous cross*.

Known as the father of English hymn writing, Watts both continued in the tradition of metrical Psalms (e.g. Psalm 90 – *O God, our help in ages past*) and began a general move away from that rather limited musical diet to a richer variety of hymnody that took root in both Nonconformity and the Church of England.

> See from His head, His hands, His feet,
> Sorrow and love flow mingled down:
> When did such love and sorrow meet,
> Or thorns compose so rich a crown?
>
> Were the whole realm of nature mine,
> That were an offering far too small;
> Love so amazing, so divine,
> Demands my soul, my life, my all!

I December

Charles de Foucauld, Hermit in the Sahara, 1916

Charles de Foucauld was born to a noble family in Strasbourg in 1858. After military training he was posted to Algeria in 1880. This dissipated young cavalry officer developed a passion for North Africa and in 1883–4 he undertook a mapping exploration of Morocco, Algeria and Tunisia, which he published to critical acclaim. The spiritual unrest which followed resulted in his conversion in 1886. He commented, 'the moment I knew that God existed, I knew I could not do otherwise than to live for him alone'.

After a pilgrimage to the Holy Land in 1888 he entered the Trappist order, with whom he spent seven years before being released from his vows in 1896. The following year Foucauld took private vows of perpetual chastity and poverty and, adopting the name Brother Charles of Jesus, went to the Holy Land. He worked for a time as a handyman for the Poor Clares at Nazareth and made pilgrimages to Jerusalem, but failed in his attempt to found a hermitage on the Mount of the Beatitudes.

Returning to France in 1901, he was ordained as a 'free priest' for the Sahara and returned to Algeria as a hermit at Beni-Abbès, an oasis near the Moroccan border with Algeria. From 1905 he increasingly spent his time at Tamanrasset in the remote Hoggar Mountains. Here he studied the language of the Tuareg, compiling a dictionary and making other translations in addition to his main work of prayer, penance and works of charity. In 1916 he was killed during an anti-French uprising – his goodness, it was said, militated against the anti-French feelings the nationalists sought to instil in the local population.

Though he wrote rules for communities of Little Brothers and Little Sisters of Jesus, no one joined Foucauld during his lifetime and it was not until 1933 that his example drew others to the Sahara. Today his world-wide formal and informal spiritual heirs treasure this prayer:

Father,
I abandon myself into your hands;
do with me what you will.
Whatever you may do, I thank you:
I am ready for all, I accept all.
Let only your will be done in me,
and in all your creatures –
I wish no more than this, O Lord.
Into your hands I commend my soul:
I offer it to you with all the love of my heart,
for I love you, Lord, and so need to give myself,
to surrender myself into your hands without reserve,
and with boundless confidence,
for you are my Father.

3 December

Francis Xavier, Missionary, Apostle of the Indies, 1552

Born in the Castle of Xavier near Sanguesa, in Spain in 1506, Francis Xavier was the son of an aristocratic Basque family. He was educated at the University of Paris, where he met Ignatius Loyola (see 31 July). Xavier was one of the group of six who joined with Ignatius Loyola in 1534. He was ordained priest in Venice in 1537 and when the Society of Jesus was founded in 1540 Xavier was its first secretary.

At the invitation of the King of Portugal to evangelize the East Indies, Xavier made his way to the Portuguese enclave of Goa in India, which became his base. After preaching with great success in Goa for five months, he moved south through India to Ceylon (now Sri Lanka), where he is said to have made tens of thousands of converts. In 1545 Xavier left India for Malacca from where he travelled down the Malay Peninsula and on to the Molucca Islands, founding Christian communities as he travelled and preached.

He was the first to note a problem that was to bedevil the work of missionaries in the following centuries as well as in his own: the oppression, exploitation and un-Christian lifestyles of Europeans were among the biggest obstacles that the missionaries had to overcome and made their task (especially when indigenous people assumed that all white people were Christians) so very much harder.

After a trip to Goa, he sailed for Japan and landed at Kagoshima in 1549. He studied the Japanese language for a year and then preached in many of the principal cities for two-and-a-half years. By 1551, when he left Japan, he had established a vigorous Christian community that was to remain faithful in time of persecution (see 6 February).

His next target was China. To gain entrance to that country, then closed to foreigners, he persuaded the Portuguese authorities to send an embassy, of which he would be a member, to the Chinese Emperor. The embassy left Goa in 1552 but got no farther than Malacca. Xavier continued alone, arriving at Sancian, a small island near Macau, in August 1552. There he died on 3 December that same year, after repeated vain attempts to reach the mainland. His body was returned to Goa for burial.

Francis Xavier died at the early age of 46, yet in his short life he proved to be one of the most effective missionaries of all time. Though the official Jesuit figure of 700,000 conversions at Xavier's hands is no doubt an exaggeration, it gives some idea of the sheer scale of his work. And if Xavier's achievements are a tribute to his total commitment to mission work they also indicate the success of his strategy, in which he sought in each area he visited to target those groups (children in South India, local rulers in Japan, etc.) most likely to be receptive to the gospel, to give it a foothold in the indigenous culture and to propagate it within their communities.

John of Damascus, Monk, Teacher of the Faith, c.749

John, born of a noble Arab Christian family, lived under Muslim rule most of his life. He received a quality education through a Sicilian monk, and held an important position in the court of the Caliph. In 725 when John's relationships with the ruling Islamic court became more difficult he resigned to pursue his vocation as a monk in the monastery of Mar Saba in the Judean desert. There he was ordained priest.

John taught and wrote a great deal, both doctrinal works and popular hymns. He strongly defended the use of images and icons in the iconoclastic controversy. This stance made him unpopular with the Byzantine Christian emperors, but as he was living outside of their jurisdiction in the Muslim-controlled territory they were unable to exert any influence upon him.

John worked to preserve and summarize the teachings of the Fathers of the Church. In his writings he draws on what is best within their work, citing them regularly, often making their sayings clearer. By doing so John was able to present a scholarly synthesis of church theology in the eighth century, and to build his own views and philosophy upon it. His work is of immense theological note, and influenced both Peter Lombard and Thomas Aquinas (see 28 January). John also sought to explain how Mary could remain free from the 'stain of sin', and in doing so was the first theologian to produce a fully developed theology of the place of Mary in the relation to the divinity of Christ.

John's spirituality revolved around the search for perfection, and a desire for the vision of God. He stressed purity of heart and love, and emphasized the need for preparation in the contemplation of the Divine. He stressed the need to imitate the walk of faith of those who have gone before, and ultimately to imitate God, as humankind was created in God's image.

His 'Hymn to the Life-giving Cross' illustrates John's life of perpetual worship:

Ceaselessly we bow
O Christ our God
Before your Cross
That gives us Life;
And glorify your Resurrection,
Most powerful Lord,
When on that third day
You made anew
The failing nature of Mankind
Showing us so clearly
The Way back to heaven above:
For you alone are Good,
The Lover of Mankind.

John Damascus: 'Hymn to the Life-giving Cross'

Nicholas Ferrar, Deacon, Founder of the Little Gidding Community, 1637

Born in London in 1592, Nicholas Ferrar was educated at Clare Hall, Cambridge, where he was elected a Fellow in 1610. In 1613 he left Cambridge for reasons of health and spent five years travelling in Europe. When he returned he began work for the ailing Virginia Company (in which his family was heavily involved), becoming its Deputy Treasurer in 1622. He was elected to Parliament 1624, possibly in order to use parliamentary influence to support the company, but all efforts were unsuccessful and its Royal Charter was revoked.

Ferrar's motives can only be guessed at, but in 1625 he left Parliament. Then with his brother, brother-in-law and their families and a number of friends, he settled at Little Gidding in Huntingdonshire, a rural estate deserted since the Black Death in the fourteenth century. The community occupied the manor house and restored the abandoned church building. Ferrar was ordained deacon by Bishop William Laud (see 10 January).

The community read the regular daily offices of *The Book of Common Prayer*, including a daily recital of the complete Psalter. A continuous vigil of prayer was always maintained in the sanctuary. Community members wrote books and stories dealing with various aspects of Christian faith and practice. They fasted with great rigour, and in other ways embraced voluntary poverty, so that they might have as much money as possible for the relief of the poor. They taught the local children, and cared for the health and well-being of the people of the district. Possibly prompted by Laud, King Charles I made several private visits to the community.

Nicholas Ferrar died in 1637 and the life of the community continued under the leadership of his brother John. But with militant Puritanism in the ascendant and the lawlessness of the Civil War prevailing in England, the days of the community were numbered and, denounced as 'an Arminian nunnery', it was forcibly dissolved by Parliamentary troops in 1646.

Though a comparatively short-lived experiment, Little Gidding was a uniquely Anglican community – open, family-friendly, with its spirituality centred on *The Book of Common Prayer*, and held together by ties that did not require monastic vows. The memory of the community survived to inspire and influence later undertakings in Christian communal living, and the name of Little Gidding was given a literary place of honour in the twentieth century as the title of the last of T. S. Eliot's *Four Quartets*.

Nicholas, Bishop of Myra, c.326

Nicholas, one of the most popular saints in both Greek and Latin Churches, is something of a mystery. All that can be said for certain is that he was Bishop of Myra, (Lycia in modern Turkey) at the beginning of the fourth century. He was buried outside of his city, facing towards the sea. His legend says that he was imprisoned during the Diocletian persecution of 303–4, and was one of the signatories of the Council of Nicea, although there is no record of his name on any of the lists of bishops at the Council.

Nicholas is the patron saint of sailors and of children. His legend speaks of him giving three girls a dowry to prevent them having to enter prostitution when their family fell on hard times. He delivered the gifts at night to avoid detection. He is also believed to have raised to life three drowned boys, and saved three unjustly convicted sailors from death.

Nicholas was honoured from early after his death, being buried in an artistic mausoleum, which became a place of pilgrimage. His legend can be traced back to the sixth century, and was embellished in the mid ninth century. His remains were translated to Bari in 1087, and his cult became popular in the West from that time onwards. His relics are still held in Bari.

He is especially popular in Russia. In Germany, Switzerland and the Netherlands Nicholas is customarily known as the provider of gifts to children on 6 December (his feast day). Dutch settlers in North America merged this legend to Nordic folklore that tells of a magician who punished naughty children and rewarded good ones, to create the modern figure of Santa Claus (Dutch for Saint Nicholas).

Ambrose, Bishop of Milan, Teacher of the Faith, 397

Born in Trier 337/9 and brought up in a Christian family, Ambrose was recommended as bishop in 374. Although he was a Christian he had not yet been baptized. After he accepted the position Ambrose received baptism, ordination and consecration as bishop within a single week. His election as bishop is a testimony to his ability in government and his personal integrity. The Church in Milan was torn between two opposing theologies concerning the nature of Christ. The Arian party denied the full divinity of Christ, whilst the anti-Arian (or orthodox) party affirmed it. The two parties could not agree on a candidate for bishop and the argument spilled over into civil unrest. Ambrose was the only candidate both parties could agree on.

In the debate Ambrose initially followed the decrees of the Emperor who was an Arian supporter. However he soon started to act for the defence of orthodoxy and pursued an anti-Arian agenda in his appointments and social affairs. One famous anti-Arian event occurred in 386 when the Arian party requested a church building in which to conduct their worship. Although agreed by the Emperor, the request was refused by Ambrose and he underlined the refusal by occupying the requested building with his whole congregation. The occupation lasted from Palm Sunday to Easter Day, and the time was passed by the singing of songs. It was the origin of Ambrosian chant in which hymns drew content from the religious events rather than just Scripture. A prolific hymn writer, Ambrose became known as the founder of liturgical hymnody in the Western Church.

Ambrose had many disagreements with the Emperor Theodosius. Although a Christian, Theodosius had difficulty ruling his empire in a Christian manner, often blindly following the advice of his largely pagan court and occasionally over-reacting in a violent manner to quell public unrest. In 390 Ambrose's power over Theodosius was demonstrated. The people of Thessalonica murdered one of Theodosius' senior officers. The Emperor had the citizens invited to the Circus and then sent in soldiers to massacre them. Records note that in three hours 6,000 citizens lost their lives. Ambrose's response was to withdraw the Eucharist from the Emperor, until he had performed public penance. Ambrose constantly challenged him over his behaviour and his policies, and pushed the boundaries of church influence deeper and deeper into the role of the State. In all this, Ambrose's main weapon was the withholding of the Eucharist from the Emperor and through this threat Ambrose claimed for the Church the right of veto over the decisions of the State.

Ambrose was a staunch defender of the Church in a time of theological unrest and debate. He was unwilling to compromise the Church's position in society. He was also willing to act for the State, making several peace missions, and intervening in civil unrest on more than one occasion. Ambrose demanded integrity in leadership from the governing class, and from the Emperor in particular. He stated quite plainly that 'the Emperor is in the Church, not over it'. He died two years after Theodosius, on Good Friday 397.

Ambrose's 'Hymn for the time of Advent' shows how he could combine doctrine and song to produce images of theological beauty:

Redeemer of the nations come,
That we may taste the virgin's fruit
And every age in wonder gaze
On such a birth, worthy of God!
No earthly father's seed played here,
But mystic Breath touched holy virgin womb:
The Word of God took human form
And human flesh blossomed divine.

Hymn for the Time of Advent

13 December

Lucy, Martyr at Syracuse, 304

The tomb of Lucy can still be found in a Catacomb at Syracuse (Sicily). She was martyred in the Diocletian persecutions of 303–4. This was the most decisive and widespread of all Early Church persecutions.

Although based on the actual martyrdom of a young girl, the record of her persecution, which so influenced her commemoration by the Church, is an account of fiction. Although the record is beautifully written, and provides a romantic view of her death, it is pure legend. Lucy is said to have been arrested whilst distributing goods to the poor at the height of the persecution, handed over to the authorities by the one to whom she was betrothed. Her judge ordered her to be raped in a brothel, and then burnt. Attempts at fulfilling both of these orders were unsuccessful, due to the protection of God. Lucy was finally killed by the sword. The record of her martyrdom was written in the fifth century.

Early fourth-century inscriptions bearing her name (Euskia) survive in Syracuse, and Lucy was honoured in Rome from the sixth century onwards. Her name means 'light' and this, together with the extravagant claims of the legend, make her the saint invoked for those with eye diseases. Her feast day is close to the shortest day of the year, and is celebrated especially in Sweden as a festival of light.

Although the detailed account of her death is legend, it is based upon the martyrdom of a young female at Syracuse in 303–4. The Diocletian persecution was intense. Lucy is an example of those who have given their lives for the sake of the gospel, and whose full story has been lost in time.

Samuel Johnson, Moralist, 1784

Samuel Johnson was born in Lichfield in 1709, the son of a bookseller. He attended the local school, and, probably more importantly, eagerly read the books in his father's shop. In 1728 he entered Pembroke College, Oxford, but left without taking a degree. It was perhaps appropriate that it was through reading that he came to faith. Boswell recalls him saying:

> I became a sort of lax talker against religion, for I did not think much against it; and this lasted until I went to Oxford, where it would not be suffered. When at Oxford, I took up Law's Serious Call, expecting to find it a dull book (as such books generally are), and perhaps to laugh at it. But I found Law quite an overmatch for me; and this was the first occasion of my thinking in earnest of religion after I became capable of rational inquiry.

In an age of generally lax religious observance, Johnson was a dutiful son of the Church of England. A strong High Churchman, in the pre-Tractarian sense of that term, he was tolerant towards Roman Catholicism though not of Nonconformity.

After an unsuccessful teaching career in Lichfield, Johnson went up to London in 1737. He was best known for his dictionary, which, after eight years in the making, was published in 1755 with around 40,000 entries. He was the subject of one of the greatest biographies ever written, James Boswell's *Life of Samuel Johnson*, published in 1791.

Some uncertainty surrounds the question of whether Johnson experienced an evangelical conversion in February 1784 in the last year of his life. There is no written record by either Johnson or Boswell, but William Cowper was clearly aware of it since he wrote to John Newton on 11 May 1784 that news of Johnson's conversion was 'a singular proof of the omnipotence of Grace'. Throughout his life Johnson suffered from depression and had a terrible fear of death and judgement and it may have been that at the last he received the assurance of forgiveness and salvation. Certainly, he received Communion eight days before his death in December 1784 and is said to have prayed:

> Grant O Lord that my whole hope and confidence may be in his merits and in thy mercy: forgive and accept my late conversion, enforce and accept my imperfect repentance ... and make the death of thy son Jesus effectual to my redemption.

John of the Cross, Poet, Teacher of the Faith, 1591

The Spanish mystic and poet John de Yepes was born in 1542 at Fontiveros, near Avila in Spain. His family had fallen upon hard times and he became a Carmelite monk in 1563 subsequently being ordained priest in 1567. Dissatisfied with the easy-going and lax ways of the Carmelites John was considering joining the Carthusians when Teresa of Avila (see 15 October) persuaded him to remain and to help extend her reforms to the male side of the Carmelite order. In 1568 he opened the first monastery of the strict or 'Discalced' Carmelites, who emphasized a life of contemplation and austerity. But as reaction set in to their initial success he was imprisoned in the monastery at Toledo in 1577 from where, after nine months of great hardships, which he alleviated by beginning to write poetry, he escaped.

The formal separation of the two branches of the Carmelite order took place in 1579–80. From 1579 to 1582 John founded and was rector of the Discalced Carmelite college at Baeza. He became prior at Granada in 1582 and Segovia in 1588. But control of the new order soon fell into the hands of extremists and in 1591 the new Vicar-General removed John from office and banished him to Ubeda in Andalusia. There he suffered inhuman treatment and died after a period of severe illness at the end of that year.

But John is best known for his writings, all of which have been translated from the original Spanish into English. They are notable for combining the imagination and sensitivity of a poet with the intellectual knowledge of a theologian trained in the tradition of Thomas Aquinas (see 28 January). The themes of his poetry concentrate on the reconciliation of human beings with God through a series of mystical steps that begin with self-communion and renunciation of the distractions of the world. His best known work, *Noche obscura del alma*, has given the phrase 'The Dark Night of the Soul' to the English language. Here he described the soul's progress in seeking and finally attaining union with God through an experience parallel to Christ's crucifixion and glory:

> By dark of blessed night,
> In secrecy, for no one saw me
> And I regarded nothing,
> My only light and guide
> The one that in my heart was burning.
>
> This guided, led me on
> More surely than the radiance of noon
> To where there waited one
> Who was to me well known,
> And in a place where no one came in view.

17 December

Eglantyne Jebb, Social Reformer, Founder of 'Save the Children', 1928

Eglantyne Jebb was born in Shropshire in 1876 and grew up at Ellesmere where she was encouraged to read, write and develop her own opinions. She studied history at Lady Margaret Hall, Oxford, where she developed an interest in social issues. After teacher training she taught at Marlborough in Wiltshire. But she found teaching too physically demanding and went to live with her mother in Cambridge. In 1906 she published her research into poverty in that city – *Cambridge: a Study in Social Questions*.

When the Balkan Wars broke out in 1912, Eglantyne went to Macedonia to aid refugees. Here she began to form views and develop strategies for long-term constructive aid as being more effective than short-term handouts. Her concern for suffering civilians was not limited by nationalistic considerations, and during the First World War she was horrified at the effect the Allied blockade on Germany and Austria-Hungary was having on their civilian populations, especially the children.

The blockade continued after the Armistice in order to put pressure on the Central Powers to sign the harsh peace treaties. So at the beginning of 1919 Eglantyne and her sister Dorothy Buxton were among the founders of the 'Fight the Famine' Council, committed to ending the blockade and establishing a League of Nations. During a rally in Trafalgar Square she was arrested and later fined for distributing an uncensored leaflet, *A Starving Baby*.

'Save the Children', launched by Eglantyne and Dorothy at the Albert Hall in May 1919, was set up to raise money for food for the suffering populations of central Europe. But as well as being a committed Christian Eglantyne was also a businesslike professional: 'The new charity . . . must be scientific; it must have the same clear conceptions of its objects and seek to compass them with the same care, the same thoroughness, the same intelligence as are to be found in the best commercial and industrial enterprises.' £400,000 was raised in 1919 alone and by 1922 Save the Children was one of Britain's biggest charities. It has since spread throughout the world.

Her Declaration of the Rights of the Child, written in 1923, was adopted by the League of Nations the following year. The present United Nations Convention on the Rights of the Child is derived from it. But ten years of exhausting work for Save the Children sapped Eglantyne's health and she died in 1928 in Geneva, aged 52.

Thomas Becket, Archbishop of Canterbury, Martyr, 1170

Born in London around 1118, the son of a wealthy Norman merchant, Becket was educated at Merton Priory in Surrey and later in Paris. About 1141 he entered the household of the Archbishop of Canterbury, Theobald of Bec, who sent him to Bologna to study law and on his return in 1154 ordained him and appointed him Archdeacon of Canterbury.

In the Middle Ages it was the Church, with a virtual monopoly on the supply of educated men, who provided the officials to administer the king's government. The new King Henry II needed a Chancellor (in effect his principal minister) and on the recommendation of Theolbald, who hoped that he would look after the Church's interests, Becket was appointed Chancellor in 1155. The next eight years he spent in unstinting service to the king and the two apparently became close personal friends. Thus in 1161 when Archbishop Theolbald died, Henry, no doubt hoping to bring the Church more firmly under his control, appointed Becket as archbishop in his place. But Henry had miscalculated. Immediately after his consecration in 1162 Becket resigned the Chancellorship, turned away from the luxuries of court to an austere lifestyle and 'from being the king's dutiful minister he became the uncompromising champion of the church'.

Good working relations between Henry and Becket soon evaporated as misunderstandings developed and conflict came to a head over the 1164 Constitutions of Clarendon, the king's attempt to extend the legal jurisdiction of his courts over clergy as well as lay people and to forbid their right of appeal to Rome. Becket saw this as a crude attack on the Church's ancient privileges and his relationship with the king deteriorated into outright hostility, as a result of which he fled to France.

Eventually, under threat of papal sanctions, a reconciliation was patched up and Becket returned to England in November 1170. But when he excommunicated some of the bishops and barons who had supported the king, Henry flew into a rage and called for the removal of 'this turbulent priest'. Four knights, who interpreted this as a coded instruction to action, made their way to Canterbury and murdered Becket before the high altar of the cathedral on 29 December 1170. Becket was canonized less than three years after his murder and Henry was obliged to do public penance at his tomb, which became a place of popular pilgrimage throughout the Middle Ages.

John Wyclif, Reformer, 1384

Because of the far-reaching effects on the Church of the sixteenth century Reformation, it is easy to forget that there were those, both in England and in Europe, who had previously expressed their disquiet with the doctrine and practice of the medieval Church and unsuccessfully sought to reform it. One of these was John Wyclif, sometimes referred to as the 'Morning Star of the Reformation'. Born at Hipswell in Yorkshire c.1330, Wyclif was educated at Oxford. Though he held the livings of Fillingham, Ludgershall and Lutterworth, he remained for most of his life at Oxford where he taught philosophy and theology. He quickly rose in the academic hierarchy from Fellow of Merton to Master of Balliol and Warden of Canterbury Hall.

Wyclif came to prominence in 1374 when he took the king's side in a financial dispute with the Pope. Wyclif soon found himself backed by two powerful patrons – John of Gaunt, Duke of Lancaster and the Black Prince – and as he began to develop unconventional theological views, they were able to protect him from the persecution that would normally have followed from his criticisms of the doctrine and practice of the medieval Church.

In what ways did Wyclif anticipate the Reformation? First he upheld the idea of a national Church over and against the international use (or abuse) of papal authority. Second, he believed in a direct relationship between humanity and God, without priestly mediation. Third, reacting against the speculations of medieval scholasticism, Wyclif sought inspiration and authority in the Scriptures and the Fathers and he initiated a translation of the Latin Vulgate Bible into English. Fourth, he repudiated the doctrine of transubstantiation as philosophically unsound and liable to cause superstition. The inevitable condemnation of his eucharistic views came in 1381, the same year as the Peasants' Revolt, for which he was unfairly blamed. He left Oxford and retired to Lutterworth in Leicestershire, where he died three years later.

Wyclif's followers became known as 'Lollards' and despite attempts to stamp them out, they remained as small illicit groups of Christian worshippers in southern England until the sixteenth-century Reformation. Wyclif's writings strongly influenced the Bohemian Reformer John Hus. After Hus's condemnation by the Council of Constance in 1415 the Council reviewed Wyclif's heresies and ordered his body to be disinterred and burned. Martin Luther (see 31 October) later acknowledged his debt to Wyclif.

The *Common Worship* Calendar – Holy Days

In the printing of the Calendar, Principal Feasts and other Principal Holy Days and Festivals are printed in bold; other Sundays and Lesser Festivals are printed in bold italics. Commemorations are printed in standard italics.

January

1 **The Naming and Circumcision of Jesus**

2 ***Basil the Great and Gregory of Nazianzus, Bishops, Teachers of the Faith, 379 and 389***

2 *Seraphim, Monk of Sarov, Spiritual Guide, 1833*

2 *Vedanayagam Samuel Azariah, Bishop in South India, Evangelist, 1945*

6 **The Epiphany**

10 *William Laud, Archbishop of Canterbury, 1645*

11 *Mary Slessor, Missionary in West Africa, 1915*

12 ***Aelred of Hexham, Abbot of Rievaulx, 1167***

12 *Benedict Biscop, Abbot of Wearmouth, Scholar, 689*

13 ***Hilary, Bishop of Poitiers, Teacher of the Faith, 367***

13 *Kentigern (Mungo), Missionary Bishop in Strathclyde and Cumbria, 603*

13 *George Fox, Founder of the Society of Friends (the Quakers), 1691*

17 ***Antony of Egypt, Hermit, Abbot, 356***

17 *Charles Gore, Bishop, Founder of the Community of the Resurrection, 1932*

18-25 ***Week of Prayer for Christian Unity***

19 ***Wulfstan, Bishop of Worcester, 1095***

20 *Richard Rolle of Hampole, Spiritual Writer, 1349*

21 ***Agnes, Child Martyr at Rome, 304***

22 *Vincent of Saragossa, Deacon, first Martyr of Spain, 304*

24 ***Francis de Sales, Bishop of Geneva, Teacher of the Faith, 1622***

25 **The Conversion of Paul**

26 ***Timothy and Titus, Companions of Paul***

28 ***Thomas Aquinas, Priest, Philosopher, Teacher of the Faith, 1274***

30 ***Charles, King and Martyr, 1649***

31 *John Bosco, Priest, Founder of the Salesian Teaching Order, 1888*

February

1 *Brigid, Abbess of Kildare, c.525*

2 The Presentation of Christ in the Temple (Candlemas)

3 *Anskar, Archbishop of Hamburg, Missionary in Denmark and Sweden, 865*

4 *Gilbert of Sempringham, Founder of the Gilbertine Order, 1189*

6 *The Martyrs of Japan, 1597*

10 *Scholastica, sister of Benedict, Abbess of Plombariola, c.543*

14 *Cyril and Methodius, Missionaries to the Slavs, 869 and 885*

14 *Valentine, Martyr at Rome, c.269*

15 *Sigfrid, Bishop, Apostle of Sweden, 1045*

15 *Thomas Bray, Priest, Founder of the SPCK and the SPG, 1730*

17 *Janani Luwum, Archbishop of Uganda, Martyr, 1977*

23 *Polycarp, Bishop of Smyrna, Martyr, c.155*

27 *George Herbert, Priest, Poet, 1633*

Alternative dates

Matthias may be celebrated on 24 February instead of 14 May.

1 ***David, Bishop of Menevia, Patron of Wales, c.601***

2 ***Chad, Bishop of Lichfield, Missionary, 672***

7 ***Perpetua, Felicity and their Companions, Martyrs at Carthage, 203***

8 ***Edward King, Bishop of Lincoln, 1910***

8 *Felix, Bishop, Apostle to the East Angles, 647*

8 *Geoffrey Studdert Kennedy, Priest, Poet, 1929*

17 ***Patrick, Bishop, Missionary, Patron of Ireland, c.460***

18 *Cyril, Bishop of Jerusalem, Teacher of the Faith, 386*

19 **Joseph of Nazareth**

20 ***Cuthbert, Bishop of Lindisfarne, Missionary, 687***

21 ***Thomas Cranmer, Archbishop of Canterbury, Reformation Martyr, 1556***

24 *Walter Hilton of Thurgarton, Augustinian Canon, Mystic, 1396*

24 *Oscar Romero, Archbishop of San Salvador, Martyr, 1980*

25 **The Annunciation of Our Lord to the Blessed Virgin Mary**

26 *Harriet Monsell, Founder of the Community of St John the Baptist, 1883*

31 *John Donne, Priest, Poet, 1631*

Alternative dates

Chad may be celebrated with Cedd on 26 October instead of 2 March.
Cuthbert may be celebrated on 4 September instead of 20 March.

April

1 *Frederick Denison Maurice, Priest, Teacher of the Faith, 1872*

9 *Dietrich Bonhoeffer, Lutheran Pastor, Martyr, 1945*

10 William Law, Priest, Spiritual Writer, 1761

10 *William of Ockham, Friar, Philosopher, Teacher of the Faith, 1347*

11 *George Augustus Selwyn, first Bishop of New Zealand, 1878*

16 *Isabella Gilmore, Deaconess, 1923*

19 Alphege, Archbishop of Canterbury, Martyr, 1012

21 Anselm, Abbot of Le Bec, Archbishop of Canterbury, Teacher of the Faith, 1109

23 George, Martyr, Patron of England, c.304

24 *Mellitus, Bishop of London, first Bishop at St Paul's, 624*

25 Mark the Evangelist

27 *Christina Rossetti, Poet, 1894*

28 *Peter Chanel, Missionary in the South Pacific, Martyr, 1841*

29 Catherine of Siena, Teacher of the Faith, 1380

30 *Pandita Mary Ramabai, Translator of the Scriptures, 1922*

1 Philip and James, Apostles

2 *Athanasius, Bishop of Alexandria, Teacher of the Faith, 373*

4 *English Saints and Martyrs of the Reformation Era*

8 *Julian of Norwich, Spiritual Writer, c.1417*

14 Matthias the Apostle

16 *Caroline Chisholm, Social Reformer, 1877*

19 Dunstan, Archbishop of Canterbury, Restorer of Monastic Life, 988

20 Alcuin of York, Deacon, Abbot of Tours, 804

21 *Helena, Protector of the Holy Places, 330*

24 John and Charles Wesley, Evangelists, Hymn Writers, 1791 and 1788

25 The Venerable Bede, Monk at Jarrow, Scholar, Historian, 735

25 Aldhelm, Bishop of Sherborne, 709

26 Augustine, first Archbishop of Canterbury, 605

26 *John Calvin, Reformer, 1564*

26 *Philip Neri, Founder of the Oratorians, Spiritual Guide, 1595*

28 *Lanfranc, Prior of Le Bec, Archbishop of Canterbury, Scholar, 1089*

30 Josephine Butler, Social Reformer, 1906

30 *Joan of Arc, Visionary, 1431*

30 *Apolo Kivebulaya, Priest, Evangelist in Central Africa, 1933*

31 The Visit of the Blessed Virgin Mary to Elizabeth

Alternative dates

Matthias may be celebrated on 24 February instead of 14 May.

The Visit of the Blessed Virgin Mary to Elizabeth may be celebrated on 2 July instead of 31 May.

1 ***Justin, Martyr at Rome, c.165***

3 *The Martyrs of Uganda, 1885–7 and 1977*

4 *Petroc, Abbot of Padstow, 6th century*

5 ***Boniface (Wynfrith) of Crediton, Bishop, Apostle of Germany, Martyr, 754***

6 *Ini Kopuria, Founder of the Melanesian Brotherhood, 1945*

8 ***Thomas Ken, Bishop of Bath and Wells, Nonjuror, Hymn Writer, 1711***

9 ***Columba, Abbot of Iona, Missionary, 597***

9 *Ephrem of Syria, Deacon, Hymn Writer, Teacher of the Faith, 373*

11 **Barnabas the Apostle**

14 *Richard Baxter, Puritan Divine, 1691*

15 *Evelyn Underhill, Spiritual Writer, 1941*

16 ***Richard, Bishop of Chichester, 1253***

16 *Joseph Butler, Bishop of Durham, Philosopher, 1752*

17 *Samuel and Henrietta Barnett, Social Reformers, 1913 and 1936*

18 *Bernard Mizeki, Apostle of the MaShona, Martyr, 1896*

19 *Sundar Singh of India, Sadhu (holy man), Evangelist, Teacher of the Faith, 1929*

22 ***Alban, first Martyr of Britain, c.250***

23 ***Etheldreda, Abbess of Ely, c.678***

24 **The Birth of John the Baptist**

27 *Cyril, Bishop of Alexandria, Teacher of the Faith, 444*

28 ***Irenaeus, Bishop of Lyons, Teacher of the Faith, c.200***

29 **Peter and Paul, Apostles**

Alternative dates

Peter the Apostle may be celebrated alone, without Paul, on 29 June.

1 *Henry, John, and Henry Venn the younger, Priests, Evangelical Divines, 1797, 1813 and 1873*

3 Thomas the Apostle

6 *Thomas More, Scholar, and John Fisher, Bishop of Rochester, Reformation Martyrs, 1535*

11 *Benedict of Nursia, Abbot of Monte Cassino, Father of Western Monasticism, c.550*

14 *John Keble, Priest, Tractarian, Poet, 1866*

15 *Swithun, Bishop of Winchester, c.862*

15 *Bonaventure, Friar, Bishop, Teacher of the Faith, 1274*

16 *Osmund, Bishop of Salisbury, 1099*

18 *Elizabeth Ferard, first Deaconess of the Church of England, Founder of the Community of St Andrew, 1883*

19 *Gregory, Bishop of Nyssa, and his sister Macrina, Deaconess, Teachers of the Faith, c.394 and c.379*

20 *Margaret of Antioch, Martyr, 4th century*

20 *Bartolomé de las Casas, Apostle to the Indies, 1566*

22 Mary Magdalene

23 *Bridget of Sweden, Abbess of Vadstena, 1373*

25 James the Apostle

26 *Anne and Joachim, Parents of the Blessed Virgin Mary*

27 *Brooke Foss Westcott, Bishop of Durham, Teacher of the Faith, 1901*

29 *Mary, Martha and Lazarus, Companions of our Lord*

30 *William Wilberforce, Social Reformer, 1833*

31 *Ignatius of Loyola, Founder of the Society of Jesus, 1556*

Alternative dates

The Visit of the Blessed Virgin Mary to Elizabeth may be celebrated on 2 July instead of 31 May.

Thomas the Apostle may be celebrated on 21 December instead of 3 July.

Thomas Becket may be celebrated on 7 July instead of 29 December.

4 *Jean-Baptiste Vianney, Curé d'Ars, Spiritual Guide, 1859*

5 ***Oswald, King of Northumbria, Martyr, 642***

6 **The Transfiguration of our Lord**

7 *John Mason Neale, Priest, Hymn Writer, 1866*

8 ***Dominic, Priest, Founder of the Order of Preachers, 1221***

9 ***Mary Sumner, Founder of the Mothers' Union, 1921***

10 ***Laurence, Deacon at Rome, Martyr, 258***

11 ***Clare of Assisi, Founder of the Minoresses (Poor Clares), 1253***

11 *John Henry Newman, Priest, Tractarian, 1890*

13 ***Jeremy Taylor, Bishop of Down and Connor, Teacher of the Faith, 1667***

13 *Florence Nightingale, Nurse, Social Reformer, 1910*

13 *Octavia Hill, Social Reformer, 1912*

14 *Maximilian Kolbe, Friar, Martyr, 1941*

15 **The Blessed Virgin Mary**

20 ***Bernard, Abbot of Clairvaux, Teacher of the Faith, 1153***

20 *William and Catherine Booth, Founders of the Salvation Army, 1912 and 1890*

24 **Bartholomew the Apostle**

27 ***Monica, mother of Augustine of Hippo, 387***

28 ***Augustine, Bishop of Hippo, Teacher of the Faith, 430***

29 ***The Beheading of John the Baptist***

30 ***John Bunyan, Spiritual Writer, 1688***

31 ***Aidan, Bishop of Lindisfarne, Missionary, 651***

Alternative dates

The Blessed Virgin Mary may be celebrated on 8 September instead of 15 August.

September

1 *Giles of Provence, Hermit, c.710*

2 *The Martyrs of Papua New Guinea, 1901 and 1942*

3 ***Gregory the Great, Bishop of Rome, Teacher of the Faith, 604***

4 *Birinus, Bishop of Dorchester (Oxon), Apostle of Wessex, 650*

6 *Allen Gardiner, Missionary, Founder of the South American Mission Society, 1851*

8 ***The Birth of the Blessed Virgin Mary***

9 *Charles Fuge Lowder, Priest, 1880*

13 ***John Chrysostom, Bishop of Constantinople, Teacher of the Faith, 407***

14 Holy Cross Day

15 ***Cyprian, Bishop of Carthage, Martyr, 258***

16 ***Ninian, Bishop of Galloway, Apostle of the Picts, c.432***

16 *Edward Bouverie Pusey, Priest, Tractarian, 1882*

17 ***Hildegard, Abbess of Bingen, Visionary, 1179***

19 *Theodore of Tarsus, Archbishop of Canterbury, 690*

20 ***John Coleridge Patteson, First Bishop of Melanesia, and his Companions, Martyrs, 1871***

21 Matthew, Apostle and Evangelist

25 ***Lancelot Andrewes, Bishop of Winchester, Spiritual Writer, 1626***

25 *Sergei of Radonezh, Russian Monastic Reformer, Teacher of the Faith, 1392*

26 *Wilson Carlile, Founder of the Church Army, 1942*

27 ***Vincent de Paul, Founder of the Congregation of the Mission (Lazarists), 1660***

29 Michael and All Angels

30 *Jerome, Translator of the Scriptures, Teacher of the Faith, 420*

Alternative dates

Cuthbert may be celebrated on 4 September instead of 20 March.

October

1 *Remigius, Bishop of Rheims, Apostle of the Franks, 533*

1 *Anthony Ashley Cooper, Earl of Shaftesbury, Social Reformer, 1885*

4 *Francis of Assisi, Friar, Deacon, Founder of the Friars Minor, 1226*

6 *William Tyndale, Translator of the Scriptures, Reformation Martyr, 1536*

9 *Denys, Bishop of Paris, and his Companions, Martyrs, c.250*

9 *Robert Grosseteste, Bishop of Lincoln, Philosopher, Scientist, 1253*

10 *Paulinus, Bishop of York, Missionary, 644*

10 *Thomas Traherne, Poet, Spiritual Writer, 1674*

11 *Ethelburga, Abbess of Barking, 675*

11 *James the Deacon, companion of Paulinus, 7th century*

12 *Wilfrid of Ripon, Bishop, Missionary, 709*

12 *Elizabeth Fry, Prison Reformer, 1845*

12 *Edith Cavell, Nurse, 1915*

13 *Edward the Confessor, King of England, 1066*

15 *Teresa of Avila, Teacher of the Faith, 1582*

16 *Nicholas Ridley, Bishop of London, and Hugh Latimer, Bishop of Worcester, Reformation Martyrs, 1555*

17 *Ignatius, Bishop of Antioch, Martyr, c.107*

18 Luke the Evangelist

19 *Henry Martyn, Translator of the Scriptures, Missionary in India and Persia, 1812*

25 *Crispin and Crispinian, Martyrs at Rome, c.287*

26 *Alfred the Great, King of the West Saxons, Scholar, 899*

26 *Cedd, Abbot of Lastingham, Bishop of the East Saxons, 664*

28 Simon and Jude, Apostles

29 *James Hannington, Bishop of Eastern Equatorial Africa, Martyr in Uganda, 1885*

31 *Martin Luther, Reformer, 1546*

Alternative dates

Chad may be celebrated with Cedd on 26 October instead of 2 March.

November

1 **All Saints' Day**

2 ***Commemoration of the Faithful Departed (All Souls' Day)***

3 ***Richard Hooker, Priest, Anglican Apologist, Teacher of the Faith, 1600***

3 *Martin of Porres, Friar, 1639*

6 *Leonard, Hermit, 6th century*

6 *William Temple, Archbishop of Canterbury, Teacher of the Faith, 1944*

7 ***Willibrord of York, Bishop, Apostle of Frisia, 739***

8 ***The Saints and Martyrs of England***

9 *Margery Kempe, Mystic, c.1440*

10 ***Leo the Great, Bishop of Rome, Teacher of the Faith, 461***

11 ***Martin, Bishop of Tours, c.397***

13 ***Charles Simeon, Priest, Evangelical Divine, 1836***

14 *Samuel Seabury, first Anglican Bishop in North America, 1796*

16 ***Margaret, Queen of Scotland, Philanthropist, Reformer of the Church, 1093***

16 *Edmund Rich of Abingdon, Archbishop of Canterbury, 1240*

17 ***Hugh, Bishop of Lincoln, 1200***

18 ***Elizabeth of Hungary, Princess of Thuringia, Philanthropist, 1231***

19 ***Hilda, Abbess of Whitby, 680***

19 *Mechtild, Béguine of Magdeburg, Mystic, 1280*

20 ***Edmund, King of the East Angles, Martyr, 870***

20 *Priscilla Lydia Sellon, a Restorer of the Religious Life in the Church of England, 1876*

22 *Cecilia, Martyr at Rome, c.230*

23 ***Clement, Bishop of Rome, Martyr, c.100***

25 *Catherine of Alexandria, Martyr, 4th century*

25 *Isaac Watts, Hymn Writer, 1748*

29 ***Day of Intercession and Thanksgiving for the Missionary Work of the Church***

30 **Andrew the Apostle**

December

1 *Charles de Foucauld, Hermit in the Sahara, 1916*

3 *Francis Xavier, Missionary, Apostle of the Indies, 1552*

4 *John of Damascus, Monk, Teacher of the Faith, c.749*

4 *Nicholas Ferrar, Deacon, Founder of the Little Gidding Community, 1637*

6 *Nicholas, Bishop of Myra, c.326*

7 *Ambrose, Bishop of Milan, Teacher of the Faith, 397*

8 *The Conception of the Blessed Virgin Mary*

13 *Lucy, Martyr at Syracuse, 304*

13 *Samuel Johnson, Moralist, 1784*

14 *John of the Cross, Poet, Teacher of the Faith, 1591*

17 *O Sapientia*

17 *Eglantyne Jebb, Social Reformer, Founder of 'Save The Children', 1928*

24 *Christmas Eve*

25 Christmas Day

26 Stephen, Deacon, First Martyr

27 John, Apostle and Evangelist

28 The Holy Innocents

29 *Thomas Becket, Archbishop of Canterbury, Martyr, 1170*

31 *John Wyclif, Reformer, 1384*

Alternative dates

Thomas the Apostle may be celebrated on 21 December instead of 3 July.

Thomas Becket may be celebrated on 7 July instead of 29 December.

Index of Names

Using the free CD-ROM

The free CD-Rom supplied with *Saints on Earth* provides two different methods for interacting with the biographies in electronic form.

Visual Liturgy

A module is provided that is compatible with *Visual Liturgy 4.0 for Common Worship*. After you have installed the *Saints on Earth* module, a number of small changes will be made to your copy of *Visual Liturgy* so that you can interact with the biographies while planning your services in VL.

In the Welcome screen and Service Overview screens, the notification of which Calendar event is to be celebrated will become a hyperlink. If you click on the link you will be shown the relevant saint's biography from *Saints on Earth*.

In the Calendar, right clicking on a Calendar event provides you with a *Saints on Earth* menu option, which also brings up the relevant saint's biography.

Lastly, an extra tab will be added to the *Visual Liturgy Agent* so that you can view the biographies there.

Please note that this module will not work unless *Visual Liturgy 4.0 for Common Worship* has already been installed.

To install:
Run **setup.exe** from the 'VLModule' folder on the CD-ROM.

PDF files

If you do not use *Visual Liturgy 4.0 for Common Worship*, the material from *Saints on Earth* has also been provided as PDF files. To browse the files, open the 'PDF' folder on the CD-ROM.

To view or print a PDF file you will need the latest version of Adobe Acrobat Reader. You can install Adobe Acrobat Reader from the CD-ROM.

To install:
Open the 'Acrobat' folder on the CD-ROM and choose the relevant installation file for your operating system.

Disclaimer

The Archbishops' Council does not warrant that this CD-ROM will meet your requirements or that its operation will be uninterrupted or error free. The Archbishops' Council excludes and hereby expressly disclaims all express and implied warranties or conditions, so far as such exclusion is or disclaimer is permitted under the applicable law.

The Archbishops' Council and Church House Publishing cannot provide technical support for issues relating to the operation of Adobe Acrobat Reader or PDF files. *Visual Liturgy* users experiencing difficulties with the *VL* compatible module should make use of the normal avenues of technical support available.